Thoughts about God and Life

Fifty-two weeks of inspirational daily readings

Thomas A. Curry

foreward by David Dick

COVER DESIGN
The picture on the cover is the tree alongside our porch where we lived in an apartment building in J.D. Nagar, Patawata, Vijayawada city, A.P., India. It brought us a great amount of peace and solitude over the years.

The actual cover design was by Lisa Anderson of Opine Design, Arden Hills, Minnesota.

ISBN-13: 978-1514268186

ISBN-10: 1514268183

DEDICATION

This devotional is dedicated to my father and mother, H. Nelson and Reba (Thomas) Curry of Liberty, Indiana. I continually benefit from their sacrifice and example in life. My father's integrity and my mother's piety have had profound influence on me. I am forever indebted to them.

ACKNOWLEDGEMENTS

Without the love and support of my wife, Rhonda, I would not have completed this task. She and Joan Ogan of Wabash, IN, were my faithful proofreaders.

Special thanks to Arthur Gay of McHenry, Illinois; Ralph Winter (deceased) of Pasadena, California; and Bishop Ezra Sargunam of Chennai, India, who have relentlessly shaped my life and ministry.

Special thanks to friends like Jim Behrendt, Steve Gettinger, Abe & Tonya Dare, Quentin Scholtz, and Don Saum whose friendship is like gold.

Special thanks to beloved friends of the congregations that I have served over thirty plus years of ministry (St. Paul's County Line Church, Andrews, Indiana; Community Church of Round Lake, Illinois; the Evangelical Church of India; and the Living Faith Lutheran Church, Wabash, Indiana). They have taught me much about truly following the Lord Jesus Christ in daily life, humbly and sacrificially serving Him.

Special thanks to my many pastor friends who have lovingly discipled me, inspired me, chastised me, and encouraged me over the years.

FOREWARD

I have known Thomas Curry since the turn of this new century. He and his wife Rhonda are committed, caring, and dedicated followers of Jesus Christ who demonstrate His character and nature through their own personal life, family, and ministry. Their love and commitment to Christ, His Church, His Kingdom, and to one another, overflow into the lives of their two adult children, and their six grandchildren. But this Christ-like self-giving and self-sacrificing quality has not stopped there. They have also pioneered a faith based not-for-profit Christian organization that in turn operates an orphanage ministry in India caring for hundreds of the poorest of the poor children, and those without the knowledge of their earthy parents, or their Heavenly Father.

Thomas and his wife Rhonda have walked the streets of villages in India where seldom, if ever, a foreign white person has ever trod before. They have given of themselves for more than ten years itinerating from the USA back and forth to India and then again for five more years living residential and serving among those they have come to call their own, mingling with everyone from the outcaste to the upper caste while earning the love and admiration of everyone in between.

I have met many leaders throughout my career, many well-known and highly respected people whom the world has recognized and rewarded with honor, prestige, power, and wealth. Thomas ranks among the best of these, yet without fame, fortune, or familiarity from the world at large. But you ask those who live in the hardest, harshest most underprivileged localities of the great sub-continent, especially among the OMS-established Evangelical Church of India (ECI), and Brother and Sister Curry will be far better known, appreciated, admired, respected, and loved than any of the well-known international personalities that frequently occupy news media space.

I recommend this devotional material to the reader because of Thomas' constant, intimate, and life transforming walk with the Lord. Don't be surprised if you see new aspects of what it means to live by faith and walk in obedience in new light as you turn each page.

David Dick, V-P at large, *One Mission Society*

INTRODUCTION

This devotional was written with my grandchildren in mind – Ethan Curry, Jonathan Curry, Olivia Curry, Bailey Thurman, Derek Thurman, (children of our son, Jim, and his wife, Jasmine) and Camden Sybrandy (son of our daughter, Jenny). I may not be able to leave them much as to land or money. My hope is that these devotional readings will inspire and challenge them throughout life, which at times can be very painful and disappointing.

The book is a good overview of the Christian faith as revealed in the Old and New Testaments of the Holy Bible. Reading through the entire year will take the reader through the whole Bible as to content, highlighting many of the great characters of the Bible. I see the Bible as God's final revelation to humanity. It has shaped and influenced the peoples of the world more than any other book ever printed in human history. It is inspired by God, fully reliable and without error.

Thoughts About God and Life is written so it can be used with any given year and therefore is not dated. It is designed to begin on the first Monday of the new year and covers the subsequent fifty-two weeks.

My usage of the word "man" refers to either man or woman and in some cases both, as used in the Bible. It is not intended to advance a patriarchal world-view.

GOD THE FATHER

WEEK #1 - LEARNING ABOUT GOD THROUGH CREATION

MONDAY – GOD IS THE SUBJECT

Scripture: Genesis 1:1-2

"In the beginning, God . . ." With these words the Bible begins. The immediate focus is God, not man, not what man has created or done. The subject of the Bible is God - who he is - what he is like - what he has done and is doing – why he is great and why he is good. It is all about him. Yes, there are many other things one can learn from the Bible, such as mankind's unique role among all living things and his search for identity and propensity towards evil, but we must not lose sight that this book first and foremost is about the Author of all life and everything we see and hear. It is about God.

Another interesting observation about these first words is the announcement of a beginning. In the book of Revelation, we learn about the end – the end of the ages, the end of the church age, and the end of sickness, suffering and death. The Bible gives us a picture of a beginning and an end. Most other religions in the world teach that this cosmos has always been and will always be with neither a beginning nor an end.

One might question what difference this makes. The difference is life having a purpose according to a plan versus life being an exercise in futility. The clarity of this purpose is rather vague in Genesis and throughout the Old Testament but is refined through Christ and the teaching of the Apostles. To live as Christ lived with the goal of doing the works of God "while it is day for night is coming" is to have an overarching purpose for one's entire existence.

PRAYER: *Father, You spoke the world into being, revealing Your greatness. You created all life revealing Your goodness. This first day of the year, I am in awe of You - God of Abraham, Isaac, and Jacob, the Father of my Lord Jesus Christ. Today and throughout the entire year, may my life be enriched by a growing awareness and knowledge of You. Amen.*

TUESDAY - GOD SPEAKS AND VOILA

Scripture: Genesis 1:3

Genesis is the foundation that the rest of the Bible is built upon. It contains numerous foundational themes. With Genesis, we quickly learn that God speaks. All other "gods" in the world are silent – not the God of the Bible. When he speaks, great things happen - light comes in the midst of darkness; land comes in the midst of large bodies of water; the earth sprouts vegetation; lights in the sky separate day from night; living creatures populate the seas and the earth; and the final pinnacle of creation comes into being – man and woman. The lead-in phrase for each day of creation is, "And God said." One can only conclude that the words of God have amazing, creative power.

It is interesting that John the Apostle, in the opening statement of his letter (John 1:1-3), presents Jesus as "the Word", who was in the beginning with God. He takes it a step further in saying that everything came into being through Jesus, the Word.

Now think about the book you have in front of you – the Bible – the Word of God. Really? The "word" of God. Open it up. Look at the words printed on page after page. It is not a rabbit's foot for good luck nor does it have mystical power as some believe a cross or crucifix might have. It is a book, yet, it is God's word. What role does God's word play in your daily life? Do you study it? Do you desire to know it better? Do you ponder its meaning? What is God saying to you through his written word, at this point in your journey of faith?

PRAYER: *Father, do it again today. Speak, Father. Speak to my heart. May Your gentle, life giving words flow through my mind and further create in me ways of being that reflect Your voice. Through Jesus. Amen.*

WEDNESDAY - GOD CREATES LIVING BEINGS IN HIS IMAGE

Scripture: Genesis 1:26-27

There is an old Scottish saying about a son and his father. "He is the spirit and image of his father." Like many sayings, over time it was somewhat corrupted to the point that many people today know the saying as "He is the 'spitting' image of his father." The point is not that words and sayings lose their meanings over time but that one of the mysteries of parent and child is how the child carries the spirit and image of the parent. Something we can see identifies the child as being connected with the parent. This is even true in adopted children as they pick up the mannerisms and thought patterns of the couple who claimed them as their own.

My wife, Rhonda, is indeed the spirit and image of her mother Helen Morrison. Ask anyone who knows them. If you know Rhonda, you know Helen, even though you may have never met Helen.

The climax of the creation story is Adam and Eve as "living beings" made in the "image" of God. This certainly tells a lot about man, but what does it tell us about God? In this sense, one could argue that humanity is an extension of God.

Out of all the creatures God created, it is Adam and Eve who bear his image, and later in Scripture, we learn that it is possible for them to possess the very spirit of their Creator. It is this fiery Spirit which motivates and emboldens them to bring life and hope into the world's darkness and chaos. Those people are precious far beyond imagination. Get to know a real-for-sure Christian, and you learn a lot about God.

PRAYER: *Father God, we praise You today that in Your infinite wisdom You created us in Your image and have filled people throughout history with Your mighty spirit. People of all races and from all times and places enjoy intimacy and human love. Because we know love, we know a little bit about You. We thank You. In Jesus' name. Amen.*

THURSDAY - GOD BLESSES THESE SPECIAL LIVING BEINGS

Scripture: Genesis 1:28

The first mention of blessing is in vs. 22 when God first creates living creatures. When he creates Adam and Eve, we find it again in the statement, *"God blessed them"*. The Hebrew word for bless is *barak* which actually means to kneel before. One gets the mental picture of a father blessing a son, kneeling before him, extending to him his special favor. Not only are Adam and Eve in the very image of the Creator, but like when he created life, God's overflowing admiration and pleasure rests upon his children.

Today we are reminded not only of God's greatness in speaking the world into being but his goodness in giving us life, bringing us into being in his image, and then carrying the honor of his blessing. This warm, intimate act by such power and majesty gives one much to ponder. In observing the God of the Bible we see a strange mixture of greatness . . . and goodness.

God's goodness many times is expressed by his love and kindness. Most people we know who are loving people are looked upon as good people, the kind we would like to have as neighbors or friends. These people would make good parents - parents whose favor and pleasure rests upon their little boy or little girl. Contrary to what some think, God is not the celestial policeman in the sky. He is not waiting for you to make a mistake and then pounce upon you, punishing you in harsh judgment. He is the intimate father who is not shy about his feeling about his sons and daughters. Much joy and pride came into his heart when he gazed upon the newly created Adam and Eve.

PRAYER: *Father God, we are constantly amazed and in awe of You. Can it really be? Can it really be? Indeed You are great, but indeed You are simultaneously good, very good, so very good that my mind can never fully grasp it. Thank You, Father, for allowing me to know You and especially to know Your goodness. In Jesus' name. Amen.*

FRIDAY - GOD RESTS AND BLESSES A DAY TO REST

Scripture: Genesis 2:1-3

Today we learn that God works and that he rests, much like any normal person. Throughout the six days of creation, there is no mention of God's creating activity as being "work". It is on the seventh day that we see God in this light.

Think of the common man who does physical labor such as the carpenter, the plumber, or the caretaker of a large estate. In the wake of much activity, our bodies cry out for rest. I remember baling hay in my childhood. We would apply much energy to lifting heavy bales from the baler to the wagon and then finally to the barn. Rest would come very easy on those nights following days where one's body was completely exhausted.

This is the picture we get of God as chapter two unfolds. Six days of creation have been completed. Does God now need some time away, a few hours of doing something other than creating, or does he need sleep? The narrative reveals only that creation was complete and that he ceased doing what he was doing. Maybe he took a walk? Maybe he took a nap. This we do not know but only that he rested.

It is interesting also to note that God looks with great favor upon this day. It is pleasing to him. He blesses it just as he did the first living creatures and as he did with Adam and Eve. Such a day in the cycle of a week was to forever be a special day.

Being made in his image, are you like him in this way? Do you have that day which is special, a day of rest built into your typical week?

PRAYER: *Father, thank You for the Bible. Thank You for the story of creation whereby we have these incredible insights of Your nature and character. Help me Lord, day by day, to be more and more like You, yes, a creature made in Your image. In Jesus' name. Amen.*

SATURDAY - GOD PROVIDES

Scripture: Genesis 2:8 & 9

The Hebrews had many names for God, one of them being Jehovah-Jireh – God the provider. In today's reading, we see God in this light. He doesn't drop fruit and vegetables from the sky, but he plants a garden and causes trees to grow. These trees were *"pleasing to the sight and good for food"*. Adam and Eve must have eaten regularly from the trees receiving all their required nourishment.

Can we assume that without God's provision of food, Adam and Even would have ceased to exist? They would not have had food nor would they have had knowledge to grow food. They were dependent on God to provide . . . and he did.

God is like that. He is our source of life in all ways. He has provided us with health and with food of all kinds. Without timely rains, the ground dries up as when major droughts have hit different parts of the world. If the sun was a little closer to planet earth, all crops would burn up. If it was a little farther away, no crops would grow as all the land would be frozen.

Jesus said to *"do not be worried about your life, as to what you will eat or what you will drink; nor for your body as to what you will put on. . . Look at the birds of the air, that they do not sow, nor reap nor gather into barns, and yet your heavenly Father feeds them. . . (Matt. 6:25 & 26)"*

God is our source of life. Without him, we die. With him, we live. Out of his love, he provides for our every need.

PRAYER: *Father, when we ponder the wonder of You as "provider" we are in awe. How do You do it? We will never know how You do what you do this side of glory but we can praise You for doing it. Thank You Father, that You are there for us, meeting our every need. In Jesus name. Amen.*

SUNDAY – GOD'S SPECIAL DAY – THE LORD'S DAY

Years ago, I decided to honor the Lord on the first day of the week, the day Jesus conquered death. The early Christians would gather together on this day and with combined voices and hearts they would honor the Lord, praise his name, and bow at his feet. They would baptize new converts and share the Lord's Supper. Christians throughout two thousand years of church history have followed this practice observing this day in a similar way the Jews would observe the Old Testament Sabbath on Saturday.

May you gather together with other Believers today. May you experience God's Spirit in your midst. May you set this day apart from all others, truly honoring the author of your being.

GOD THE FATHER

WEEK #2 - LEARNING ABOUT GOD THROUGH NATURAL REVELATION

MONDAY – GOD CAN BE UNDERSTOOD THROUGH THE OBJECTS OF HIS CREATION

Scripture: Romans 1:20

Think of an old clock that rings on the hour and half hour. My grandparents had one that sat on the fireplace mantel. It was known as a "seven day" clock, as it required winding once every seven days. If you looked inside the clock casing, you would be amazed at how those many gears and parts could possibly move in such precision as to accurately move through every minute of every day. Surely, only a person of high intelligence could have manufactured such a machine.

The Apostle Paul makes the argument in his opening remarks to the Christians at Rome that one can see the invisible attributes, the power and divine nature of God by observing what God has made. Much like observing a precision machine and marveling at the engineering ability on display, as the clock just described, God has put on display much about himself that everyone who has eyes to see can observe.

Being in India for the past five years, my wife and I have missed seeing the four seasons of North America. This past few weeks during the month of October is the first time in years we have seen tree leaves turn fiery red, pumpkin orange, and rust brown. It was a sight to behold. Never before in our lives did we appreciate something as simple as dying leaves. In seeing such indescribable sights, we thought of just how amazing it is that one being could possibly create such beauty. How could this be? The word great seems to fall short of such accurately describing such a being, such power, such awesome ability all wrapped in one, divine person.

Prayer: *Father, we are humbled today by Your greatness. No human could even begin to compete with an intelligence and power that is a hundred times that of man, and yes, even a thousand times or ten thousand times of the most intelligent human ever born. Abba Father, You are our God. All honor and praise to You. In Jesus. Amen.*

TUESDAY – GOD CAN BE UNDERSTOOD BY OBSERVING LIGHT

Scripture: Genesis 1:3; I John 1:5

First thing on the creation agenda for God was light. All of the cosmos was darkness - penetrating, cold darkness. Darkness is the natural state of the universe. Where there is nothing, there is darkness. Light penetrates darkness; it dispels darkness. Darkness cannot exist in the presence of light. Light requires outside intervention, and in Genesis 1, God is that source of intervention.

Throughout Scripture light is a metaphor for good and darkness for evil. Jesus is described by the Apostle John as the *"Light of the world"*. In the first epistle of John we learn that God is light and that in God there is no darkness. It is quite interesting then that as the Bible begins with total darkness, it ends in total light. The picture we see in the Bible's final chapter is absolute light with darkness being forever dispelled by God as light.

Every morning we should be reminded of life's most stunning truth – the existence of God. As the sun appears, night is no more. Ever notice how your fears are amplified at night? I can lay in bed tossing and turning worrying about this and that but when the sun comes up, something very special happens as light bursts through the darkness. Our fears subside and we are off running with the hopes and dreams of a new day.

When Jesus comes to bring in God's Kingdom in its fullness, as described in the final chapters of Revelation, all darkness and all evil will vanish. There will be no sickness, no death, no pain, no fear, and the absolute purity of God will be forever our existence. Every time you see the sun, think about that. *"Come Lord Jesus"*.

Prayer: *Thank You, Lord, that there is no darkness in You. We all have our dark moments, but in You we are drawn to the Light. Thank You God for light. Thanks for giving us light day after day after day. Jesus, thank You that You are the Light of the world. In Your name. Amen.*

WEDNESDAY – GOD CAN BE UNDERSTOOD BY OBSERVING THE SEAS

Scripture: Genesis 1:10; John 4:13-14

On day three after creating the seas, we read, "*God saw that it was good*".

Water is the only substance found on earth naturally in three forms: solid, liquid and gas. Each of these forms is a different substance yet each form is fully water. How can these three be of different form yet of the same substance? This is a mystery yet it is true, a fact no scientist would deny.

A common analogy for the three forms of God is??? You guessed it – water. The Bible describes God as three persons: Father, Son, and Holy Spirit. Each form is indeed fully God. The Father is God. The Son is God. The Holy Spirit is God. These are separate forms of the same one substance – God.

Over the years, many very brilliant and highly intelligent Biblical scholars have written volumes trying to explain how God is one, yet three persons. In theological terms, this is called the Trinity. Like water, this is a mystery. With Bible in hand, we know it is true, but our little minds will never fully grasp its depth.

Years ago our family spent a few days in South Carolina along an Atlantic Ocean beach. The roaring of the waves and the magnitude of the sea was awesome. One could sit in the sand hour after hour and be entertained. This reminded me of the magnitude of God's greatness. I thought, "How great must God be to create all this." Yet he did it - and not just this one beach and one little piece of the sea but all the seas and oceans in the entire world. It was overwhelming, like God was displaying his greatness for me to behold.

Prayer: *Father, how can any one living being be so great, so awesome, so beyond what the mind can think or comprehend? When I take the time to look up, I want to drop down to my knees to adore You. Thank You today, Father, for putting Your greatness on display for all people in the world to see. In Jesus' name. Amen.*

THURSDAY – GOD CAN BE UNDERSTOOD BY OBSERVING PLANTS AND ANIMALS

Scripture: Genesis 1:11, 20; Psalms 104:24, 25

Another aspect of the creation story are plants, trees, and two days later, swarms of living creatures in the seas, on land, and birds. Like other aspects of creation, God calls this good. Life has always and forever will be a mystery to us humans, whether it be plant life or animal life.

The mystery surrounding life should make us all stand up and take notice. Just this past Saturday, we were with family as my niece's little pet dog was attacked and killed by another much larger dog. One could argue that it was "just an animal", but for my niece it wasn't "just another animal". It was a living being that could receive her love and, in turn, give her love - a finite being that had a beginning and an end. At one time his little heart was pumping warm blood all throughout his hundreds and maybe thousands of tiny blood vessels. Then at one given moment it stopped and quickly got cold. His lungs were no longer breathing, and his heart no longer beating.

With every plant, one cannot begin to imagine how it can sprout up from a tiny seed in the ground, receive light, warmth from the sun, and water and exhibit real life. Who has ever seen one of the giant trees in the Pacific Northwest and not have been in absolute awe? For example, one Douglas fir is 300 ft tall, while a Mountain hemlock is an amazing 49 ft wide. Imagine that?

It doesn't take a rocket scientist nor brain surgeon to be in awe of the God of the universe; look around and observe the work of his hands.

Prayer: *Father, You are truly amazing, truly far beyond my ability to comprehend all the mysteries around me today. Thank You, Father. I behold You today. I give You my praise today. In Jesus' name. Amen.*

FRIDAY – GOD CAN BE UNDERSTOOD BY OBSERVING THE HEAVENS

Scripture: Genesis 1:14-16

Though light was created on the first day, "lights" were created on the fourth day, i.e. - the moon and the stars.

A brief study of our solar system is quite revealing. For example, the sun contains 99.9% of the matter in our solar system and its temperature is 27 million degrees. The earth orbits the sun as the moon orbits the earth, being its only natural satellite. The sun and moon cause the earth to constantly change its rate of speed.

Upon landing on the moon as the first human beings ever to walk on another planet, July 20, 1969, American astronauts, Buzz Aldrin and Neil Armstrong, read the words of Jesus from the Gospel of John and celebrated communion (Life Magazine, August 1969). They wanted to read the words publicly but Houston refused to allow it. They read to one another and shared the bread and cup. Why did the astronauts turn to the words of Jesus? Was it not that they were overwhelmed with gratitude to God for his greatness in creating such a stunning solar system? Was it not that they were very aware of who was responsible for this vast universe?

When a small boy, I would frequently see the television commercial for Frosted Flakes breakfast cereal with the animated character of Tony the Tiger describing Frosted Flakes as "Grrrrrrrrrrrrrrrrreat". The message was that this breakfast cereal was much greater than just great. It was great many times over. This is the message I get about God when I give serious thought to the universe. Is he great? Of course he is. But observing all that he created tells me he is great many times over, many, many times over.

Prayer: *Father, You are grrrrrrrrrrrrrrreat! The sun and moon and stars give testimony to Your greatness. How can it be that You being so great care about every single person on this planet? We praise You. We praise Your word, the means You chose to create everything we see around us. In Jesus' name. Amen.*

SATURDAY – GOD CAN BE UNDERSTOOD BY OBSERVING HIS GREATEST CREATIVE ACCOMPLISHMENT

Scripture: Genesis 1:26-27; Colossians 1:15-16

In the creation story, we see God's greatest accomplishment on the last day of creation. It is with the creation of man and woman that God goes into great detail. It is here that God himself is first referred to in the plural, a clear reference to the other two persons of the Trinity – Jesus and the Holy Spirit.

Man is the only living creature created in God's likeness. Almost a third of chapter one is dedicated to the creation of mankind. Then throughout all of chapter two, the Lord goes back to the creation of man and woman and expands the details even further describing their existence in the garden called, "Eden". From this point on the Bible unfolds with the story of God and his plan for mankind (men & woman).

So what does this teach us about God? If man is "like" God, made in his "image", then we should learn something about God by observing men and women. Most Bible scholars would understand "image" to mean figuratively, not physically. They interpret this to mean man has the capacity for spiritual fellowship with God i.e., having the capacity for love, for relationships, for knowing truth, wisdom, holiness and justice.

People of all religions and races marvel at the birth of a child. This is another mystery that our finite minds cannot begin to grasp. This newborn baby girl or baby boy, made in God's image, bursting with life and energy, holds the most incredible possibilities for relationships, for kindness, for purity of heart and life and for compassion. And, like God, he can create new ideas, new discoveries, new advancements and technologies and new ways of thinking and solving problems. Wow.

Prayer: *Father, You wow us with the whole story of creation. Your ability to do things far beyond us is on display. We praise You for human life made in Your image. May we, Your image bearer, make You proud today. In Jesus' name. Amen.*

SUNDAY – GOD'S SPECIAL DAY – THE LORD'S DAY

"They were continually devoting themselves to the apostles' teaching and to fellowship and to the breaking of bread and to prayer." Acts 2:42

GOD THE FATHER

WEEK #3 - LEARNING ABOUT GOD THROUGH SPECIAL REVELATION: JESUS CHRIST

MONDAY – GOD CAN BE UNDERSTOOD THROUGH THE INCARNATION

Scripture: Matthew 1:20; Philippians 2:5-8

Incarnation comes from the word incarnate, a verb that means to represent an entity in bodily form. For example, the Devil or Satan would be the incarnation of evil. In a similar way, Jesus is the incarnation of good, or we believe him to be the incarnation of God. In other words, Jesus is God personified. Thus one can learn a lot about God by looking to Jesus. The first four books of the New Testament all tell, in a general way, the same story – the birth, life, death and resurrection of Jesus. We call these four books or letters, the Gospels.

Matthew, in his Gospel, records the words of the Angel Gabriel to young Mary declaring that the baby in her womb was not conceived like all other babies but was, in fact, conceived by the spirit of God or known throughout Scripture as the Holy Spirit.

The Apostle Paul in his letter to the Philippian church describes Jesus' prebirth state as existing in the form of God being equal with God but then upon birth taking the form of a man, a common servant. He writes that Jesus "emptied Himself" upon coming to earth. For his time on earth, Jesus surrendered his divine state or position by taking on human flesh.

Christ's incarnation teaches us much about God. We learn that God took a huge step down so that we could step up. This aspect of God's nature is a behavior that we can choose to adopt. We can learn to be humble and unassuming. We can set aside any opportunity for wealth or prestige that comes our way for the sake of the salvation of other men and women, boys and girls.

Prayer: *Father, when Jesus was born some 2,000 years ago, You visited us, You visited the human family. By doing that, You revealed Yourself in ways that would be impossible to understand simply by observing nature. Today Lord, we thank You for such revelation, for coming to earth for our sake. In Jesus' name. Amen.*

TUESDAY – GOD CAN BE UNDERSTOOD THROUGH THE LOVE OF CHRIST

Scripture: John 3:16; I John 4:16

No doubt, the most popular verse in the Bible (John 3:16) proclaims God's love for the world. Twice in the Bible we read that *"God is love"*. Both of these verses are in one of John's letters called I John. Numerous places in the New Testament speak of God's love. Though, the Old Testament is three times larger than the New Testament, it rarely references God's love to us. We get this message full blown in the New Testament through Jesus Christ and his subsequent followers.

It is thus true that more love and compassion has been shown to the world through Christianity than any other religion. This is no surprise, given the huge emphasis on God's love for mankind and then as a result, man's instruction to love one another like God loves us. All religions make some claims about spiritual truths, but the one claim most obvious of the Christian religion is it portrayal of God having the ability to love and targeting the human family with that love.

Love is the foremost attribute of God's goodness. Love defines God. Anyone who can understand love can begin to understand what God is like. This is profound yet very simple.

Love is the most powerful force known to man. The withholding of love to a small baby can have devastating effects upon that child's life which will last throughout adulthood. Love shown to a child will build self esteem and give the child much confidence to face the challenges of life. Love is the single most important ingredient in the development of a child, regardless of what culture the child was born or what period of history the child was born into. God is love.

Prayer: *Father, Your love for us is indescribable. It is the reason You sent Your son, Jesus, into the world. It is reason enough for me to serve You today and love You with my whole heart. I love You Lord. Amen.*

WEDNESDAY – GOD CAN BE UNDERSTOOD THROUGH THE TEACHING AND PREACHING OF CHRIST

Scripture: Matthew 11:1; Acts 15:35

Without question, one of the most noted things about the three years described as Jesus' ministry is his teaching and preaching. One could say that teaching is the giving of instructions or the revealing of facts whereby preaching is the art of persuasion. When Jesus spoke, we see both elements. In reading the Gospels, we quickly observe Jesus instructing the common people (including the Jewish priests and religious leaders) about the nature of God - what he is like - what he loves and what he hates - what type of life is acceptable to God and what is not – and what to do to please God.

When Jesus spoke, in addition to giving instructions about God, he also challenged and persuaded people to abandon empty, selfish pursuits and to embrace a lifestyle devoted to God and his kingdom. He told stories so people would see through vain, small dreams and recognize a higher, more lofty goal. More than anything else, Jesus wanted people to enjoy the intimacy with God that he enjoyed. This appears to be the goal of his preaching and teaching.

One of the big pluses of my life has been the relationship I enjoyed with my father. I grew up following him around the farm almost every day, learning how to work, laugh, and even play. During my adulthood though I lived and worked hours away, I spoke with him on the phone at least once weekly. This relationship has significantly influenced my life. This is precisely the type of relationship God wants with all his children. Intimacy with God will profoundly shape the life of every man and every woman who responds to the call of Christ and lives by his words.

Prayer: *Father, we learn so much about You by Jesus coming into the world. Thank You today that we can know You as our heavenly Father, that You desire a relationship with us which has greater depth than any other relationship we will ever know and that will not end with death. In Jesus' name. Amen.*

THURSDAY – GOD CAN BE UNDERSTOOD THROUGH THE MIRACLES OF CHRIST

Scripture: John 11:39-44

The Bible is a book of miracles starting with the creation story in Genesis. The Gospels record Jesus doing thirty-five miracles (Nave's Topical Bible). For sure, the Bible portrays Jesus as a dynamic worker of supernatural events. Events such as changing water into wine at a wedding feast, feeding 5,000 people with a few loaves of bread and a few fish, and raising someone from the dead attracted much attention back then and would today as well. When people see things they have never seen before or that are beyond man's intellectual understanding, they stop in their tracks and take note.

Making the connection between God and Jesus inevitably leads to a much greater knowledge of God as it relates to his personal concern for individual people and his ability to defy basic laws of nature by his power. Though he was busy, maybe the busiest person to every life, he took the time to reach out to the sick, the hungry, and the lonely during his short time on earth. Indeed, this tells us something about God.

Knowing that God has the ability to do the kind of things Jesus did, one can pray with a much higher level of confidence as to seeking his intervention in human situations and problems. The Christian knows God cares and that God has the power to bring about change.

Every night before we go to sleep, Rhonda and I pray for each one of our children and grandchildren, asking God to protect them from the evil that sometimes surfaces in dreams. We know he cares, and we know he has the power. We have learned how to ask him in the name of Jesus.

Prayer: *Father, Your power is reality yet it is really difficult for our small minds to grasp. Thank You for caring about me, about my struggles and problems and challenges in life. Thank You for the power of prayer today. In Jesus' name. Amen.*

FRIDAY – GOD CAN BE UNDERSTOOD THROUGH THE CRUCIFIXION OF CHRIST

Scripture: John 19:17 & 18; I John 4:10

The cross has become the symbol of the Christian faith around the world and throughout history. Though the cross employed to crucify Jesus was a cruel, barbaric means of a tortured death used by the Roman Empire, only for the worst of criminals, it is cherished and even proudly displayed by all who follow Christ today. A large section of each of the four Gospels tells in detail the story of Christ's crucifixion. It is the picture of God himself providing a way of compensation (atonement) for all men and women throughout time. Without the shedding of Christ's blood, there is no forgiveness of sins. With his shed blood, he took our sin to be his sin and paid the price that we could never pay.

What does the crucifixion of Christ tell us about God? In the Old Testament, we get occasional glimpses of his compassion and grace, such as at the end of the story of Jonah. With the New Testament, God's compassion and grace is on display big time in the crucifixion of his Son for the sins of the world. It is repeated in detail four times immediately before we read of the birth of the church in the book of Acts. I don't think God wanted the reader to miss this part of Christ's story.

I have often wondered where I would be if God hadn't given me a second chance. By his grace, through the shed blood of Jesus, he broke the barrier that separated him and me. My sins were an obstacle to my eternal life, an obstacle that I could never overcome my own. The cross tells me of God's grace.

Prayer: *Father, all the righteous deeds in the world would not be enough for payment of my sins, but Your payment through the blood of Son is enough. For that, oh Lord, I will forever thank and praise You. In Jesus' name. Amen.*

SATURDAY – GOD CAN BE UNDERSTOOD THROUGH THE RESURRECTION OF CHRIST

Scripture: Mark 16:4-6; I Corinthians 15:17

Like the crucifixion, detailed accounts of his resurrection are given in all four Gospels. God clearly wanted this event made known. How can a man live if he dies?

We have all seen death either by loss of a loved one, friend, or loss of a pet. We know what happens when death is experienced. It is not pretty. No one wants to die. Many people refuse to even give it thought and the vast majority of people want to avoid the subject. If a person would be dead for three days and then come to life, all cable tv news channels would cover it as well as headlines of all papers.

The Disciples themselves refused to believe, until Jesus appeared to them. Imagine what that did to their faith. Is it any wonder they travelled to the four corners of the world to their death carrying the message of salvation through Christ?

No other Biblical event displays God's power quite like the resurrection of Jesus Christ. It is the culmination of all miracles to date. As a result, Jesus has impacted human civilization more than any other person.

Ponder for a moment the potential of your relationship with God. In Christ, you have the opportunity to enjoy intimacy with God as a heavenly Father, a closer relationship possibly than you have ever known in your life. Again, think about being in relationship with God. He created the world and all life, by his word. He split the Red Sea. He gave us the Ten Commandments. He came to earth as a common peasant, a carpenter's son, and did miracle after miracle until he finally conquered our most feared experience – death.

Prayer: *Father, Your power over death has given me life, and for this I am eternally grateful. There will come a moment when my body will turn cold, blue and stiff, yet by Your power, I will live again. Praise be Your name. In Jesus. Amen.*

SUNDAY – GOD'S SPECIAL DAY – THE LORD'S DAY

"And let us consider how to stimulate one another to love and good deeds, not forsaking the assembling together as is the habit of some, but encouraging one another; and all the more as you see the day drawing near." Hebrews 10:24-25

GOD THE FATHER

WEEK #4 - LEARNING ABOUT GOD THROUGH HIS INTERACTION WITH PEOPLE

MONDAY – GOD INTERACTS WITH JOSEPH

Scripture: Genesis 39:2-3; 50:18-19

Approximately 25% of the book of Genesis is devoted to the life story of Joseph and how the Lord used him to bring the Israelite people to Egypt. As with all Biblical characters, Joseph had his share of faults. His inflated ego caused much jealousy and hatred among his brothers. In spite of this, we read on several occasions the comment, *"the Lord was with Joseph"*. Even an Egyptian high ranking officer, Potiphar, recognized a divine presence with Joseph.

Sold into slavery by his brothers, falsely accused of rape by his master's wife, and subsequently jailed for several years, Joseph had every reason to hate his brothers, hate the Egyptian people, and even hate God for allowing all these bad things to happen to him . . . but he didn't. He forgave his brothers and consistently believed in the power of God in his life and in the lives of others. At the end of his life we learn one of the most amazing aspects of Joseph's life, his ability to forgive his brothers and to see the hand of God at work even when they treated him harshly with evil motives.

I want to direct your thoughts to God and his personal involvement in this young man's life. Few young men would refuse the sexual advances of a beautiful woman but because of Joseph's awareness of how this would deeply offend God, he firmly resisted the seductions of this vivacious beauty. This gives us a picture of God in the very first book of the Bible which tells us that God wants to know the inner thoughts and desires of our hearts and cares about our moral decisions. He is a personal God.

Prayer: *Father, You are so much more than Creator. You care about individuals, which means me. You care about the times I am tempted to do things which can bring great shame upon You. Father, give me Your presence today and every day that by Your power, I can be the person You want me to be. In Jesus' name. Amen.*

TUESDAY – GOD INTERACTS WITH MOSES

Scripture: Exodus 3:1-2, 5-6

The story of God redeeming his people from their plight of suffering in Egypt is the subject of the next four books of the Old Testament – Exodus, Leviticus, Numbers and Deuteronomy. The main character of this massive movement of people is Moses.

Moses was raised in the royalty of the house of Pharoah, the highest public official in the nation. As a Jewish baby adopted into wealth and power, he maintained an awareness of the Jewish people and God's special promise to them. As a young man who stood for his people, he was banished into exile and became a sheepherder. It was there while tending sheep one day, the Lord appeared to him and revealed his will to him in leading his people out of Egypt. Moses resisted, as he had a speech problem and did not see himself as this bold, dynamic leader qualified for such an enormous, leadership task. Moses' lack of ability was not a problem for God. Finally after making excuses, Moses obeys, and the rest is history. I hope someday you have the time to read the amazing story in its entirety.

In this grand narrative, we learn that God did not forget his promise to the Jewish people. He was aware of their suffering and pain. He rescued them through a man who had his share of ordinary, human weaknesses.

We almost always focus on our weaknesses not the Lord's power. God makes promises, and when he does, he does not forget his promises and never has broken even one. We live among people who are forever telling half-truths and sometimes blatantly saying things which aren't true. God is not like that.
Aren't we glad?

Prayer: *Father, You see the big picture always. When we say yes to Jesus, You promise eternal life to us. You promise to be with us in hardships and disappointing times. Thank You Lord. In Jesus' name. Amen.*

WEDNESDAY – GOD INTERACTS WITH RUTH

Scripture: Ruth 1:16; 3:11

Most ancient societies were male dominated yet occasionally a woman surfaces in the pages of history who was unusually influential in some way. Such is with the story of Ruth who was not born a Jew but by marriage was brought into the Israelite family. Upon the death of her husband, she chose to care for her mother-in-law and to find her identity with the people of the God. A leading man of the village was attracted to this pious young lady and married her. As it happens her great grandson was none other than the famous King David. It is quite unusual that we find a Gentile woman listed in the ancestry list of Jesus but such is the case in Matthew 1:5.

The role of women in the church and in society has been very controversial over the years. With equal regard for holding true to the Bible as the Word of God, some believe men only should be church leaders and others believe the Bible supports women as church leaders. Today's story is an example of God using a devout and virtuous woman in ways outside the box of expectations. In ancient Israel women were viewed as property or in a significantly lower light than men, but here in the Old Testament is a story of a *"woman of excellence"*.

We make a big mistake when we think we have God so figured out that he would almost have to ask our permission to do something outside the realm of our expectation. God is God. We need to know that. We can see how he works in general ways, but we need to be very careful about limiting what he can and cannot do.

Prayer: *Father, thank You for occasionally stretching our understandings of what You can and cannot do. Thank You for Ruth and the thousands of women like her throughout history who quietly loved and served You. In Jesus' name. Amen.*

THURSDAY – GOD INTERACTS WITH JONAH

Scripture: Jonah 1:1-2; 3:5

Listed as one of the Old Testament Prophets, Jonah gives us the greatest missionary story in Hebrew history. When God makes his covenant with Abraham in Genesis 12, he promises to bless all the nations of the earth. Over time, the Jewish people lost sight of God's plan for the world and unfortunately viewed their own race as the only people favored and loved by God. The "other" people of the world – Gentiles – were looked upon as quite inferior. The story of Jonah shatters that view of people. God sends Jonah to Nineveh, which is a Gentile city. Though at first resisting God's call, he finally obeyed, and preached repentance to the people of Nineveh. They repented and God spared the city from destruction. In the final chapter, we read of God as being *"gracious, compassionate, slow to anger and abundant in lovingkindness"*.

Many Christians are much like the Old Testament Jews. They take pride in being God's people and think the grace of God is exclusively for them, failing to see how much he yearns and desires for all the peoples of the earth to know him, enjoy fellowship with him, and to be saved.

With all the wars and violence in the Old Testament, it is easy to see the God of the Old Testament as being almost a different God from the God of grace in the New Testament. Not so. Today's story is proof. God deeply loves every race, every ethnic group, every language group and people of every religion. Through Christ, his grace and message of eternal salvation is there for them all – every man, every woman, every boy and every girl. They are all precious in his sight.

Prayer: *Father, forgive us when we think that we as Christians, as Your covenant people, are better than other people. Forgive us when we don't feel love in our hearts for peoples of other nations and cultures. Give us Your heart of love. In Jesus' name. Amen.*

FRIDAY – GOD INTERACTS WITH ESTHER

Scripture: Esther 2:17; 4:14

Though not a prophet, nor mother or grandmother of a King, the orphan girl, Esther, stands tall in the history of the Israelite people. She lived after Israel and Judah were destroyed by warring nations, after Jerusalem was burnt to the ground in 586 B.C. and its people taken captive in Babylon. Persia had later conquered Babylon and thus was a world power when the story of Esther took place. Because of jealousy and hatred toward the Jews, the Persian King Ahasuerus, ordered the destruction of all Jews scattered about the Persian Empire. His beautiful, young wife had kept her Jewish identity secret. When faced with the eminent destruction of her own people, she risked her life disclosing her identity and appealing to the King to save her people. Out of his respect for her, he provided for the safety of the Jews and to this day, Jewish people all over the world celebrate the deliverance of their people through Esther with a holiday called "Purim".

Many stories remind the reader of God's faithfulness to Christians living as "covenant" people or people of promise. God refers to those people as his own and as his elect. They are people chosen by God yet they are people who choose God. Today they exist in virtually every nation on the planet.

The Jews who witnessed their Temple burnt, city destroyed, and many loved ones killed must have wondered many times while captive in a foreign land, "Where are you Lord?" The Christian life is like this at times. Just when we are about to be destroyed by the circumstances around us, God intervenes and does the impossible. We see again his faithfulness and his commitment to his people.

Prayer: *Father, when You chose me and I chose You, I couldn't imagine the extent of Your commitment to me as Your child. Thank You, Lord, for faithfulness to me, when I didn't deserve it. Thank You Lord. In Jesus' name. Amen.*

SATURDAY – GOD INTERACTS WITH PAUL

Scripture: Acts 9:15-16; Galatians 2:20

Out of twenty-seven books in the New Testament, the Apostle Paul is the author of thirteen of them. He is known as the last Apostle and the first missionary. He was educated as a Pharisee and known to be an expert in Jewish law. Comfort, wealth, leisure, and easy living would not be words one would use to describe Paul's life. He was determined and bold in his stand for faith in Jesus Christ and promoted the message of Jesus Christ throughout much of the Roman Empire. The book of Acts ends with him in prison in Rome. Legend has it that he later was executed by the Romans.

Paul chose to live as Christ lived. He called this life the "crucified" life. He wrote in today's Scripture reading, "*I have been crucified with Christ*". He could have stayed in Jerusalem and lived a very comfortable, dignified life as a Pharisee, but he didn't. And even some 2,000 years later, you and I benefit from that choice he made.

Some preachers today describe the Christian life as blessing, blessing, blessing – meaning God will solve all your problems, heal your diseases, and make you rich and famous. Those preachers need to take a closer look at Biblical characters like Paul. Many times when people tell the truth and are honest, they and their families suffer for it. Many times when Christians speak the Gospel message they are ridiculed and scorned. When looking at Jesus, we see sacrifice and suffering bringing life to many people for eternity. This is our God. He stooped down by coming to earth. He is a sacrificing God and those people who chose to follow him will also learn the secret of sacrifice and suffering.

Prayer: *Father, many times the opposite of what we think is actually true. The crucified life would not appear to be appealing but it is a far greater life than one ruled by selfishness and greed. Lord, help me to take the higher road, to live the crucified life to Your glory. In Jesus' name. Amen.*

SUNDAY – GOD'S SPECIAL DAY – THE LORD'S DAY

"But we request of you, brethren, that you appreciate those who diligently labor among you, and have charge over you in the Lord and give you instruction, and that you esteem them very highly in love because of their work. Live in peace with one another." I Thessalonians 5:12-13

OUR BIGGEST NEED – SPIRITUAL RECONNECTION

WEEK #5 - THE LOST CONDITION OF MANKIND

MONDAY – MAN'S NATURE IS POISONED

Scripture: Genesis 3:1-3; Romans 7:21-23

The entire chapter 3 of Genesis has been monumental in the church's historic understanding of the nature of man. Theologians use the phrase "total depravity" or "original sin" to describe how man was poisoned in his thinking. Here we see man losing his innocence because of the "serpent" or the Devil. At the beginning of the chapter, Adam and Eve were walking in fellowship with God, enjoying his presence, with no guilt and no worry about their needs, having access to the tree of life and thus possessing eternal life. At the end of the chapter, they have hidden themselves from God, are cursed by God, and banned from the tree of life thus not possessing eternal life. The rest of the Bible is the story of man regaining what he lost. The Bible ends with man having fellowship with God through his Son, Jesus, and subsequently having access to the tree of life and living forever.

As medical science and technology increased during the later 1800's and early 1900's many people believed that mankind was becoming more civilized and advanced and thus had the ability to bring the Kingdom of God to earth, putting an end to all social evil. WW I and WW II was then quite the wake-up call with approximately 60 million people dying. Such massive loss of life is staggering by any imagination. Wars, violence, and deception is the story throughout human civilization.

The Apostle Paul writes, "Oh wretched man that I am. Who will set me free from this body of death? (Rom. 7:24)" Through the shedding of Christ's blood, one is free from the penalty of sin, but his sin nature still remains.

Prayer: *Father, all around we see the result of man's sin. Our heart longs for the day when the curse of Adam will finally be no more and righteousness will reign throughout the land. Come, Lord Jesus. Amen.*

TUESDAY – THE FISH BITES THE WORM

Scripture: Genesis 3:4-6; James 1:14-16

If the fish only knew that imbedded in the worm is a sharp hook, he would certainly think twice before biting the tasty looking worm. Unfortunately, the desire of the flesh wins in many cases resulting in death. If Eve only knew the price she would pay for giving in to temptation, she would have run the other way as fast as she could run upon hearing the voice of Satan. If the drug addict only knew . . . ; if the alcoholic only knew . . .; if the schoolboy cheating on the exam only knew . . . ; if the businessman cheating his customers only knew . . .

The story of Joseph being tempted by the beautiful wife of his Egyptian master is a lesson for us all (Gen 39:1-9). Attracted to Joseph, she made sexual advances toward him, a young man. How did Joseph react? By the power of God he resisted and explained, "How could I do this great evil and sin against God?" He realized this would not only be a sin against her, her husband, his parents and family, but most of all, it would be a sin against God. His behavior would have blatantly offended God.

We are tempted to live like animals being led around by the desires of our bodies, whether it be through food, drink, sex, selfishness, greed, dishonesty, arrogance, or envy . . . and the list could get quite long. When we come to faith in Christ and experience his grace, the Holy Spirit takes control of our lives and though we still have the animal urges and are not perfect, those animal urges no longer direct our lives.

Prayer: *Father, it is because of the cross that we no longer live a life of defeat and guilt. Yes, we may occasionally sin, but sin is not our Master. You are. Thank You for claiming us for Your own. In Jesus' name. Amen.*

WEDNESDAY – WHERE ARE YOU?

Scripture: Genesis 3:8-10; Luke 19:10

What is the reaction when the child is caught taking the cookie out of the cookie jar? Does little Johnny quickly look mom in the eye and tell the truth? Or does he try to quickly exit the room, or possibly hide the cookie, or hang his head in shame avoiding eye contact? It is so amazing how human nature has not changed in thousands of years. Avoidance is a definite part of the story in the "fall of mankind".

When God came to the garden to be with Adam and Eve, they were hiding. They were avoiding him. They felt the guilt and didn't want to face him. Adam had a good excuse for hiding . . . because he was naked. God immediately knew what had happened as previously they were naked and not ashamed. The real issue was not a lack of clothes but disobedience, guilt and shame.

As far as we know, animals don't feel guilt. Guilt is a human thing. Through training, man can induce guilt on pets, such as with a dog, but it is only natural with humans. It is true that we will never stop hiding, never stop running, until we run into the arms of God and experience his forgiving grace.

No other religion offers a solution for guilt. I spoke with a Muslim young man on the steps of the Taj Mahal one day and inquired about his life. He was quite open and briefly shared how he tried to please Allah but still sinned and felt much guilt. I asked him if there was anything in his religion that would take away guilt. He could not answer me, and I knew why. . .

Prayer: *Father, thank You for providing the solution to our biggest problem. Thank You that through Christ, there is forgiveness and with forgiveness, no more living a life of guilt and shame. In Jesus name. Amen.*

THURSDAY – BLAME IS THE GAME

Scripture: Genesis 3:12-13; I John 1:9

The first three chapters are foundational to the whole Bible. If you haven't read the Bible much, make sure you know the content of these chapters before you read much else.

Another interesting aspect of our humanity is the tendency to blame others for our wrong actions. Adam's first response when God found him was to blame Eve. Then what does Eve do but blame the Devil. Both follow the precise same pattern. Like Adam and Eve, we are tempted to blame others and make excuses, doing everything but accepting responsibility for our own actions.

When Moses came down from the mountain with the Ten Commandments and found the Israelite people worshiping a golden calf, did Aaron, their leader, take responsibility? Not. Though he had instructed them to bring him the gold from their jewelry and had himself fashioned the golden calf, yet he told Moses that he threw the gold into the fire and "out came this calf". Oh really?

This problem we all have not only leads us to sin but it also leads us to blame others and avoid taking responsibility. Though I have known the Lord Jesus since the age of thirteen, my first reaction when in an awkward situation, through my own doing, is to shift blame. It is then the Holy Spirit speaks to my heart and, most of the time, I do the humbling task of owning up, apologizing to those involved and apologizing to the Lord, seeking his forgiveness.

Taking responsibility is one of the most important things to learn. Though many people around us might display a victim mentality, God wants us to man up and walk a higher road – a road which will yield maturity, depth and purpose.

Prayer: *Father, thank You for the work of the Holy Spirit in our lives, when he taps us on the shoulder and moves us to resist blaming others and making excuses. Thank You that in Jesus, we don't have to stoop to low-life behavior. In Jesus' name. Amen.*

FRIDAY – RAMIFICATIONS OF EPIC PROPORTIONS

Scripture: Genesis 3:16-17; Revelation 22:2-3

After hearing all the excuses given by Adam and Eve, God cursed the devil, spoke judgment to Eve, and then to Adam. God condemned the serpent (the devil or Satan) to crawling on the ground and then told him there would be strife or harsh feelings between him and the woman. It is interesting that in general, women are not as likely to fall prey to criminal activity. They seem to recognize Satan's tricks a little quicker than men. Pain in childbirth is Eve's punishment.

When God speaks to Adam, he curses the ground and informs him that from now on things are going to radically change, as to living off the land. Only by hard work and sweat will the ground now yield fruits and vegetables. The natural state of the ground will be weeds, thorns, and thistles. For both man and woman, life is going to become quite a struggle and then back to dust it is.

I have often wondered if the ground were not cursed, would its fruits and vegetables be so pure and full of nutrition that people would live forever? Years ago I read a study of the human heart which concluded that technically the human heart should live forever. There is seemingly no explanation why the heart ages. It appears we actually were made for eternal life, but then something mysterious happened. I think our chapter today might speak to that mystery.

History reveals a picture of intense and exasperating struggle for human survival. It is a struggle to give life, as a woman giving birth. It is a struggle to sustain life for the man. And at the end of it all is a grave.

Prayer: *Father, we live under a curse that will only be lifted when Your Kingdom comes. We know this will happen only through Jesus and with his coming again. We praise Jesus today for giving us this precious hope. Come, Lord Jesus. Amen.*

SATURDAY – ACCESS TO THE TREE OF LIFE IS BANNED

Scripture: Genesis 3:22-23; Revelation 22:2

The final part of Genesis 3 is God speaking to Jesus and the Holy Spirit. Here we learn why man was banned from the "garden of Eden". In the garden was the "tree of life". Apparently whether we say this tree is symbolic of a source of life or if we say it is a literal tree, either way it was life-giving, eternal life-giving. If man now being a sinner by nature could eat of this tree, God's Kingdom would be forever polluted. God could not allow that so the picture we see is God driving man out of the garden and God making it impossible for man to enter the garden, in his fallen state.

Now let's move to the last book of the Bible, the last chapter, and we find a more detailed description of the tree of life, when there is no more curse and the ban to the garden is lifted. Here we read that this tree will be a significant factor in the healing of the nations (peoples). When Jesus comes and brings the Kingdom in its fullness, there will not be strife, hate, violence and war. These horrendous wounds will be forever healed. In the previous chapter, it states there will be no more death, mourning, crying or pain.

It is really amazing how the Bible ends with a similar picture as its beginning - mankind in perfect fellowship with God enjoying life in its purest form – no envy, no jealousy, no bullying, no deceit, no arrogance, no false pride, no hate, no poverty, no sickness, no lust, and no selfishness. When I seriously ponder life in that way, I think to myself, "Can it be true?" "Can it really be true?"

Prayer: *Father, thank You that it is true. It is really true. Thank You for Your presence with me in this life, until Your Kingdom finally comes in its fullness. In spite of all that is wrong, thank You for all that is right and good. In Jesus' name. Amen.*

SUNDAY – GOD'S SPECIAL DAY – THE LORD'S DAY

"I will tell of Your name to my brethren; in the midst of the assembly I will praise You." Psalms 22:22

OUR BIGGEST NEED – SPIRITUAL RECONNECTION

WEEK #6 – FORGIVENESS WITH A PRICE

MONDAY – JESUS IN THE OLD TESTAMENT: ABRAHAM OFFERS HIS ONLY SON

Scripture: Genesis 22:9-13

Christians read the Old Testament through the lens of Jesus Christ. We try not to read into the text something that is not there, but there are obvious references to Christ throughout the book. One such obvious reference is found in Genesis 22 with the story of God instructing Abraham to take his son to a mountain and offer him as a sacrifice. Abraham knew the Lord would provide a lamb and was thus faithful to follow God's instructions. It wasn't until Abraham had the knife over his son that God intervened and miraculously provided a lamb.

The picture of a father offering his only son as a sacrifice certainly reminds us of God the Father sending his only Son into the world, knowing that he would die on the cross a sacrificial death. Jesus is thought of as the "Lamb of God". He is the Lamb God provided for us. We should be on the cross for our sins, but God intervened and provided a sinless, sacrificial Lamb.

I am convinced that nothing good happens without sacrifice. My wife's father worked two jobs during much of his adult life so his three daughters would have the opportunity to go to college. All three went to college. His sacrifice was great.

Sacrifice is a key component of our faith, and it begins with God. Grace is freely given but the price paid for us to be forgiven is a high price. God gave his only Son for a reason. Jesus' shed blood was payment for my sin, for your sin. He was the sacrifice given whereby through forgiveness of sin, we could be reconnected to God, be brought back into fellowship with God, and enjoy him forever.

Prayer: *Father, thank You for the sacrifice You have made and for the sacrifices made of all the people before me so that I could walk in newness of life. Help me to learn the secret of sacrificial living. In Jesus' name. Amen.*

TUESDAY – JESUS IN THE OLD TESTAMENT: THE BLOOD OF THE LAMB IS POWERFUL

Scripture: Hebrews 9:22; I John 1:7

The old hymn by Lewis E. Jones says it well, "Would you be free from the burden of sin? There's power in the blood, power in the blood. Would you o'er evil a victory win? There's wonderful power in the blood." As a child growing up in rural Union County, Indiana, I sang that song with my family in church many times.

When the Hebrew people were in Egypt as slaves, God used Moses to lead them out of Egypt and into their own land. Pharoah, the leader of Egypt, resisted such an exodus until God sent ten plagues upon the Egyptian people, the last one being a plague of death. In this last plague (Genesis 12), God sent the angel of death throughout the land killing the firstborn of all the people. He wanted to redeem the Hebrew people, so he told Moses to have each family kill a lamb and paint the blood of the lamb over their doorposts and wherever the angel of death would see the blood of the lamb, the angel would pass over that home.

The spilling of innocent blood for the forgiveness of sin was instructed by God to Moses for the Hebrew people and was practiced all throughout the history of Israel. Blood is thought to contain the life of the animal. To shed its blood is to bring about death. Because sin always results in death in some way, the shedding of blood because of sin was a very powerful and moving, awkward reminder of the seriousness of sin. All of this shedding of blood for the forgiveness of sins was a foreshadow of the shedding of Christ's blood as a once and for all sacrifice for all sins.

Prayer: *Father, through the blood of the Lamb of God, may the angel of death pass over me and my family. When I take communion in church and take the cup, remind me, Lord, of Your power in the blood of Christ. In Jesus' name. Amen.*

WEDNESDAY – JESUS AS THE LAMB OF GOD

Scripture: John 1:28-29; Revelation 5:11-13

John the Baptist made the connection between the Old Testament concept of the sacrificial lamb, when John first saw Jesus. He was baptizing in the Jordan River and Jesus came to him. Picture Jesus walking down a hill to a small lake where John was standing and all of a sudden, there stands Jesus. Jesus must have been silent as nothing is recorded about him speaking. Evidenced by the word, "Behold", John is overwhelmed. In today's terms, he might have said, "Holy smokes!" More than any other person on the planet, John knew who this man was, who was standing before him. His words? "Behold the Lamb of God who takes away the sin of the world!"

In this bold proclamation, we learn of Christ's reason for coming to earth – take away sin. Because of God's instructions to the Hebrew people, this could not be done without the shedding of blood in a sacrificial manner. Jesus was to be that sacrificial lamb . . . and John knew it.

The picture at the end of history is a scene in heaven with every created thing that had ever lived – people, birds, cows, dogs, cats, rabbits, pigs, horses, elephants and fish – they are speaking - all in unison speaking. Imagine that scene! What do they say? "To Him who sits on the throne, and to the Lamb be blessing, and honor and glory and dominion forever and ever."

The more I learn about who Jesus really is, the more I want to be with God's people every Sunday, and I mean every Sunday. I want to stand in that company and honor him as he truly is – the Lamb of God who takes away the sin of the world.

Prayer: *Father, it is such a privilege to use our mouths to offer You praise. We stand in awe at the Biblical story. Who are we to inherit such things? Who am I to be Your child? For all eternity, Father, we praise You. In Jesus' name. Amen.*

THURSDAY – JESUS IS THE FINAL SACRIFICE

Scripture: John 19:28-30; Hebrews 9:11-12

When dying on the cross, Jesus said, *"It is finished."* For a long time in my Christian life, I wondered what was the "it". What is finished? Was it his life? Was it his mission? Was it the punishment by Roman soldiers?

Many scholars say Jesus was referring to his mission – the completion of the task the Father has put before him. That may be true, but I have thought in recent years it could possibly have been the Old Testament complicated and complex system of blood sacrifice. Ever read the book of Leviticus? It is the priestly laws, as given by God, to Moses for the blood sacrifice of bulls, goats, lambs, and birds, doves, and pigeons. It also includes grain sacrifices given as burnt offerings for sin, offerings for guilt, and offerings for peace. There are detailed instructions for the type of linens the priests are to wear, even down to the type of underwear that is to be worn and how to properly consecrate all these things. Each time I read it, I thank God that we are not saddled with the burden of performing and doing all of these many things precisely as God had instructed the Jews. It was a burden that even they couldn't bear.

When Jesus' blood was shed, it was the culmination of all the innocent blood shed of creatures, thousands and thousands of them, over a period of some 2,000 years. When the blood of Christ was shed, that was enough. His blood was that powerful. No more. No more innocent creatures dying. No more shedding of blood. It was finished.

When we take communion, we remember God's final sacrifice - *"Do this in remembrance of Me"*.

Prayer: *Father, again, thank You for Jesus. Thank You that we can simply repent and believe to receive eternal life. Thank You that we can be baptized and partake in the Lord's Supper. Thank You, Father. In Jesus' name. Amen.*

FRIDAY — JESUS PAID A DEBT THAT YOU COULD NOT PAY

Scripture: Colossians 2:13-14; Hebrews 10:11-12

Most of us know what it is to be in debt. Some might have had or presently have credit card debt and some might have debt on a house or car. Some teen-agers borrow ten or twenty dollars from a friend and have learned what it is to "owe" another person. When you owe someone a debt and can't pay them, you usually avoid them. It is awkward being in their presence as you don't know what to say. Owing someone when you can't pay them usually creates distance between you and them.

With the great gift of life God has given us and with being made in his very image, we owe him a lot. We want to live right and do right only we wind up falling short, and this bothers us. We avoid God but don't understand why. As the years go by, our hearts get harder and more calloused, and we become farther away from God.

We look around and see that we are morally just as good as this or that person who goes to church so we rationalize and think, "Why go to church?" The truth is that our conscience bothers us, and going to church is not a pleasant thought.

The devotions of this week have been quite "heavy". We have learned that God has provided us the very answer to our biggest problem — sin and death. Let's get personal. Jesus died for every bad thing you have ever done or said. And he died for everything you should have done and didn't do or didn't say. And yes, some day you will die. The question is how will you die? Will you die in guilt? Will you die making excuses? Or will you die forgiven?

Prayer: *Father, thank You for paying my debt. My debt was too much for me to ever pay, and You loved me enough to provide the way for me to be free of guilt. I don't have to avoid You. I can be intimate with You and enjoy Your fellowship forever. In Jesus' name. Amen.*

SATURDAY — JESUS BREAKS THE CHAINS OF DEATH

Scripture: Mark 16:4-6; Philippians 3:10-11

The Apostle Paul speaks about knowing him, meaning Christ, and knowing the power of his resurrection. Paul obviously believed both of these things were possible and no doubt had witnessed many others who had experienced this kind of life transformation.

Because of the resurrection, we know Jesus lives. Throughout some two thousand years of history since his death, thousands and even millions of people have testified that he is alive, and they know him. How can anyone argue with that? Usually if two or three people say they have seen something, we believe them, but thousands and millions? With the sin problem solved, the door is open to know Jesus and thus to know God. It is not rocket science.

It is instinct in every creature to fear death. Being raised on a farm, I have had to cull weak pigs. This means killing them. It always bothered me to see a little pig struggle to live. What does it have to live for? Yet, it wants to live. God has put this desire for life in every living creature. We want to live, not die.

Jesus came to break the curse of Adam so that we can live in the power of his resurrection. We were not born to die, but to live. We were not born to go day by day beating ourselves up in guilt or thinking we are victims of a bad childhood or prejudice or lack of education or poverty or sickness. The list goes on and on. Through faith in Jesus, God gives us real power — power greater than death — resurrection power - power to say yes to every day, in spite of all that is wrong with us or our world.

Prayer: *Father, You have the key to real life, and we see it more and more. Oh Lord, through the crucifixion and resurrection, we learn so many things about living. We praise You and honor You for life and all the possibilities it holds. In Jesus' name. Amen.*

SUNDAY — GOD'S SPECIAL DAY — THE LORD'S DAY

"I have proclaimed glad tidings of righteousness in the great congregation; behold, I will not restrain my lips, O Lord, You know. " Psalm 40:9-10

OUR BIGGEST NEED – SPIRITUAL RECONNECTION

WEEK #7 – THE CALL TO REPENT

MONDAY –   IT BEGINS WITH A CALL

Scripture: Matthew 3:2; Acts 2:38

The thinking of most Jewish people throughout history is that religion is by birth or blood. You have no choice if you are born a Jew. You would understand yourself to be Jewish and therefore a child of God. The concept of becoming right with God by hearing a call to repent was foreign to the Jewish people of Jesus' day.

When John the Baptist, Jesus, and the Apostles called people to repent, they appealed to them. The people first had to hear and understand this call. In the case of John the Baptist, it was to a group of people whereby Jesus called people to repent individually. In the book of Acts we find the first example of a call to repent coming forth in a sermon to a very large crowd.

A few minutes ago, the telephone in my office rang. Yes, it was what we think of as a "call". A voice from another person came to my ear. My brain processed the words from that voice, and I responded appropriately. In my church denomination, a congregation will issue a "call" to a pastor, which means the people have communicated their desire to the pastor for him to come and be their minister.

Today the call to repent, believe, and be baptized can be issued either individually or corporately, but it requires understanding that a specific appeal or request has been made to the unbeliever or non-Christian. The call, whether verbal or written, is usually issued by a believer, or in many cases by a preacher, but it is recognized to be from God. God speaks, not just man. God has a request. God is calling, and this is no ordinary call.

Prayer: *Father, You desire us to come to You. You call us to come to You. You are not satisfied when people are distant and stand aloof. May many people today hear Your call in their hearts. In Jesus' name. Amen.*

TUESDAY – IT LEADS TO DROPPING THE FACADE

Scripture: John 4:15-18

A façade is defined as a showy misrepresentation intended to conceal something unpleasant. In growing up, we quickly learn how to put on a façade. When having a difficult day and someone asks, "How are you today", what do you say? Most people simply smile and say "Fine", when really they are not fine. People can actually feel very crappy and be mad at the world and still smile as if everything is great, when it is not. We see this all the time. We even can do it with God, when God calls.

When Jesus reached out to the Samaritan woman at the well, he took the conversation to a deeper level. He inquired about her husband. He knew she presently did not have a husband. When she responded that she did not have a husband, to her surprise, Jesus said, ". . . *you have had five husbands, and the one you have now is not your husband . . .*" At that moment, all the pretense and show went out the window. Her façade meant nothing, and she knew it.

To truly hear God's call in your heart is to come to the point when you realize the game is over. Your façade is no longer working. The Lord sees you as you really are. For some people, this is quite frightening and intimidating.

You can never truly respond to God's call to repent if the façade is not dropped. True repentance always involves standing before the Lord as you are with all warts showing. No, he will not condemn you or make you toast. He is standing with arms wide open waiting for you to get real.

Prayer: *Father, thank You today that I can trust You enough to let down my guard and for a few brief moments allow myself to be seen as I truly am. Thank You for Your call for me to repent. It is the beginning of a new day. In Jesus' name. Amen.*

WEDNESDAY − IT IS AS EASY AS SAYING, "I AM SORRY"

Scripture: Genesis 50:16-17

"I am sorry" are three words that can significantly change about any relationship − father/son, mother/daughter, brother/brother, sister/brother, friend/friend. Why are these three words so hard to say? What is there about seeking forgiveness that goes against the grain of our humanity?

One of the most touching stories in the Bible is in Genesis 50 when Joseph's brothers come to him seeking forgiveness for their nasty, despicable behavior. Joseph had every right to disown them as they tried to disown him, selling him as a slave. He had every right to be angry at them and to give them back a little bit of what they had given him. In this story, they appeal to him to forgive them. They end their appeal by admitting that they did him wrong. What is Joseph's response? He wept. It was obvious that he received their apology and did forgive them with much love shown. How rare this happens in families but how beautiful it is when it does.

God doesn't ask that you be born of certain lineage to be his child - to be included in his covenant people. He doesn't ask that you make a large contribution to the church or to clean up your act before coming to him. He knows your every thought, both good and bad. He knows every shameful thing you have ever said or done. There is nothing you could tell him about yourself that he doesn't already know. He only asks that you admit your wrong and seek forgiveness through the shed blood of Christ. Why is that so hard? If you have never done that before, today may be a very special day in your life.

Prayer: *Father, there are so many things in my life that have gone wrong. I want to get this right. I want Your forgiveness through Christ's shed blood on the cross for me. Forgive me Lord for . . . .*
I receive You, Jesus, in my heart. I believe You are the only Son of God and commit my life to You today.
Thank You for taking me and including me in Your special family. In Jesus' name. Amen.

THURSDAY — IT INCLUDES CONFESSION

Scripture: Matthew 10:32; Romans 10:9

Most all churches who put a great emphasis on Bible teaching will also guide new believers into a "confession of faith" or some call it a "profession of faith". Many times this is done when a person is baptized or when joining a church.

Standing before people and putting one's belief and faith into words is easy for some people but more difficult for others. Some of the most touching professions have been by people who everyone knew to be quite shy and for them to speak in public in any form would require a miracle.

The distinct memory of a young lady from my first pastorate near Huntington, Indiana, comes to mind. When explaining to her the importance of confessing Christ, she protested saying the last time she stood up to speak in front of others, she vomited. "Do you want me to vomit in church before everyone", she argued.

I challenged her to trust God that he would empower her to do something she could never do without him. Driving home that day, I panicked. "Lord what if she does trust you and then she vomits in church?" You know the rest of the story. She confessed Christ. That young lady experienced first-hand the power of God.

Confessing Jesus before others moves our faith from the private world of "me and Jesus" into the public realm. This was important to Jesus. How are people going to hear the amazing story of Christ unless people speak it, write it, and live it? Jesus makes it clear that he is concerned about all the peoples of the world. He wants the message of salvation to penetrate every crack and crevice of human civilization.

Prayer: *Father, thank You for all of Your people who have confessed their faith to their families, their friends and neighbors, their church, and to the world. They are precious in Your sight. In Jesus' name. Amen.*

FRIDAY – IT IS MORE THAN WORDS

Scripture: I Corinthians 4:20; James 2:14-17

Yesterday's devotion put a great emphasis on confessing Christ, which is hugely important. With that said, we need to also be reminded of putting too much emphasis on words. The Apostle Paul certainly reminds us of this very thing when he states that the Kingdom of God does not consist of words.

We all know talk is cheap. We have all been deceived by clever people who know how to use words to further their own selfish agendas. In our excitement over someone who says the right words about our Lord, we need to also keep in mind that if logical actions do not follow words, then most likely the words were hollow and empty.

Discipleship is a journey allowing the Holy Spirit of God to purge selfish ways of thinking and acting. Discipleship is learning to adopt Christ's mind and heart and subsequently making lifestyle changes and adjustments that reflect the reality of God's Kingdom in our lives. Discipleship is allowing the mind of Christ to penetrate every aspect of our minds so that others around can say, "She has the mind of Christ" or "He has the mind of Christ".

Lifestyle changes do not usually come about quickly. Worldview changes do not come about quickly. Yes, we can quickly hear the Lord's call, quickly be convicted of our sin, quickly repent of our sin and receive forgiveness, and quickly confess Jesus to be our Lord. When the old self begins to drop away, the new self emerges, not instantaneously, but over a period of time – weeks, months, and years. After the new believer begins to mature, fruit of the Spirit will surface. For most of us, this happens after much push and pull of life.

Prayer: *Father, thank You for beginning a work in us. Thank You for Your patience and perseverance in molding and shaping us in the image of Your Son, Jesus. In His name. Amen.*

SATURDAY – IT WILL ALWAYS CHANGE YOUR DIRECTION

Scripture: Luke 13:3; II Corinthians 5:17

Which direction is your life going? It is up or is it down? Hopefully it is up. By the fact you are reading this devotional, and have made it this far, is indication that your direction is up, not down.

Out of all the Biblical characters, which one do you think mentions hell and eternal punishment more than any others? Did you guess Moses? David? Ruth? Paul? Mary? Wrong. It is Jesus. He mentioned it time and time again because he knew its reality more than any other person to ever live. He knew the results when men and women choose to ignore his call and go the path of selfishness and deceit. Evil is not pretty. When man embraces evil, human misery runs rampant. Think of Adolf Hitler and Joseph Stalin. Think of the murders, the child abuse, the cheating and stealing, and the adultery. It all lays at the feet of evil. Satan sends the spirits of darkness into this world dressed in the garb of entertainment and fun, but the bottom line is anything but entertainment and fun. It is broken people, broken families, and broken dreams.

When sins are forgiven through Christ and the relationship with God is restored, the new believer has a fresh and living hope which is eternal. His life now is centered in God, not centered in self. The life without Christ is like a circle with self sitting on the throne in the center of the circle. After conversion has happened and salvation has come, the picture has radically changed. Self is no longer on the throne. It is off to the side. Christ in God is on the throne now. True spiritual life has begun.

Prayer: *Father, thank You for taking people who were once southbound and turning them completely around. Thank You for all the people who have opened the doors of their hearts wide open to You. In Jesus' name. Amen.*

SUNDAY – GOD'S SPECIAL DAY – THE LORD'S DAY

"I will proclaim your name to my brethren, in the midst of the congregation I will sing your praise." Hebrews 2:12

OUR BIGGEST NEED – SPIRITUAL RECONNECTION

WEEK #8 – THE CALL TO BELIEVE

MONDAY –   IT IS SOMETHING VERY PERSONAL

Scripture: John 11:23-26

Remember the comic strip Peanuts? Remember the voice of the parent? It is always a muffled sound, something like "wah, wah, wah". One gets the feeling that the characters of Lucy and Charlie Brown never really listen when the parents speak. Yes, they hear the words but the words have this monotonous, hum drum, flat kind of effect. Many times the spiritual truths we hear, attending Sunday School and worship throughout childhood, get to be something like "wah, wah, wah".

When reading the story of Jesus interacting with Martha, as she was grieving the tragic death of her brother, I think of the comic strip Peanuts with the parents speaking. Jesus tells her a most amazing, profound truth in stating that her brother would *"rise again"*. By Martha's response, Jesus' voice was like "wah, wah, wah". She didn't begin to comprehend the truth of what he had just said. Jesus responded the second time with much more detail and then point blank, almost as if to get in her face, he said, *"Do you believe this?"*

In August of 1978, my heart was ripped apart with the pain of grief, through the loss of our baby girl, Joni Annette. I attended church the following Sunday but didn't hear a word the preacher said. I remember nothing about the funeral message. It was not until weeks and months later that the words I had heard many times over throughout my childhood began to sink into my mind concerning resurrection of the dead. It was no longer a matter of doctrinal truth like wah, wah, wah. Jesus got my attention, and his words were the same as to Martha, *"Do you really believe this?"*

Prayer: *Father, You give us words of life, words which are true, words which are alive and bursting with real hope. Thank You that we can believe and by believing our lives are changed and made whole. In Jesus' name. Amen.*

TUESDAY – IT IS MADE POSSIBLE THROUGH OTHERS

Scripture: John 17:20; I Thessalonians 1:5

For most of us born in the western world, where we put great value on individual decision making and independent thinking, it is more difficult for us to see that believing involves other people. Our society is highly individualistic, much different than eastern countries like China and India, where decision making always involves others, such as family.

The picture of believing in Jesus as the only son of God, believing the Gospel story, as given to us in the Bible, involves more than just the individual. Though it is within his power, God does not speak the Gospel story to people by means of an audible voice from the sky. The story of Jesus always comes through the means of human beings. Regardless of whether it is by radio, tv, a sermon, or a book, receiving the Gospel always includes the human aspect. This is God's plan. This is how he chose to give us the message.

Think of yourself. When was the very first time you heard about Jesus? Who did God use for this precious task? Was it your grandmother? Your father? Your mother? Your Sunday School teacher? Your pastor? Someone prayed for you and took the bold step of telling you the Gospel. Have you thanked that person? If they are not alive, have you thanked God for that person?

Remember this thing of believing is not just about you. It is also about others. It is also about you being that really special person in someone else's life. The obvious requirement is knowing the story of Jesus, knowing enough about the story to explain the simple steps of repentance, believing, and trusting. The circle gets bigger and bigger every day.

Prayer: *Father, thank You for all the people around the world who will be Your messengers today. Thank You for the person in my life that shared the Gospel with me the very first time. In Jesus' name. Amen.*

WEDNESDAY — IT IS USUALLY CONNECTED TO BAPTISM

Scripture: Acts 2:38; I Corinthians 12:13

As recorded in Acts 2, the very first Christian sermon to be preached, after Jesus' resurrection and ascension to heaven, was preached by Peter, on what was known as the Jewish festival, "Day of Pentecost". His final appeal at the end of the message was for his hearers to *"Repent and let each of you be baptized . . ."* At the conclusion of Peter's message, the Bible states that 3,000 souls were baptized. The practice of baptism was quite evident as the church was born and people from many different cities and nations came to Christ. Baptism was closely associated with the initial step of faith in believing.

In the Roman Catholic Church, children born of Christian parents are baptized. Many Protestant groups also baptize infants, believing this to be the practice of the early church. It is true that in several places in Acts, when adults were baptized, children are mentioned also. Lengthy arguments have been made on the subject of the appropriate age for baptism. Many Protestant groups believe that only those old enough to understand the Gospel and repent should be baptized. Both groups appeal to certain Biblical texts as justification for their beliefs.

My thinking is that if God wanted to make it crystal clear as to infant vs adult baptism, it is within his power to do so. This I know, when I preach a sermon calling people to repentance, I want to mention baptism also. I think there is a connection between believing and baptism. Though you are saved by grace through faith, you are instructed by the Bible to be baptized. When were you baptized? Are you at peace that your baptism was according to Scripture?

Prayer: *Father, thank You for giving us these signs that speak powerful messages to our hearts as well as to our friends and neighbors. You give us specific things to do as Your people. Thank You again, Lord. In Jesus' name. Amen.*

THURSDAY — IT IS COUNTERED BY UNBELIEF

Scripture: Mark 9:23-24

Believing and having faith are essential elements of the Christian life. One cannot be a follower of Christ without believing in Jesus as the Son of God. Believing is something you do. It is an exercise of the mind.

Our story today in Mark is about Jesus healing a demon possessed boy. The father wasn't sure if Jesus had this kind of power but had probably heard that Jesus was a miracle worker. When the father expressed doubt, Jesus said, *"All things are possible to him who believes."*

The father's answer is quite candid. He said, *"I do believe. Help my unbelief."*

I must have been age twelve when the elderly, woman pastor at Greenwood Evangelical United Brethren Church (a United Methodist Church now), personally instructed me to repent and follow Jesus.
At that time, I believed in Jesus, but how much did I believe in Jesus? I wish I could say my belief was big, but actually it was quite small. My unbelief haunted me. I had moments when huge doubts about God loomed in my mind.

When reading the story in Mark of this father and his unbelief, I quickly identify. Many times in my forty-nine years of following Christ, I have cried out to God in a similar way, "I do believe, help my unbelief." Remember how the story ends? Jesus heals the boy. Jesus answered the father's prayer. He did help his unbelief. Jesus has helped me in the same way at crisis moments of doubting when I cried out to him with complete honesty and transparency. He can handle our doubts and fears. He is even powerful enough to give us faith and bolster our belief if we would but ask him.

Prayer: *Father, thank You for not casting us away when we express doubts and fears. Thank You for caring so much that You take us where we are and do a mighty work in our hearts. In Jesus' name. Amen.*

FRIDAY – IT IS BEFORE YOU EVERY MORNING

Scripture: II Chronicles 32:31; II Corinthians 2:8-9

My faith and belief in the presence and power of God is not static. It does not rise to a certain level and stay there throughout life. It is fluid. A seed doesn't become a plant without stress. During dry spells, the plant is forced to sink its roots deep, which in turn brings great benefit to the growth of the plant.

One of the most Godly Kings of Israel was Hezekiah. At the end of Hezekiah's life, for a short period of time, he became proud and no longer appreciated all the Lord had done. In today's verse, we read that God left him alone to test him. It states that God wanted to know all that was in Hezekiah's heart. Though he was a very Godly man, Hezekiah's faith and belief in the Lord had its share of ups and downs.

I don't believe a person is saved one day, and then because of a disobedient moment, loses his salvation. I think saving faith is believing in the Lord Jesus Christ as Savior, the Son of God. Upon that faith, one becomes a member of God's covenant family. Like a father who sees the need to discipline a disobedient child, I see God as a Heavenly Father disciplining his children, when needed. In the case of Hezekiah, God left him alone to test him. Even though God is all knowing, God wanted to see Hezekiah's unbelief flushed out in the open. It was then that Hezekiah would take a good look at himself.

Maturing as a child is not without its ups and downs. Maturing in the faith, likewise, is not a series of mountain tops, but the valleys are there as well.

Prayer: *Father, make me grow up spiritually. Make my faith and belief become stronger and deeper amidst the storms and disappointments of my life. In Jesus' name. Amen.*

SATURDAY – IT MEANS MORE THAN YOU THINK

Scripture: Joshua 24:15; John 20:30-31

A Presbyterian radio preacher, Steve Brown, many years ago described becoming a Christian in this way. "You make the first step. God makes the second step. And by the time you get to the third step you realize it was God who made the first step." Most all this week we have been looking more closely at belief and faith, but we need to keep in mind that God first chooses us.

Jesus said, *"You did not choose Me, but I chose you. . . (John 15:16)"* By Christ's death on the cross, we have been chosen by him to believe in him and have eternal life. God will help you believe. You only have to want to believe. God will do the rest.

The decision to follow the Lord is the biggest decision a person will make in this life. It is a bigger decision than whether to marry or not to marry or whom to marry. It is a bigger decision than going to college or pursuing graduate level college. It is bigger than whether to have children or not. There is no decision that will have a greater impact on who you are and what direction you go in life than choosing to follow the Lord Jesus Christ.

Once a person truly hears the story of Jesus, he will never be the same. He either will respond with "yes" and go forward in repentance and belief, or he will resist that inner voice to his death. The person who does not have eternal life cannot blame God for his eternal state. He said "no" to Jesus, "no" to eternal life, and God has given him what he chose – eternal death.

Prayer: *Father, thank You today for choosing me. Because You chose me, I have chosen You and have determined to follow You all of my earthly days until You call me home. In Jesus' name. Amen.*

SUNDAY – GOD'S SPECIAL DAY – THE LORD'S DAY

"Let the word of Christ richly dwell within you, with all wisdom teaching and admonishing one another with psalms and hymns and spiritual songs, singing with thankfulness in your hearts to God."
Colossians 3:16

OUR BIGGEST THREAT – THE ENEMY

WEEK #9 – THE REALITY OF EVIL

MONDAY – NOT THE MAN IN THE RED SUIT

Scripture: Genesis 3:1; Rev. 12:7-9

Many people today resist talk of the Devil or Satan and jokingly dismiss such thinking as medieval, old-fashioned, and unenlightened. Artists of the middle ages would depict Satan as this man with horns and a pitch-fork, dressed in red tights. "Modern man" is thought to have moved on to a more educated understanding of reality.

The Bible certainly does not dismiss the reality of evil. It is interesting that evil is highlighted in the first few chapters of the Bible and also very much in the last book of the Bible. As I have mentioned before, Jesus spoke more about the Devil than any other Biblical character.

In Revelation 12, we learn of a war in heaven, a rebellion among God's angels. The angel leading this rebellion is referred to as "*the great dragon*", the "*serpent of old*". The picture we see is God throwing the Devil and his angel followers out of heaven and casting them down to earth. In the Old Testament book of Job, we read of a day when the sons of God came to present themselves before the Lord and Satan shows up. The Lord asks Satan where he came from. His answer? "*From roaming about on the earth. . . (Job 1:7)*" The Bible is consistent in it description of the Devil.

In the Scriptures we see evil appearing in many forms, all of them quite appealing and unrecognizable by humans. Eve failed to recognize the serpent as the Devil. King David failed to recognize the Devil when tempted to commit adultery. Satan is crafty, cunning and quite deceitful. He very much prefers that you and I not recognize him and that we not admit the possibility of a personal devil or evil.

Prayer: *Father, we are so vulnerable and so easily deceived by many things and certainly by evil. Lord, give us discerning eyes, ears, and minds. Help us to not be easily deceived but to recognize the truth and know the truth. In Jesus' name. Amen.*

TUESDAY – APPEARANCE IN THE GARDEN

Scripture: Genesis 3:1-5

One can learn many things about the Devil from Genesis chapter 3. The first thing is that he is "crafty". Some translations describe him as shrewd, clever, or subtle. When I think of someone being crafty, I think of someone who is skillful at deception. This is our first picture of the Devil.

The serpent approaches Eve and begins to engage her by quoting from God. How interesting is that? He knew she had intimate fellowship with God and viewed God's words in a very favorable light. His obvious desire was to trick her into believing that if she ate from the tree she would not die, but in fact would become wise. She failed to recognize him as someone or thing who could bring her harm, and she believed him. The truth was that if she and Adam ate from that tree, their oneness with God would be broken, leaving them alienated and fearful, quite vulnerable to the serpent's control from that point on. He knew their disobedience to God would mean spiritual death and even physical death. He didn't care.

Through Jesus, that cord linking us to God is restored, and we rise above Satan's temptations and schemes. Satan still comes to us, unrecognizable, seeking to deceive us into doing things that separate us from God and bring shame, embarrassment, and pain to ourselves and to our loved ones. We need to remember that he is always out to trick us, to make us believe something other than what is really true, that what we are thinking about will indeed give us pleasure. His deception on earth began with Adam and Eve and continues to this day.

Prayer: *Father, we look around and see so many people deceived. We see people who have believed that their choice of a lifestyle will make them happy when in truth it makes them anything but happy. Again today, we thank You for Jesus and for giving us truth to bring light to our path. In His name. Amen.*

WEDNESDAY – OBJECT OF GOD'S CURSE

Scripture: Genesis 3:14-15

Upon learning of Adam and Eve's disobedience, God immediately speaks to the serpent. He already had quite a history with this rebellious angel that had been cast out of heaven to earth. He condemned the serpent to an existence on the ground, eating dust, and then utters an amazing prophecy. Most all Christian scholars see chapter 3 verse 15 as the first prophecy of Jesus Christ.

God has put an instinctive fear in women, in general, of snakes. He not only has done this with this specific form of reptile, but there is another truth here also. God has given women a spirit that is more discerning as to Satan's ways. It is no secret that women are more likely inclined to spiritual things than men. It is no secret that men are more prone to criminal, violent acts than women.

The second part of this curse has to do with Satan and the woman's "seed". Some translations use the word offspring, but most use seed. The Hebrew word there is singular, not plural. God is fast-forwarding history, pointing to one person in history who would be struck on the heel by Satan but the "seed" of the woman would strike Satan on his head. What happens when you strike a snake on his head? We all know if you want to kill a snake you don't go for his tail but his head.

Christian scholars use this reference to point to Jesus' victory over death as being the final blow to Satan. Through the crucifixion, Satan struck Jesus on the heel, but through the resurrection, death was destroyed. If someone asks the question, "Where is the first reference to Christ in the Bible?", you now know the answer.

Prayer: *Father, thank You for giving us a glimpse of ultimate victory early on in Genesis where it appears that Satan is the victor. Thank You for victory over evil and death. In Jesus' name. Amen.*

THURSDAY – MORE THAN A TEMPTATION TO IMMORALITY

Scripture: Matthew 25:44-45

Feeding the hungry, caring for the homeless, for those in prison, and for the sick has been a top priority for Christians throughout history. Nations that have been heavily influenced by Christianity are the nations who do more to provide care for hurting people and victims of injustice. In Matthew chapter 25, the people who do these things are the ones who really care for Jesus. They are the ones whose faith is more than talk.

This story strongly suggests that people as a collective group have a responsibility to provide justice, to care for, and to assist the weaker elements of society. Jesus uses the strongest wording possible when he said that those societies who are not compassionate and caring in this manner will be cast into hell. This is much more than a rebuke.

Many Christians think only of the devil's temptation being on a personal, moral level, such as with stealing or adultery. They tend to ignore the responsibility that we in a society care for those in our midst who are not doing well such as the mentally ill, those with disabling illnesses and physical handicaps. Severe child abuse can emotionally damage a child for the rest of his or her life. They may never be able to work a job or be free from severe depression. Who will be the champions for these people? Who will commit the time and energy to creating assistance in ways that actually help? Jesus is saying if we look the other way, if we go on about our own lives, caring just for ourselves and our own families, we are turning our backs on God and the price to pay for doing that is big.

Prayer: *Father, help us to hear the cries of the poor and the weak. Help us to resist Satan's lie that those people deserve to be that way. Help us to help them. Help us to be Your eyes, and Your arms, and Your hands. In Jesus' name. Amen.*

FRIDAY – A CONNECTION TO EVIL AND LOVE OF MONEY

Scripture: I Timothy 6:9-10

Most of us would not see the goal of getting rich as anything necessarily evil. Good capitalists that we are, we might even view such a desire to conquer as healthy. In a 1976 motion picture, *All the Presidents Men*, a catchphrase was used that has since become somewhat popular, "Follow the money". The suggested meaning is that the flow of money is a common denominator for almost all corruption and suspicious activity.

The Apostle Paul in writing to a younger pastor, Timothy, clearly warns him about wanting to "get rich" and later states that those who want to get rich fall into temptation and a snare. He went on to state the well known verse, *"For the love of money is the root of all sorts of evil . . ."* Take note he did not say money is the root, but the <u>love</u> of money is the root.

This connection between evil and love of money should raise our eyebrows. Here we find something that appears on the surface to be quite innocent, such as love of money, yet it actually can be the entry point to the worst kinds of evil imaginable. Paul doesn't mention Satan in this text, but when mentioning evil, Satan is always in the background.

How many marriages are destroyed by arguments over financial matters? How many workaholics justify their greed by trying to make a living? How many lives destroyed by drugs only because some pimps were in the background making big bucks? How many young boys' minds are poisoned each year because some porno tycoon is making his millions? Here we see it - something that appears innocent leading to death.

Prayer: *Father, we see so much that falls short of what You intended for Your people. Lord, keep me from this seductive love of money that has inflicted so much evil on others. In Jesus name. Amen.*

SATURDAY – HELL - THE FINAL PLACE OF DEATH AND DARKNESS

Scripture: II Peter 2:4; Matthew 25:41

One of the most politically incorrect topics for conversation in our society is hell. Engaging people in conversations about spiritual truths is difficult and considered off limits by some, but any discussion of hell would be at the bottom of the list of spiritual topics. This is not a subject open for discussion in any circle.

Because it is mentioned in the Bible is enough reason for me to include it as a devotional theme. Jesus mentioned it numerous times as recorded by the Gospel writers. In one place already mentioned this week, he refers to it as an eternal fire reserved for those who refuse to be compassionate and generous. In telling a parable about a rich man and a poor man, Jesus describes it as a place of intense heat. The Apostle Peter mentions hell and describes it as *"pits of darkness"*.

Maybe this is the main reason I do not want to be cremated. I wouldn't voluntarily go into a room of intense heat, and I wouldn't willingly jump into a fire, and being in total darkness for much longer than a few minutes is not my idea of fun.

I don't follow Christ out of fear of hell but rather am attracted to a life of discipleship because of God's love for me and for the people of the world. The reality of hell, though, when one seriously gives it thought, is rather unnerving. When I seriously think about being in agony for eternity, it is quite overwhelming. Could it be true? Could people who clearly refuse God's offer of grace in Christ be destined for an eternity of pain, which is so off the charts, that it is unimaginable?

Prayer: *Father, Your truth is not always warm fuzzies, but it is truth. The reality of many things in this journey is difficult to grasp. Thank You again today for Jesus and our hope of heaven. In His name. Amen.*

SUNDAY – GOD'S SPECIAL DAY – THE LORD'S DAY

"For where two or three have gathered together in My name, I am there in their midst." Matt. 18:20

OUR BIGGEST THREAT – THE ENEMY

WEEK #10 – THE SCHEMES OF THE DEVIL

MONDAY – LIES AND DECEIT

Scripture: John 9:44

Many years ago, when I was in the first grade, living in Greely Colorado, while playing outside during recess on a cold day, a young girl told me that by sticking my wet tongue onto the pipe of the swingset, I would get a special thrill. Two other girls agreed that it would be great fun. What do you think I did? Yes, I did it . . . and you probably know the rest of the story. My tongue immediately stuck to the frozen pipe, and the girls ran away laughing. I had been played a fool. At an early age, I learned the disastrous consequences of deceit. Though I didn't realize it at the time, I got my first object lesson on the nature of evil.

In today's text, John records Jesus giving a detailed description of the devil. In a rather heated debate with Jews, Jesus challenged their religious arrogance. Like all Jews, they took great pride in thinking they were "sons of Abraham". They were above Gentiles, non-Jews. Abraham was their "father". Forgetting their own sinful nature, they saw themselves as children of God and were quite proud of such elite status. Jesus gave them a powerful lesson on truth by telling them their father was the devil, the father of lies. You can imagine how well they received that. Jesus also called the devil a murderer, a liar, and that there is no truth in him.

By nature, every child knows how to lie. He needs no special instruction. His true father is the father of lies. That is obvious. By God's grace through Jesus, this can change. The father of truth can reign. Praise be his name.

Prayer: *Father, I know my nature is to lie and distort the truth. I sometimes even think it is ok to tell "white" lies. Father, forgive me for every lie I have ever told or wanted to tell. Give me a love for the truth. In Jesus' name. Amen.*

TUESDAY – QUOTING GOD

Scripture: Matthew 4:5-6

Remember how everything came into being? God spoke and it happened. God's word has unimaginable power. Remember again how the serpent approached Eve? The first recorded words of the devil are in Genesis 3, where the serpent quotes God. I find that rather interesting. Knowing the power of God's words, the serpent used God's words to deceive Eve. Unfortunately, it worked, and humanity has paid the price throughout history.

Our text today is quite revealing. It is the story of Jesus being tempted by the devil in the wilderness, immediately after his baptism. Here the devil is called the "*tempter*". He tempts Jesus three times. The story is that the devil takes Jesus to Jerusalem to the pinnacle of the Temple and then to a very high mountain. We don't know if this is a vision or somehow a literal manifestation, but we do know that the devil quoted Scripture to Jesus in seeking to seduce him to surrender his life to evil. In response to all three temptations, Jesus uses Scripture, the word of God, to combat the devil. At the end of the last temptation, Jesus commands the devil to leave, calling him "*Satan*".

It is quite amazing that even the devil knows the power of God's word. We need to remember, when facing our temptations in life, that Satan knows the Bible very well. He will quickly use it to further his own agenda. When Satan uses Scripture, he always twists it and distorts its meaning. This is why every Believer should have a solid knowledge of the Bible, reading the Bible every day. This is why every Believer should find a Bible teaching church. There is power is God's word.

Prayer: *Father, thank You for Your word that is written and easily available. Help me, Lord, to develop a hunger and a desire for Your holy word. In Jesus' name. Amen.*

WEDNESDAY – ACCUSATIONS ALL AROUND

Scripture: Revelation 12:9-10

When rereading today's text, I was so inspired that I read it to Rhonda, though we both have read the Bible many times. This *"great dragon"* is called the serpent of old, the devil, and Satan. Moving into verse 10, Satan is now presented as the *"accuser of our brethren"*. He is accusing these Believers before God day and night. Wow.

At the beginning of Job we see a similar picture. Satan is making accusations against Job before God. In the book of Jude, we read of Satan arguing over the body of Moses.

I have come to believe that every soul matters to God and matters a whole lot more to the grand scheme of God's plan than most of us will even begin to understand in this lifetime. I believe there is a war fought for the soul of every person. Satan wants me. He wants you. He is there to point out before God every time we lie, every time we fall prey to sexual lust, every time we gossip, every time we envy someone else's new laptop, notebook, smartphone, house or car, every time we fail to help someone in genuine need, or to be the champion for the underdog, every time we cheat on a test or on our taxes, and every time we know to speak up or stand up and we stay silent. I think Satan will argue with God for your soul until he sees that your eternal destiny is settled.

Ever wonder why you hear a subtle voice in your mind that says, "You are no good." "You do not deserve to live." Ever wonder where that came from? I don't.

Prayer: *Father, thank You that we can overcome because of the blood of the Lamb. Thank You for the testimony of the Believers gone before us who have overcome. In Jesus' name. Amen.*

THURSDAY – SPIRITS OF DARKNESS

Scripture: Luke 8:35-36

Travel all around India and you will find the majority of people (Hindus) live in absolute fear of evil spirits and curses. Travel in Africa, where animism is the norm among tribal people, and one sees the same picture – witch doctors coming forth with bizarre treatments to do what – keep the evil spirits away. Go to the regions of the world dominated by Islam. What do you see? What do you find? Here again, one finds the majority of people, though proudly Muslim, living in fear of demons and curses. In China and much of the far East, such evil spirits can come from offended ancestors. Bottom line is an inherent recognition of supernatural beings who have the power to inflict diseases or bad luck.

The New Testament, especially, gives a clear picture of these beings and information about their origin. In Revelation 12, we read they are actually angels who were thrown to earth in a revolt led by Satan, against God's authority. The four Gospels give us many incidents where Jesus exercised his authority over demonic power, casting out these dark angels who had possessed people.

When our son was age 4, he was troubled by what some doctors call "night terrors". Though that was more than thirty years ago, I will never forget seeing his little body trembling and the look of fear in his face, as he stood in his bed screaming. With the simple mention of the name of Jesus, he stopped screaming, settled down, and went to sleep. Rhonda and I will always believe he saw something that night that for whatever reason, we could not see, but it left the room when the name of Jesus was spoken.

Prayer: *Father, thank You today for the power over evil You have given every one of Your people through the name of Jesus. Thank You that no ghost, demon, or evil spirit can touch those who are kept by the blood of the Lamb. In His name. Amen.*

FRIDAY – DEMON POSSESSION

Scripture: Mark 9:25-27

It is strange that almost every pastor in India casts out demons as a regular part of his ministry, but such a practice is rare among American pastors. Is it because there are less demons here in America? Is it because the evil spirits here disguise themselves in more attractive venues and are much more subtle in their approach? Is it because pastors in India are more in tune with doing ministry as Jesus did ministry? I wish I had a definite answer. This I know, the demon possession in India is very real. Seeing is believing.

My father struggled with a mild form of bi-polar condition, a form of mental illness many people have but are able to cope and live what most would call normal lives. In my years of pastoring, I have seen much mental illness, some of it severe to the point of complete disability. I believe there is a difference between mental illness and demon possession.

The young boy in our story today was demon possessed, and Jesus knew it, recognized it, and was not timid about taking immediate action. This evil spirit had found a home in the soul of that young lad and would not leave, and most likely would have held him hostage to his death, if not for Jesus. This story is especially interesting because Jesus' disciples had tried to cast out this demon without success. After the boy was healed, in private, they asked Jesus why they could not cast out this demon. Jesus' response - prayer.

The challenge is to be more and more discerning as to our ability to recognize demonic activity and to be deep enough in prayer to pray with God's power.

Prayer: *Father, forgive us when we soft peddle the power of evil. Forgive us when our prayer lives are so shallow and void of true Holy Spirit power and boldness. In Jesus' name. Amen.*

SATURDAY – DIVISION AMONG CHRIST'S PEOPLE

Scripture: John 17:20-21; II Corinthians 2:11

Nothing threatens the future of churches as does their willingness to see beyond selfish agendas and individual weaknesses, showing one another the love and forgiveness of Christ. This was very much on the heart of the Apostle Paul when he wrote to the Corinthian church. In the very context of forgiving one another, he states the reason for doing this – *"so that no advantage would be taken of us by Satan, for we are not ignorant of his schemes."* Without question, he saw division in the body of Christ as a scheme of the Evil One. Brothers and sisters of the faith who refused to forgive and love one another as Christ loved them were being tricked by the same force that deceived Eve in the Garden and by the same force which possessed that little boy in yesterday's devotion.

In Jesus' final prayer, chapter 17 of the Gospel of John, Jesus makes the connection between the oneness of Believers and world evangelization. He does this twice – once in verse 21 and then again in verse 23. Jesus prays that his followers would be one, not divided in two groups, three groups, fifty groups, one hundred groups or ten thousand groups – one.

He also prays that they would be perfected in unity. Many Believers think they will be perfected by their church attendance, by their offerings, by the number of Bible verses they memorize, by the length of their prayers, by their ability to preach, or teach, or sing, or speak in tongues. This unity, which is evidence of our spiritual maturity, is at the top of the list as to whether the world will hear our message. It is time we become informed as to Satan's schemes.

Prayer: *Father, we don't want to be among those who are ignorant of Satan's plans and strategies to destroy your people. Help us to be a unifying force among the body of Jesus Christ. In His name. Amen.*

SUNDAY – GOD'S SPECIAL DAY – THE LORD'S DAY

"Let them extol Him also in the congregation of the people, and praise Him at the seat of the elders." Psalm 107:32

OUR BIGGEST THREAT – THE ENEMY

WEEK #11 – THE EVIDENCE OF EVIL

MONDAY – AVOIDANCE

Scripture: John 8:31-32; 18:37-38

When Adam and Eve were nowhere to be found in the Garden, and God was calling for them, imagine how they were feeling? They had blatantly disobeyed God, and they didn't want to face the truth. Their fellowship with God was broken by the Devil's lie and now they were in their prison of shame and guilt.

In the movie, "A Few Good Men", filmed in 1992, Lieutenant Colonel Jessup, played by Jack Nicholson, is put on the stand in a military court marshal for the murder of a Marine. When in a heated moment of testimony, he boldly responds to the young attorney questioning him, "You want answers? You can't handle the truth!" Many people don't want to hear the truth, don't know the truth, and live in a complicated web of avoidance.

When Jesus was questioned by the powerful, Roman ruler, Pontius Pilate, he revealed why he had come into the world saying, "For this reason I have come into the world, to testify to the truth."

Pilate's response was typical of most politicians who have long lost their ability to know truth. He said, "What is truth?" Pilate was avoiding the truth at all costs.

Because of our poisoned nature, our first reaction to most situations is to avoid truth. Jesus said those who would continue in his word would know the truth, and the truth would make them free. They would no longer live a life of avoidance. Think about it. The Devil's work began in the Garden based upon an untruth. Jesus comes to testify to the truth. He came that people would know the truth and thus no longer exist in their prisons of avoidance.

Prayer: *Father, thank You that You are truth, and that You have given us truth to make us free. Thank You that by Your power, we no longer avoid the truth but walk in the truth. In Jesus' name. Amen.*

TUESDAY - DISHONESTY

Scripture: Exodus 20:16; Colossians 3:9

Dishonesty is closely related to avoidance. When little Johnny tells a lie, he usually avoids eye contact. Dishonesty and avoidance are like first cousins or siblings - all in the same family. Dishonesty is actually the sin where avoidance is usually the result of sin.

Since God is truth, to speak the truth or to possess the characteristic of truth-telling is understood to be Godly. People like this trait. People appreciate the truth, even though at times they don't want to hear it. People dislike people who are not truthful. Dishonest people are people who trick and mislead. Guess who does the tricking and misleading in the Garden? The Devil being the *"Father of lies"*, as described to us by Jesus, is the Master deceiver, the driving force behind all dishonesty.

In the Ten Commandments we find the instruction to not bear false witness, which is to be dishonest. In Colossians, the Apostle Paul instructs the early Christians to *"not lie to one another"*. The Biblical teaching on this subject is crystal clear.

We live in a day where "situational ethics" is popular. Situational ethics simply means that your ethics is to be determined by your situation. Ethics is your principles of right and wrong. The one who believes in situational ethics believes that you can change your principles if the situation demands it. Thinking like this, one would easily justify being dishonest one time and honest the next time, depending on the situation. This is not a Christ-like view. Granted, there might be extreme situations that would cause a person to kill or to lie, but for the follower of Christ, living in the truth and speaking the truth is the way of life.

Prayer: *Father, thank You for putting my feet on solid ground as to my desire to be a person of truth. Thank You for clear instruction through Your word to resist the temptation to speak anything other than the clear truth. In Jesus' name. Amen.*

WEDNESDAY – INSECURITY

Scripture: John 8:12; 14:6

One other common aspect of our fallen condition is our insecurity – our identity crisis. The big question, "Who am I?" usually emerges during our teen years and is like a dark shadow that follows most people around throughout life. This changes when God's grace comes. The identity anxiety lessens when we see ourselves through the lens of faith in Christ and continues to lessen the more we mature in faith.

I am amused by stories and movies of people going to India or Nepal or Tibet to "find themselves". They usually locate some Buddhist monk or Hindu priest in the Himalayan mountains and learn some new way to stare at their navel. I have been in those mountains, seen the monks, and seen the Hindu priests. I have found them to be some of the most confused people on the planet. They are the ones who would give what wealth they had to some idol in a Temple while their neighbor starved to death. Go figure.

Jesus was the only person ever born who didn't have an identity crisis. In John's Gospel, he is repeatedly saying "*I am . . .* " He says, "*I am the bread of life*"; "*I am the light of the world*"; "*I am the door of the sheep*"; "*I am the good shepherd*"; *I am the resurrection and the life*"; "*I am the way, the truth and the life*"; and "*I am the vine; you are the branches*". The dark shadow identity crisis was absent in Jesus. It is absent in those who walk in his ways.

As a pastor, I have witnessed many people truly "finding themselves" in Jesus. The dark shadow leaves. It is something that never ceases to amaze me.

Prayer: *Father, thank You for freeing us from insecurity. Thank You for giving us security and for the knowledge of who we really are. Thank You for Your light which gives us light. In Jesus' name. Amen.*

THURSDAY – ALIENATION

Scripture: II Corinthians 5:18-19

One sees broken relationships everywhere. Studies have shown that loneliness is the root cause of many illnesses. A growing number of retirement facilities are now allowing their residents to have pets which helps to combat loneliness. As we are made in God's image, we are made to give and receive love in relationships. When this doesn't happen, we suffer.

In our Scripture text today, the Apostle Paul teaches that since we have been reconciled to God, we should be about the business of reconciliation. Since they themselves have experienced reconciliation, Christians should know how to reconcile and should be agents for reconciliation.

Two people who have been alienated from one another over this disagreement or that need to be reconciled. They need to put away their differences, forgive one another and come together again as friends. This is reconciliation, which is the opposite of alienation.

We see alienation in the Garden of Eden as Adam and Eve were alienated from God. We see alienation everywhere in our world – in schools, businesses, organizations, and families. It is one of the many results of evil and man's fallen condition.

Alienation among family members reduces the quality of life immensely. It is in my family and every family I have ever known. Because of envy, jealousy, and an unwillingness to overlook weaknesses, brothers who once played and laughed together now hold harsh feelings toward one another. Sisters who deeply loved one another in childhood, later on in life seldom visit one another or inquire as to how life is going. Alienation has set in. It is not from God. It is not God's will for his people. It is the opposite of life-giving, supportive, forgiving relationships.

Prayer: *Father, we grieve the alienation in our own lives, in our own families and in the world. The devil enjoys and inspires it. We grieve it and suffer. In living for You, help us to be Your agents of reconciliation in all parts of life. In Jesus' name. Amen.*

FRIDAY – DYSFUNCTION IN FAMILIES

Scripture: Genesis 27:34-35

At the root of all dysfunction is the same sneaky serpent who approached Eve. Read the story of Isaac and Rebekah and their twin sons, Jacob and Esau, and you will learn about a highly dysfunctional family. You will read of a wife who instructed her son to deceive his father and lie to his father to steal his brother's inheritance.

The above story is being replayed time and time again in our highly educated and highly civilized society. Ask anyone who has pastored a few years and he will probably say that he could write a book with all the sad stories of dysfunctional families, but he dare not.

The breakup of American families is a shameful testimony of a nation that is looked upon as "Christian" by the rest of the world. It is very possible to have good basic morals, do honest work every day, and even go to church on Sunday, but in reality to be selfish, greedy, controlling, and manipulative people, inflicting huge dysfunction into their family systems. People can look very good on the outside and on the inside be something much different. Jesus called these people "white washed tombs". Jesus also called them "hypocrites" and "sons of the devil". They knew how to play the religious game very well. They knew how to paint themselves white. They knew the memorized prayers and wore the proper attire, smiled and waved to the crowds and kissed the babies, but one problem – it was all a big show.

The people of God today had better harken to the words of Jesus. Many are being duped by the same serpent of old, and their families suffer the most.

Prayer: *Father, help us to be the real thing. Satan is destroying marriages and families all around us. We see the pain and alienation. We see the hypocrisy. Help us, Lord. In Jesus' name. Amen.*

SATURDAY – DYSFUNCTION IN CHURCHES

Scripture: James 4:1-2; I Peter 4:8

Many times congregations become quite dysfunctional, split apart by fighting and quarreling. If the devil can cause people of a church to envy, to fight and quarrel, he will stop the advancement of God's Kingdom.

A congregation is an organization, not unlike the Chamber of Commerce. An organization is made up of people who by nature are selfish, dishonest, envious, greedy and manipulative. Do you see a train wreck coming here? It doesn't take much for any organization to disintegrate.

Usually because of a high level of commitment to a common goal, the people of an organization choose to overlook all the bad things about one another in order to accomplish that common goal, whether it be to advance the cause of local businesses or to meet the needs of a special group of disadvantaged people. When the fervency and passion for the common goal weakens, the warts of the individuals surface and become noticeable. At that point the organization begins to break down.

A congregation is comprised of many individuals as is described above. Because of their fervent commitment to advancing God's Kingdom, they overlook and tolerate one another's weaknesses and inconsistencies. When that commitment begins to lessen, these people who worked together now begin to have problems. The difference between a church organization and a secular organization is the real presence of God's Spirit among them and the ability of the people to love one another and forgive one another.

When Christ's love is shown one to another, the Spirit of the Lord encamps. God blesses this with his Spirit. When people of a congregation place personal agendas above love and forgiveness, the Lord withdraws his Spirit and the congregation becomes dysfunctional.

Prayer: *Father, thank You for the ability You give us to extend your love and forgiveness to one another. Thank you for blessing Your people, who truly walk in Your ways, with Your sweet Holy Spirit. In Jesus' name. Amen.*

SUNDAY – GOD'S SPECIAL DAY – THE LORD'S DAY

"O magnify the Lord with me, and let us exalt His name together." Psalm 34:3

OUR BIGGEST THREAT – THE ENEMY

WEEK #12 – THE JOURNEY OF OVERCOMING

MONDAY – POWER

Scripture: Ephesians 6:10-11

Power has always impressed me. When a child on the farm, I remember my father purchasing a tractor big enough to pull a four bottom plow. The thrill of pulling the throttle open was exciting. Later on as tractors got bigger and trucks got bigger, I was mesmerized by engines that could do great things. In recent years, I stand in awe as I see a large jet leaving the ground and try to wrap my mind around the amount of raw power going before my very eyes.

When facing an enemy whose intelligence and wit far exceeds mine, I feel overwhelmed at times. I need more than Tom Curry strength to survive the storm. As I look around, I'm not alone. The Apostle Paul's instruction to us is to be strong, not just in our own strength, but in the *strength of His might*. He also says to put on God's full armor.

Having proper equipment and military garb is essential in war. I can't imagine American soldiers going into Iraq with civilian clothes. They knew their enemy was deadly and real. They knew the bullets would come from all directions. They knew the importance of being prepared. And they were ready.

Christians today should be doing life as if their enemy is real, because he is. He is smart and deadly. He wants their marriage, their children, their church, and even the family pet. He thrives on death and darkness. He has many tools at his disposal, and though you may be young, energetic and tough in many ways, you don't stand a chance against him on your power. With the Lord's power, you will win. With his strength, you will overcome.

Prayer: *Father, I need You today in many ways. I need the power of Your Holy Spirit in my life. I need to rise above all the southbound ways of living and thinking around me. Come upon me, Father. Breathe on me, breath of God. Fill every part of my being with Your light and love. In Jesus' name. Amen.*

TUESDAY – TRUTH

Scripture: Ephesians 6:14

Previously we addressed the subject of honesty and dishonesty. We saw that deceit is the devil's main strategy. If he can keep us from the truth, he will control us and imprison us. Remember Jesus' statement that the truth will set you free? Remember, Jesus said he came to give testimony to the truth? Also, remember how Jesus battled Satan - with God's truth - his word?

It shouldn't surprise us that the first piece of God's armor given in the analogy of a soldier is the belt of truth. The text actually states, "*having girded your loins with truth*". A strong belt is a key part of the soldier's armor. It may not be the most visible piece of armor, but it is a very key piece. Without it, the armor falls apart.

One of God's blessings to me has been my bad eyesight. You might wonder how bad eyes can be a blessing? Let me explain. My mother was legally blind. Years ago, an eye doctor told me that I had my mother's eyes and would most likely lose my sight in my older years. This motivated me to memorize Scripture, thinking that there may come a time that I will not be able to read the Bible. This caused me to have as a goal to know enough Scripture to preach, in case I lost my sight. Within my first year, I had memorized forty verses and have since added to that number to where it is well over one hundred verses. Keeping these fresh requires regular practice. This means I roll these verses around in my mind to the point that they have stuck in my mind. A huge hunk of God's truth is stored in my mind - what a blessing.

Prayer: *Father, thank You again for truth. Thank You that we can battle our demons by knowing truth and using it in our lives. Thank You that by Your power, we can overcome. In Jesus' name. Amen.*

WEDNESDAY – RIGHTEOUSNESS

Scripture: Ephesians 6:14

Again today we are looking at the same verse in chapter 6 of Ephesians. In the analogy of a soldier, Paul not only mentions the belt but also mentions the *"breastplate"*. The breastplate of a medieval warrior protected his vital organs from attack.

If someone is thought to be good, moral, upright, just, or virtuous, we could also say he is righteous. We could refer to his character as righteousness. It is interesting that most people who have ever lived in history, regardless of their ethnic or cultural background, have somewhat of a common understanding of righteousness. Righteous people would be people who are unselfish, compassionate, kind and who have high standards of conduct. They wouldn't be liars, murderers or thieves or rapists. Their ability to discipline their mouths and other body parts would be known to all. We look upon these people as righteous.

My father-in-law, Don Morrison, was a "righteous" man. All who knew Don looked upon him in that light. This character that he possessed was a major chunk of God's armor in his life. Though he wasn't perfect and didn't claim to be, the character that he had developed protected him on many fronts. He had a high respect for womanhood and likewise hoped that I, as his son-in-law, would share that same standard. This was a good challenge for me as a young, married man. Though nothing intentional was ever said, I knew that he expected me to treat his daughter the same way he treated his wife.

The righteousness of a man will protect the vital organs of his family. His moral character will be a thick shield to protect his wife and children from the dark shadows of evil.

Prayer: *Father, thank You today for all the people in my life who have displayed and modeled righteousness to me. Give me that protective shield, Father. Put in my heart a desire to live upright, to be compassionate, unselfish, honest, and kind. In Jesus' name. Amen.*

THURSDAY – PEACEMAKING

Scripture: Ephesians 6:15

The third piece of the soldier's armor mentioned by the Apostle is the shoes. He describes the shoes as the *"Gospel of peace"*. Since I am by nature a rather feisty, argumentative person, this analogy stretches me in ways that I need to be stretched.

Irish people take pride in being feisty. For centuries in western Europe, they were primitive, warring, tribesman. The Notre Dame sports teams are known as the "fighting Irish". Currys are Irish, and my temperament fits that mode quite well. I am one that without the Lord, I would have on the back of my car the bumpersticker, "You toucha my car. I breaka you face."

I am reminded that Jesus said, *"Blessed are the peacemakers . . . "* (Matt. 5:9). Isaiah, the Old Testament prophet, made a very obvious reference to Jesus stating that he would be called the *"Prince of Peace"*. History shows that the presence of Christianity in societies and countries has contributed greatly to the lessening of tension, violence, and wars.

Learning to be a peacemaker and learning to bring reconciliation into families, organizations, and communities is an important aspect of the Christian's opposition to evil. Peace has to first come into one's heart before it can flow from one's life to others.

A shoe which does not fit properly can bring havoc to the whole operation of the body. A Christian who does not have God's peace, or a desire for God's peace, is easy prey for the devil. He can bring havoc into his church and family and community. Overcoming evil with good should be the picture of our life. Being God's instrument for peace is one of the secrets of overcoming.

Prayer: *Father, I look around and see the need for peace in many areas. We live in a world of violence. May You, Jesus, be truly the Prince of Peace in my life and in my family. In Your name. Amen.*

FRIDAY – FAITH

Scripture: Ephesians 6:16

The next item listed of the warrior's equipment for fighting is a shield. Such a shield would be used for basically one thing – to protect the warrior from swords and arrows. The swords and arrows would be intended for the warrior's death. The Apostle Paul describes this shield in the Christian's armor as a *"shield of faith"*.

We know that faith is a fundamental aspect of the Christian life. The Bible tells us that Abraham's faith was credited to him as righteousness. God spoke to Abraham. Abraham believed God. Because of this belief or faith, God declared him righteous. In Romans 4 we read that *"man is justified by faith"*. Faith is defined in Hebrews 11 as being *"the assurance of things hoped for, the conviction of things not seen"*.

Jesus asked people to believe in him. He said in John 14, *"believe in God, believe also in Me"*. Because of the obvious faith in Jesus shown by this woman (Luke 7), Jesus said, *"Your sins are forgiven. . . Your faith has saved you. . . "*

As in the Garden with Eve, we know the devil is suggesting and telling us things which are not true. God is telling us many things through his word. Who do we believe? Who do we have faith in? It is of paramount importance that we put our faith in the Lord and in his word. The lies whispered in our ears by the devil are described as *"flaming arrows of the evil one"*. When these flaming arrows come, the Christian is to immediately believe God. He is to use the shield of faith to extinguish those instruments of death coming at him at a high rate of speed.

Prayer: *Father, you know very well just how much we need a shield when we go to battle. Thank You, Father, that we can believe You and have faith, the same faith that Abraham had. Thank You that we can hold high the shield of faith. In Jesus' name. Amen.*

SATURDAY – SALVATION AND GOD'S WORD

Scripture: Ephesians 6:17

The helmet and the sword are two very important pieces of the soldier's equipment. Likewise, salvation and the Scriptures are two very important aspects of standing firm against the devil.

Salvation can be firmly in place without hesitation or uncertainty. Much to my amazement, I have heard people, who have attended church for many years, express uncertainty about their salvation. John, in his first letter, makes the connection between knowing one has eternal life and the things written down in the Bible. We have God at his word about repentance and belief in Christ. Don't we believe that? If we do believe, there comes a level of confidence in the faith of the Believer that is noticeable and attractive. It is not possible to be passionate about faith without this strong assurance.

When the storms of life come, when unfortunate things happen, when people disappoint you and you find yourself facing huge discouragement, the devil is always there at your weakest moment to tempt you where your armor is the weakest. These are defining and revealing moments. The real you comes forth, which for some people is quite frightening. Having a faith that is shallow or plastic is like a soldier wearing a helmet that is plastic, or like having a sword that is made of plastic. It might look nice, but when the real battle begins, it becomes obvious very quickly that you are in trouble.

Yes, I do wish there was no evil, no hell, no devil, no Satan, and that nothing bad would ever happen. I wish all this talk about warfare would not be true, but it is true. And the evidence is everywhere you look.

Prayer: *Father, everything about You is true and trustworthy. You are my refuge, Father. I run to You, and seek to live and exist only in sweet fellowship with You. Thank You for the power of overcoming. In Jesus' name. Amen.*

SUNDAY – GOD'S SPECIAL DAY – THE LORD'S DAY

"I was glad when they said unto me, 'Let us go to the house of the Lord.'" Psalm 122:1

SPIRITUAL DISCIPLINES

WEEK #13 – THE DISCIPLINE OF BIBLE READING

MONDAY – OUR BIBLE - SCRIPTURE

Scripture: II Timothy 3:14-17

Christians see the Bible as being the product of God's Holy Spirit moving in the hearts and minds of some forty men over a period of one thousand five hundred years. The Holy Spirit didn't speak in an audible voice, as these men simply recorded what they heard. But the Spirit was stirring and moving within them in such a way as to perfectly guide them. Because God did not dictate the actual words in a specific language, scholars have felt the freedom to translate the Bible into many different languages, resisting the idea of any one language being holy as such.

This contrasts with the Islamic view of the Koran. The Koran was written by one man, Mohammed, who claims to have heard the audible voice of an angel speaking the precise words to record in Arabic. This "dictation", as claimed, has made it very difficult to translate the Koran in any other language, making Arabic a holy language with all other languages being sub-standard and secular. This fuels the thinking of the Arabic people to see themselves as a holy people with all other peoples of the world as less than holy. This also leads Muslims to see the actual book as somewhat super holy, even worthy of their worship, as it is the very words that God spoke. If anyone would damage a Koran, it is therefore a very serious offense worthy of imprisonment or death in some cultures.

Jesus said the *"truth will make you free"*, not *"a book will make you free"*. The Christian is to seek the truth, and because the Bible is absolute truth, inspired by God, it is Holy Scripture. This "truth" can be expressed in every language.

Prayer: *Father, we live in an age of so many books and so many words. Thank You for this book and these words You have preserved for us as Your written revelation. In Jesus' name. Amen.*

TUESDAY – OUR BIBLE – THE INSPIRED WORD

Scripture: Hebrews 4:12

Christians believe God's truth in the Bible is inspired, but all languages are somewhat fluid with words meaning different things to different people at different moments in history. For example, the word "gay", when the King James Version Bible was written, meant happy and joyous. It does not mean the same to most English speaking people today, thus the ongoing need for updating the Bible in modern language.

Most evangelical, Christian groups over the years have stated that the Bible, as it was written in the original languages, is inspired. The Old Testament was originally written in Hebrew. The original Hebrew writings were inspired and without error. The New Testament was originally written in Greek. The original Greek writings were inspired and without error.

The Bible on my desk could actually have a few punctuation errors or a few misspelled words. I can believe in the inerrancy of the Bible but still recognize that the English Bible that I happen to be reading from at the moment could have some minor errors. As I study the Scriptures, it is good to seek the meaning of the text and not be hung up over the specific words used by any one translation.

For hundreds of years, the Roman Catholic Church only recognized one translation as true Scripture – the Latin Vulgate Bible. For hundreds of years, some Protestant groups would only recognize the King James Version English Bible as the only true Bible. It has taken some time for Christians to finally begin to see that there is no one translation which is forever "the Bible". God wants us to study, to seek, and to struggle to find his truth which cannot be copyrighted by any one language, church, government, or culture.

Prayer: *Father, Your word is living and active. It does inspire, challenge, and correct. Lord, give me a greater desire to know Your word and to understand the depth of its truths. In Jesus' name. Amen.*

WEDNESDAY – GOD'S WORD IN YOUR HEART

Scripture: Psalm 119:11

Today's chapter in Psalms is the longest chapter (176 verses) in the book; it is divided into 22 sections with each section named after a letter of the Hebrew alphabet and contains numerous references to God's word. Our verse for today opens the door to the possibility of treasuring God's word in the heart.

I treasure the memory of my father and mother in my heart. I treasure the memory of my grandparents in my heart. The heart, when spoken of in this manner, is not the blood-pumping organ on the left side of the chest. It is the secret place in your soul where things most tender to your being reside.

The writer of today's Psalm says that he has treasured God's word in his heart. It is impossible to treasure God's word in one's heart without being transported from worldly thinking and living to Godly thinking and living. Such an accomplishment will significantly shape the direction of one's life. It will transform people of any age, but think of the difference this would make in a young person's life. It will put him on a road which will reward him huge benefits for many years.

At age 13, I began to read a verse or two from the book of John every night before I went to sleep. It was then that my desire to know his word began to grow, and I began a life-long journey of treasuring his word in my heart. To treasure God's word is to grow to love God's word. Just as it is impossible to treasure the memory of someone in your heart without loving that person, it is impossible to treasure God's word in your heart without loving his word.

Prayer: *Father, I want to be like the author of Psalms. I want to treasure Your word more and more in my heart. Help me, Father. Help me to study, to ponder, and to meditate on Your most powerful truths. In Jesus' name. Amen.*

THURSDAY – GOD'S WORD AS PREVENTION

Scripture: Psalm 119:11

Today we look at the same verse, only at the later half. The Psalmist indicates that treasuring God's word in his heart will work as protection against sin. This is a huge side effect of treasuring God's word.

We normally think of side effects when using certain drugs and as somewhat negative. The last time I purchased drugs at a pharmacy, I opened the bottle and found a small piece of folded paper with words in tiny print. After reading all the fine print about the potential side effects, I wondered if I really wanted to take the medicine. If I put these pills in my body, these horrible things might happen to me.

Remember when Jesus was tempted by the devil in the wilderness? Remember the key role quoting Scripture played in Jesus' defense against the devil's attacks? Jesus had treasured God's words in his heart and was able to use God's words at those moments when the temptation was the greatest.

All of us are tempted in various ways. This is quite real to life. None are exempt. Sin always is appealing. Something inside us really wants to do this or that or say this or that. What will stop us? Will sheer self will? Maybe. But having God's word tucked away in the secret recesses of your soul will compose a defense that will stand strong when temptations are the greatest and human will is the weakest.

Again I think of Joseph when he was seduced by a beautiful, rich woman. I wish Joseph were here to teach us today. I have a feeling he would quickly agree that even though his human will was weak, God's word in his heart was super strong.

Prayer: *Father, it is amazing how powerful Your word really is. Thank You, Lord, that Your power is available to us through Your word. Thank You that we are not condemned to animal life, whereby our physical urges are the primary forces which drive us. In Jesus' name. Amen.*

FRIDAY – GOD'S WORD AS REVIVAL

Scripture: Psalm 119:25

One cannot be revived unless one has already been vived at some point. The Psalmist in our verse for today describes his soul as cleaving to the dust, which was always associated with death, as when the body goes to dust. This reminds me when God showed Ezekiel the valley of dry bones (Ezekiel 37). God told Ezekiel to prophesy or to speak his word over these dead, dry bones. God told him to say, "*O dry bones, hear the word of the Lord.*" You probably know the rest of the story. The bones began to clatter as muscles and tendons appeared on the bones, as God breathed on them through his Spirit, and the people came alive.

Every Christian will go through times when the fervor and energy to serve the Lord appears to be getting less. Once you were "vived", animated with great plans and passion, and possibly through unfortunate circumstances you find yourself facing disappointment and possibly even disillusionment. That which was vived now needs to be revived. The answer is "*hear the word of the Lord*". The answer is like the Psalmist who prayed, "*revive me according to your word*".

In August of 1978, every star in our heaven came down when our baby girl died. At the time, we were farming near Liberty, Indiana. Our energy to live was suddenly gone. Rhonda and I struggled to do the most basic things. People were concerned. They could see our depression. Our parents were worried. Finally through early morning prayer and study of the word, God began to revive my soul. I needed to hear from God, and I did. Since that time many years ago, I have never ceased in my daily Bible reading.

Prayer: *Father, You created everything through Your word. Your only Son is known as "the Word". That which gave us life and continues to give us life today is Your word. Oh Father, breathe on us every day and give us life. In Jesus' name. Amen.*

SATURDAY – GOD'S WORD AS LIGHTING THE WAY

Scripture: Psalm 119:105

When thinking of the Bible, think of a flashlight or lamp when in absolute darkness. Years ago on our honeymoon, Rhonda and I visited Mammoth Cave in Kentucky. During the tour, the guide turned off his light and suddenly the darkness was upon us. It was overwhelming. We could not even see our hands. After a couple of minutes, which seemed like eternity, he lit a match. What a difference a little light makes when in complete darkness. If you have ever experienced total darkness, you know the feeling.

There are many wonderful things in this world, yet in many ways, with all the uncertainties and unexpected curves, when going through life, it is almost like trying to go through a dark room without a light. The average person faces many times when decisions must be made and either way one chooses seems to be less than what God wants. Knowing how to think and what to do in life is a seismic challenge.

The Psalmist uses the analogy of a light in describing God's word. He not only states that his word is a "lamp" but even gets more specific in stating that his word is a lamp *"to my feet"*. Our feet carry us many places and down many paths. With a lamp, it is much easier to find the right path for our feet.

For the Christian, the Bible is truly that lamp. The Bible is there to commit to memory, to ponder, and to study. It is not enough for your parents to know the Bible, or for your youth leader to know the Bible, or for your pastor to know the Bible, but what about you?

Prayer: *Father, I need that lamp to light my path. I know I will face many challenging moments, and I know how dark it can seem. Thank You today for the light of Your word. In Jesus' name. Amen.*

SUNDAY – GOD'S SPECIAL DAY – THE LORD'S DAY

"The heavens will praise Your wonders, O Lord; Your faithfulness also in the assembly of the holy ones." Psalm 89:5

SPIRITUAL DISCIPLINES

WEEK #14 – THE DISCIPLINE OF WORSHIP

MONDAY – A SPECIAL WAY OF GIVING THANKS

Scripture: Psalm 105:1-3

Many years ago when I was in my late teens, I was with my father as he was taking a semi load of cattle to the Cincinnati Stockyards. It was a bitter cold, January morning, down around zero degrees. We were involved in a bad traffic accident. Nearby the scene was a house where a lady allowed us to stay to get warm and to make phone calls, without the expectation of any pay. She even served us coffee and donuts. A few weeks later, my father and I stopped at her home to say "thanks" and to offer a gift as a token of our appreciation. We felt as though it was the least we could do, in response to her kindness to us, when we were in great need.

I did nothing great before I was born that made it so that God owed me life. God's gift of life to me was not because he owed me something, but it was simply because God is good. The least I can do is to thank him.

There are many ways to give thanks. In the story above about me and my father, we thanked the lady with words of thanksgiving and with a gift. The Hebrew people and the early Christians gave thanks to God in spoken words and also in song. Yes, they would bring him a gift of material value but their greatest gift to God was the fruit of their lips in singing to the Lord.

The giving of thanks is a big theme throughout the book of Psalms. In most instances, where the giving of thanks is referenced, singing is mentioned. It is medicine for the soul and greatly pleasing to the Lord.

Prayer: *Father, we thank You for the great examples of thanksgiving we have in the many chapters of the book of Psalms. We thank You again that You are good and worthy of our praise. In Jesus' name. Amen.*

TUESDAY – STARTING SMALL

Scripture: Psalm 9:1-2

We live in a world of instant gratification. We don't want to start out on the bottom and work our way up. We want to start out on top. We don't want to start by saving pennies, slowly acquiring more. We want to start out with a big bank account. Many couples who get married don't want to start out with less expensive, second hand furniture. They want the best and nicest so they borrow money to get it. Many people who are somewhat attracted to the things of God want to start out by going to a big, fancy church with much hype. They don't want to start praising God in the privacy of their home.

Learning to give genuine praise and thanksgiving to God in song is more than singing a song about God and more than going to a Christian concert, where you see other people praising and giving thanks. It took me many years to really *"get it"* as to individual worship. I enjoyed singing hymns with other people but never would sing to God in praise when alone. My worship was limited to the larger setting.

It was only after personally yearning for ways to express my feelings of gratitude to God that I began to worship him by singing praises in my private devotional times. This took me to a whole new level of worship. It changed how I sang songs to God in church and with others. When my worship and praise in the public realm was an outgrowth of what was happening in the private realm, it became quite exciting and inspiring. I not only wanted to sing. I wanted to shout for joy to the Lord.

Prayer: *Father, thank You that we don't need an expensive church building to worship and praise You. Thank You that we can worship You while alone in our prayer closet. Forgive us, Lord, for thinking that we can only come to You to make requests. We praise You and glorify Your name. Through Jesus. Amen.*

WEDNESDAY – FROM THE CLOSET TO THE CONGREGATION

Scripture: Psalm 22:22-23

The idea of a loner Christian is completely foreign to the Bible. After one has experienced worshiping the Lord in the closet, the next huge blessing is to stand in the midst of people of like faith, joining voices with them in a chorus of praise. This is the picture we get at the end of the age, described in Revelation, as the saints of God gather around his throne with thousands and thousands of angels singing to God and praising him in song.

Throughout the book of Psalms, we find the word "assembly" or "congregation". In the New Testament in the book of Hebrews (10:24-25), the author reminds the reader to ". . . *consider how to stimulate one another to love and good deeds, not forsaking the assembling together, as is the habit of some* . . ." There must have been "some" who had forsaken the assembly, "some" who did not see the need to be in relationship with other Believers. Jesus was their Lord. They had repented and were baptized. They were assured of eternal life. What more did they need? The author of Hebrews had specifically those people in mind when he wrote the above words. Remember, those words are in the Bible and are relevant for Believers in any period of history.

Today we can see the same tendency in people who think they want to have Jesus but not the Church. Those people need to open the Bible and read it again. They have missed a huge aspect of the Christian faith. They have bought into *"Christianity light"*. They may very well be saved but they have short-changed themselves as to the quality of life God has in mind for his people.

Prayer: *Father, it is really exciting to see what You have visioned for Your people. With all our problems and hang-ups, we gather with others to glorify Your name - awesome. In Jesus' name. Amen.*

THURSDAY – A DECISION FOR A LIFETIME

Scripture: Psalm 30:10-12

It is somewhat of a paradigm shift to go from the mindset of *"being saved"* to the mindset of a *"worshiper forever"*. You see this especially in the last book of the Bible. You see people who have been washed with the blood of the Lamb, standing in God's presence clothed in white robes - people from all races, tongues, nations, and tribes - worshiping the Lord forever. Heaven is not a holding pen for the "saved". It is a place where those who were born to be one with God are now enjoying God, glorifying him with all their being.

People were born to worship something. This is one of the distinctives of the human being. Have you ever seen a cow in the field bowing down to worship a tree or the moon? Have you ever seen a dog or cat trying to make a god so they can sacrifice to that god? Worship is a human thing. Study the history of civilization and you will see that people of every ancient civilization had their gods, regardless of where they were in the world, or their language spoken, or their race. Worshiping is not a choice we have. We will worship something or someone. The question is not whether we will worship but who or what we worship.

Marriage is a big, life decision and so is the choice of one's career or profession. A decision that is bigger yet is your decision to become a life-long worshiper. Years ago, I decided that I would go to my grave worshiping. Psalm 30:12 could be my chosen life theme – *"that my soul may sing praise to You and not be silent. O Lord my God, I will give thanks to you forever."*

Prayer: *Father, what joy it is to behold Your presence and to know that we can do that forever and ever. We join the saints in glory and those here on earth giving You great praise. In Jesus' name. Amen.*

FRIDAY – PRAISING IN THE TOUGH TIMES

Scripture: I Peter 1:6-7

A famous Baptist preacher from London, Charles Spurgeon, once said, "If you can't trace his hand, you can trust his heart."

One of the great things about walking with the Lord many years is that one has seen how he works in life situations, and has seen his faithfulness in the hard times when life doesn't make much sense. I have done many funerals where I had no answers as to the big "why" that haunts so many people when suddenly a young person or child dies.

It is good, though, to remember that God's greatness is not determined by how smooth my life or your life is going right at the moment. We praise God for his greatness, not for this chaotic life where sickness, hate, violence, and death rules the day, many times. We praise God for his promises to us in the grand purpose of life and not because he has promised us an easy road with no pain and no disappointment.

When you are in the woes of grief, you praise God with tears coming down both cheeks. Yes, you are sad. Knowing the Lord doesn't change the fact that your loss is real. But in your sadness, you can raise your head and look up and remember that God's greatness is not any less and that His love for you is just as great.

Pain and disappointment does test our faith. It forces one to take a hard look at one's faith. Questions surface like, "Do I really believe?" In today's Bible verse, the Apostle Peter refers to these times of trial as times of testing, like fire tests gold, and that it can result in praise and glory and honor.

Prayer: *Thank You, Father, that my willingness to praise You is not determined by circumstances in this life. I know my faith will be tested many times. Help me, Father, to keep my head up always and never to allow the evil in this world to keep me looking down. In Jesus' name. Amen.*

SATURDAY – THE MYSTICAL POWER OF PRAISE

Scripture: Acts 16:25-26

Today's text gives us Paul and Silas praying and singing hymns of praise to God, while they were in jail, after being arrested and beaten for sharing the good news of Jesus Christ. As they were praying and singing, a miracle happened. A great earthquake hit, and the jail doors were flung open.

I remember being put in jail in Chicago one Saturday night, falsely accused of a crime. I had been with a **Jews for Jesus** team passing out Gospel tracts in the ritzy Million Dollar Mile (Michigan Ave.). That evening I had taken a youth group to the **Pacific Garden Mission** to help serve the homeless. While boarding a commuter train late at night, I was arrested and jailed.

After a long night on the 14th floor of the old downtown lockup, I was finishing my glass of water and a bologna sandwich when it occurred to me that it was time for our church service to begin. Though I had been having a pity party, I realized that God's greatness was not any less so I started to sing praises to the Lord. I was not bashful, as I sang the first verse of maybe 8 or 10 old hymns. A jailer came to my cell and said, "Excuse me. You don't belong here, do you?"

I responded, "No Sir, I don't".

He said, "Tell me about it." After hearing my story, he said, "Wait five minutes, and I will get you out." And he did. While walking out of the jail, I realized that if I had not been singing praises to God, I most likely would still be in jail. Praising God can do miraculous things.

Prayer: *Father, following Jesus leads to a white knuckle ride through life. Jesus and many precious saints have faced similar circumstances. What a privilege to know You, and what a privilege to praise and give honor and glory to Your name. In Jesus. Amen.*

SUNDAY – GOD'S SPECIAL DAY – THE LORD'S DAY

"Let us go into His dwelling place; let us worship at His footstool." Psalm 132:7

SPIRITUAL DISCIPLINES

WEEK #15 – THE DISCIPLINE OF PRAYER

MONDAY – KNOWING THE POWER OF PRAYER

Scripture: Luke 11:1

The Disciples were raised praying. All young Jewish boys would have heard great stories about Abraham, Joseph, Moses, Samuel, and David. They would have witnessed the Priests praying in the Temple and, no doubt, their own parents and relatives praying. So why ask Jesus, *"Lord, teach us to pray . . ."*

Could it be that they had seen Jesus pray, . . . and it was different? When Jesus prayed, the blind man's eyes were opened; water was turned to wine; a young boy was healed; demons were sent away; and the dead were raised. Prayer had become exciting and full of surprises. When Jesus prayed, God came into the situation, and his power was visible. The Disciples were attracted to Jesus' prayers. They had tasted God's power and presence and wanted more.

One of the most revealing verses about Jesus and how he prayed is found in Hebrews 5:7. Here it states that Jesus offered up prayers with *"loud crying and tears"*. This tells me his emotions were heavily involved in his praying. I can imagine his heart crying when he prayed. All pretense was dropped. Jesus was probably not worried about impressing anyone around him and spoke to his Heavenly Father with every fiber of his being.

Few churches today have these kinds of prayers offered. We have polished prayers, written in the finest of prose, but where do you find the broken-hearted, weeping before God for the healing of others, for deliverance from addiction or other forms of evil? Where do you find this level of caring? Many times pastors will even give out funds to people seeking assistance without crying out to God for the person's needs. "Lord, teach us to pray."

Prayer: *Father, I want to pray like Jesus. I want to have a deep intimacy with You and be able to tap into that intimacy when approaching You in prayer. I know this is possible. Oh Father, help me. In Jesus' name. Amen.*

TUESDAY – MAKING TIME

Scripture: Luke 5:16

Luke gives us great insight into the spiritual disciplines of Jesus. In today's verse, he writes that Jesus *"would often slip away to the wilderness and pray"*. Why would he do that? Do you think he would feel guilty if he didn't, so as a way to avoid guilt, he would create time to pray? Do you think he was bored and didn't have anything else to do? I tend to think he knew where his inner source of power and life came from and felt a need to tap into that inner source often. He knew he needed to cultivate, on a personal level, his relationship with God through prayer - by talking with God, by expressing his doubts, his fears, by confessing his need of God's presence with him. At one point, we read that he spent a whole night in prayer. Prayer was not a footnote to Jesus' day. It was the main thing. It was the key to his spiritual life.

We live in a busy world with many commitments and competing voices. But the last time I checked, we each had the same amount of time in our day, and it hasn't changed – 24 hours. Most of us still have control of our time. The things that are really important, we make time for them.

Let's shift the focus now to you. What is your day like? Do you carve out time to expressing your hopes and fears to God, to admitting your need of him, to seeking his power to live in victory? Every great Christian leader who has ever lived will agree that carving out time with God in prayer is a struggle, but the key to a successful Christian life.

Prayer: *Father, I want to know You, really know You. I don't want to have a surface relationship but one of depth. I want to know Your heart and Your mind. I want to walk in Your power and presence, just like Jesus. In His name. Amen.*

WEDNESDAY – PRAYING IN JESUS' NAME

Scripture: John 16:23-24

The name of Jesus is powerful and special. Jesus instructs Believers to use his name in prayer, to ask in his name. Upon asking in his name, Jesus clearly indicates that these prayers will be answered. Such a scenario would bring great joy to the Believer.

The Apostle Paul, in Philippians (2:9-10), declares that God has highly exalted Jesus and given him a name which is above every name. At the end of the age, every knee will bow, upon the mention of the name of Jesus, and every tongue confess Jesus to be Lord.

Many songs and hymns have been written about the name of Jesus. People give testimony to evil fleeing at the mention of Jesus' name. All the prayers in this devotional are ended *"in Jesus' name"*. When instructing his followers to pray, Jesus tells them to pray, *"Our Father . . ."* This is why I pray to God as "Father" but in Jesus' name.

Luke, in Acts 3:16, records a man being healed based upon faith in "the name of Jesus". The early church did miraculous things in the name of Jesus.

The Hebrew name, Joshua, also was pronounced Jesus. It was a common Hebrew name in Jesus' day. Many men had the name of Jesus. It was obviously not a magical word to be used as such but a name referring to the person of Jesus of Nazareth. He is the focus, not necessarily his name. When one prays in the name of Jesus, he is to be praying using the mind of Christ. For example, to use Jesus' name to pray for more ability to lie and deceive would be obviously contradictory to Jesus' teachings, not truly praying in his name.

Prayer: *Father, thank You for giving us the mind of Christ, making it possible to pray in his name. Help us to learn more about how to use his name for Your glory. In Jesus' name. Amen.*

THURSDAY – ASKING, ASKING, ASKING

Scripture: Luke 18:3-7

There is much to be said for perseverance in most things. Many people lack a willingness to persist when seeking something. They give up easily and miss a great blessing.

Today's story is one to remember. It teaches us a lot about prayer. It drives home the point of persistence and perseverance in praying. Jesus said in vs. 7, "*. . . will not God bring about justice for His elect who cry to Him day and night . . .*"

In my daily prayers, I pray for the salvation of family members. I believe this is God's will for them to be saved and thus I cry out to God for their souls daily. One could easily argue, "*Why do you ask God for something that you asked him for yesterday? Don't you think God has a good memory? Don't you think he remembers that you made that same request just yesterday?*" It is enough for me to know that Jesus told a story to illustrate the point of perseverance in prayer.

Many years ago, I started praying for the salvation of a specific nephew. Every day, I ask God to open the door of heaven for him, to move his heart to repentance, to speak to him, and to send Godly people in his life. I did this for more than twenty years. Though I faithfully prayed and prayed, I slowly had resigned myself that I may not see this happen in my lifetime. One day the phone rang. You guessed it. It was my nephew. He was excited about his newly found faith in Christ and couldn't get enough of Bible teaching. I was shocked and overjoyed. God had indeed answered my pleas.

Prayer: *Father, thank You for answered prayer. Thank You for Jesus' word to keep on and keep on, when we pray. Thank You for hearing us. Thank You for Your perfect timing, oh Lord. In Jesus' name. Amen.*

FRIDAY – THE LORD'S PRAYER

Scripture: Matthew 6:7-9

When praying, Jesus puts forth one big flashing, yellow light of caution - "*meaningless repetition*". Since the beginning of time, religious groups have used "mantras" or the continual repeating of a phrase or poem as if it is a magical formula, a secret potion for mystical power. This is still practiced in Hinduism and Buddhism and, surprisingly, among some Christian groups. After issuing this caution, he gives us what has been known throughout the ages as "The Lord's Prayer".

Unfortunately, many Christians who say this prayer in a worship service say it in such a way that it is "meaningless repetition". It is said and not truly prayed. It is repeated at such a high rate of speed that no one is giving any thought to the meaning of the words, making the words "meaningless" - the very thing Jesus warned against. Can't you picture Jesus, at times, throwing up his hands in disgust saying, "*What are you thinking?*"

The prayer can be seen in three basic parts – praise, petition, and praise. It begins with reverential praise and ends on the same note. In the middle are specific, practical petitions. The one big petition will be addressed all throughout next week. It is his request that "*Your kingdom come*".

The Lord's Prayer is addressed to God as "Father". Some pray to Jesus. Some pray to the Holy Spirit. I am not opposed to praying to either, but keep in mind, Jesus instructed us to pray to God. Jesus is our path to God. The Holy Spirit takes our prayers and presents them to God. Prayer as Jesus taught involves all three parts of the Trinity – Father, Son, and Holy Spirit.

Prayer: *Father, thank You for such wonderful instruction as to prayer. Thank You that true prayers are not hocus-pocus, magical tricks. Help us, Lord, to never pray words we don't really mean. In Jesus' name. Amen.*

SATURDAY – THE COMING OF THE KINGDOM

Scripture: Matthew 6:10

The Gospel of Matthew (3:1-2) introduces John the Baptist by telling of his message, *"Repent, for the kingdom of heaven is at hand."* We read on and we find that Jesus came preaching the kingdom of God. Much of his teaching is about this "kingdom". Many of his parables explain in detail about the "kingdom".

When Jesus healed people and cast out demons, he said things like, *"The kingdom of God has come upon you."* In today's text, The Lord's Prayer, a key petition is *"Your kingdom come"*. At the end of Jesus' ministry, he tells of the last days when there will be wars and rumors of wars, an increase in earthquakes and famines, and finally, signs in the sky. He then makes a very revealing statement about his return. He said, *"This gospel of the kingdom shall be preached in the whole world as a testimony to all the nations, and the end will come.* (Matthew 24:14)" Isaiah spoke of the coming of this great day. The theme of God's kingdom coming is a major theme in the later Old Testament prophets and the entire New Testament. The Bible ends with a detailed description of God's kingdom and then a three word prayer, *"Lord Jesus, come"*.

You may have prayed The Lord's Prayer, but have you really prayed for the Kingdom of God to come? All next week, our devotions will focus on different aspects of God's kingdom and relating those aspects to the focus of our prayers.

Rhonda and I give thanks to God before every meal. When blessed with so much, we also remember those in the world who are in need and then end our prayer with the request, *"Come, Lord Jesus"*.

Prayer: *Father, the coming of your kingdom in its fullness is my heart's desire. I long for things to be right, but when I look around, I see so many things wrong. Come, Lord Jesus. Amen.*

SUNDAY – GOD'S SPECIAL DAY – THE LORD'S DAY

"Enter His gates with thanksgiving and His courts with praise. Give thanks to Him, bless His name." Psalm 100:4

SPIRITUAL DISCIPLINES

WEEK #16 – THE DISCIPLINE OF PRAYER

MONDAY – PRAYING FOR THE HOLY SPIRIT

Scripture: Luke 11:13; Acts 10:38

In thinking of the one Biblical character most associated with the Holy Spirit, one would have to think of Jesus. He was conceived of the Holy Spirit, and then at his baptism, the Holy Spirit descended upon him. His teaching and preaching was anointed by the Holy Spirit. The miracles he did were made possible by the Holy Spirit. One cannot imagine Christ's life or ministry without the Holy Spirit.

Jesus, in Luke's Gospel, gives specific instructions concerning prayer. After sharing with them the Lord's prayer, he tells a story about a man seeking assistance from his neighbor and how through perseverance, the neighbor finally gives in to help him. He offers the analogy of a son seeking gifts from his father and how the father desires to give good gifts to his son. Jesus makes the obvious comparison of the father to God, and the son to us. He ends with a very pointed question appealing to their logic about earthly man, with all his weaknesses, giving good gifts to his children, and God, being pure and perfect, desirous and willing to give the Holy Spirit to those who ask him.

It is interesting that God is waiting for us to ask him for the gift of the Holy Spirit. For many years in my Christian life, I failed to ask God for this gift - the Holy Spirit. I have since employed the habit of expressing to God my desire for his Spirit on a regular basis. Like the neighbor who would not give up asking for assistance, I have decided to not give up in my pursuit of God to anoint my life with his precious Spirit, as he anointed Jesus and thousands of Believers before me.

Prayer: *Father, I ask today that You anoint me and fill me with that same Spirit that gave birth to Jesus and anointed his ministry. Breathe on me, breath of God. Give me life in Your Spirit. In Jesus' name. Amen.*

TUESDAY – PRAYING FOR CHRIST'S CHURCH TO BE ONE

Scripture: John 17:20-21

As we all have families, we can relate to the truth that strong families are those who rise above their differences to maintain mutual respect and love. Families who do this have a sense of oneness and are families that others esteem. I have never known a parent who didn't desire his children to get along, work out their differences, and love one another.

The greatest need in congregations happens to be the subject of a key component of Jesus' prayer in John chapter 14 – unity in the Church. This entire chapter is Jesus' prayer to the Father immediately before he was taken to Pilate and then crucified. Here we see Jesus pleading with God for his followers to share in the same intimacy and oneness that Jesus shared with God. A big concern on the mind of Christ, in his final hours, was that these people who had said "yes" to following him would be one with each other and thus be one with him and the Father. His prayer "that they may all be one" should be our prayer as well.

Thirty-three years of ministry has taught me this. Without a miracle of God, people in a congregation will be divided. Without a miracle of God, selfishness, lust for power, jealousy, and envy will rule the day. Without a miracle of God, a congregation will be a hornets' nest, bringing pain to many people, rather than a haven of God's love and grace. There is no institution which holds the potential for bringing hope and life to people like Christ's Church, where the members are respectful of one another, caring for one another, and supporting one another. Christ's Church is God's instrument for changing the world.

Prayer: *Father, thank You for the Body of Christ on earth – Your Church. Because You love Your Church, I should also love Your Church. I join my Lord Jesus, today, in His prayer for Your people to be one. In His name. Amen.*

WEDNESDAY – PRAYING FOR PROTECTION, HEALTH, AND HEALING

Scripture: Matthew 6:33; James 4:3

Jesus teaches us to seek first his kingdom and his righteousness, and things like food, clothing, and personal, practical needs, will be given to us. He then tells us to ask, and promises it will be given to us. In James (4:3), he reminds the early church that the reason their prayers weren't answered is because they asked with wrong motives and indicated their prayers were self-centered. We also know that Jesus asked the Father to protect his people from the evil one (John 17:15).

Knowing how or what to pray for, as to personal needs, is a challenge. We should always look to the Scripture for guidance. God already knows our needs before we ask him. It is also true that if our primary focus is on God's kingdom, he will take care of our needs. Bearing in mind God's desire for intimacy with us, I have concluded that if something is weighing heavy on our hearts, we should bring it before the Father in prayer. If it is a selfish want, when we bring it before the Father, the Holy Spirit will convict us or put a check in our spirit. More than anything, God wants us to release our inner desires, wants, and fears to him regularly.

Rhonda and I pray for the Lord's protection from the devil for our children, grandchildren, and loved ones every night before going to sleep. In our morning prayers, we pray for them again, only more for spiritual growth and maturity. In my private time, I pray for health for me, Rhonda, and all my family as well as for practical, daily needs. These things are on my mind and heart. I release them to the Lord daily.

Prayer: *Father, thank You for guidance in the Scriptures, as to something as fundamentally important as prayer. Lord, I want my connecting link to You to be strong and healthy. Lord, teach me to pray as Jesus prayed. In His name. Amen.*

THURSDAY – PRAYING FOR THE NEED OF THE HOUR

Scripture: Matthew 9:38; Acts 13:2-3

A common problem in churches is the lack of real knowledge as to the specific things to pray for, as given by our Lord. One of these things is the challenge to pray for kingdom workers.

Think of a basketball game or football game. There are basically two groups of people at the game – the players and the spectators. Unfortunately we see the same thing when looking at most churches – two groups of people – those in the arena with sleeves rolled up doing the work of the kingdom and those on the bleachers watching and doing occasional cheers. Jesus gave the Church specific instructions in asking God to change that scenario. He saw a harvest that was seismic, but he also saw a very serious problem – too few workers to bring in the harvest. He then instructed his people to *"beseech the Lord"* to send out workers. This is one of the few things Jesus specifically instructed people to ask of God.

Our reading from Acts gives us a picture of church leaders who took this challenge seriously . . . and as a result, the Holy Spirit spoke a message. Maybe a more correct way to view this is that those church leaders heard the Holy Spirit's message. I think the Holy Spirit is speaking today but people are not hearing. They don't take the time and put forth the effort in prayer and fasting to hear God.

As a result of fasting and praying by the leaders of the Antioch church, the first missionary team was sent forth – Barnabas and Paul – and the harvest was huge. Praying for harvest workers is a challenge to be realized and personalized for every church and for every Believer.

Prayer: *Father, I have heard Your call to pray for more workers. I see the harvest, and I see the problem. Oh Lord, give us more and more humble workers, men and women, who are sold out to You. In Jesus' name. Amen.*

FRIDAY – PRAYING FOR THE LOST, THE POOR, IMPRISONED, LONELY, HURTING

Scripture: Luke 10:8-9

Our Lord pointed the way for his followers to care for others, as he cared for others, as he took notice of the poor, the sick, and the marginalized. Jesus could have kept the focus on himself, being the King of Kings, the Lord of Lords, the Son of God, but instead his focus was on others. He noticed those who were unnoticed by the power brokers of his age. He noticed the weak and hurting people around him. He proved his love by his consistent efforts to reach out to them. When he sent seventy of his followers out to minister in his name, he told them to *"heal the sick"*.

As people who claim to know the Lord God, we should be like Jesus. We should take notice of the unnoticed. We should give our attention to marginalized people, those who for whatever reason cannot press their own agenda. The people of God today should be the people to stand up and extend their hand to help the helpless. Our focus should not be inward but upward and then outward.

The prayer life of a Believer should be much more than a laundry list of selfish needs. The "me and Jesus" mentality is far from the Jesus of the Bible. A significant chunk of our prayer life should be devoted to bringing the lost, the least, and the lonely before the Lord. Given the enormity of our task to "make disciples of all nations", we must genuinely seek the Lord's love and power to accomplish such a God-sized mission. When the Lord comes crashing into our hearts for the hurting people around us, we can effectively go forth in boldness to show them the love of God.

Prayer: *Father, I want to be the hands and feet of Jesus to the lost, the least, and the lonely. Give me more and more of Your love for others. Help me to see ways to help them. In Jesus' name. Amen.*

SATURDAY – PRAYING FOR THE LORD'S RETURN

Scripture: Revelation 22:17, 20

The Bible ends with a three word prayer followed by a benediction (vs. 21). That three word prayer should be on the lips often of God's people. It is simple, *"Come, Lord Jesus."*

Jesus spoke of the end of the age and his coming again numerous times. The last account of Jesus here on this earth is in Acts 1 where he ascends into heaven. Upon his ascension, two angels appeared and said that Jesus will "come in just the same way as you have watched him go . . ."

For many years, I never prayed to Jesus for him to come. Now I do at every mealtime. I remember the lost, the least, and the lonely when I thank the Lord for my food and then end my prayer, *"Come, Lord Jesus."* I have an increasing desire for all the evil and pain on this planet to end.

When everything is going good, why pray for Jesus to come? If you have health, wealth, and plenty of "things", you might think you already have your heaven here on earth. It doesn't take long, though, to look around and see unspeakable disappointments, tragedies, injustices, suffering, and pain. In many parts of the world, cruel governmental systems rob people of basic human rights and freedoms. Atrocities occur daily, only to go unreported. In America, we live in a very soft, protected bubble. Reality for most of the world is quite different.

My heart yearns for a better kingdom, as described at the end of the Bible. When Jesus healed people, they tasted of God's kingdom. When he raised the dead, they tasted of God's kingdom. That is the kingdom Jesus will bring, when he comes. Oh happy day.

Prayer: *Father, put a desire in my heart for Your kingdom to come in its fullness. Come, Lord Jesus. Amen.*

SUNDAY – GOD'S SPECIAL DAY – THE LORD'S DAY

Enter his gates with thanksgiving and his courts with praise. Give thanks to Him, bless His name.
Psalm 100:4

GOD THE SON – HIS NAME IS JESUS

WEEK #17 – THE PERSON OF CHRIST

MONDAY – NOT PLAN B

Scripture: John 1:1-2; 14

Some people have viewed Jesus Christ as God's "Plan B", his "Plan A" being the Jewish people in the Old Testament. In this thinking, Jesus was God's backup plan, if the Jewish people messed up. The Apostle John in compiling his Gospel, begins by giving great clarity on the preexistence of Christ. John begins his Gospel with the exact same wording as we find in Genesis 1:1 – "*In the beginning . . .*" John describes Jesus as "the Word" and boldly states that all things came into being through him. Later in the chapter (vs. 14), John makes one of the most profound statements in the Bible, "*And the Word became flesh . . .*" You may be highly intelligent and achieve great levels of understanding in a specific field or science, but you will live your lifetime and never fully wrap your mind around that verse, "*And the Word became flesh*".

Our universe, created by "The Word", is vast beyond anyone's imagination. It was through the medium of words that God brought everything into being. John presents us Jesus, as "the Word". This truth is fundamental in the Believer's understanding of the person of Jesus Christ. He is the eternal Word, the second part of the Trinity – God the Father, God the Son, and God the Spirit.

In Revelation 19:13, John sees Jesus on a white horse. He is pictured as clothed in a robe dipped in blood and is called, "*The Word of God*". Christian faith is centered in the person of Jesus Christ, not in an ecclesiastical structure, not in any mythological god or goddess, and not in spiritual feel-good ecstasies. May we not forget, it is all about Jesus.

Prayer: *Father, thank You for Jesus. Thank You that he did become flesh. Thank You that I can know Him. How awesome. Every prayer to You is in His name, a name that is far greater than any name I could possibly ever have. In Jesus' name. Amen.*

TUESDAY – BORN OF THE SPIRIT

Scripture: Matthew 1:18; Luke 1:35

Some Christians believe that the only way Jesus could have been born sinless was if Mary was sinless. If Mary had the original sin nature then logically Jesus would also have had a sin nature. Viewing Mary as sinless has led to her exaltation as the *"mother of God"* and has even led to her worship, as such, by some.

If you were stranded on an island and all you had as a means to understand Christianity was the Bible, you would most likely never view Mary as anything other than human. The Gospels of Matthew and Luke make it very clear that Jesus was conceived in a special way, through the work of the Holy Spirit. His mother is never referred to as "sinless", but as his father is God, and God is completely pure, Jesus is therefore completely pure and without sin. No other human ever born is thought of as conceived by the Holy Spirit.

Many things about the Christian faith are not fully comprehendible. The birth conception of Jesus is one of them. Virgins don't have babies. This simply does not happen and is not within the realm of rational thinking. It truly is one of the great mysteries of the Christian faith. One could even view it as the "magic" of Christmas. A multitude of angels gave praise to God upon this miraculous birth.

Historic, orthodox Christian faith teaches that Jesus is fully God yet fully man. This is pictured in his birth. Because he was born through the birth canal of a woman, as any human is born, we say he is full human. Because he was conceived by the Holy Spirit, we say view him as fully God. Wow.

Prayer: *Father, when I contemplate the Word becoming flesh, I step into this world of wonder and again marvel at the birth of Your Son. How You did it is far beyond the understanding of my little mind. I praise You again and again for sending Jesus. In His name. Amen.*

WEDNESDAY – PREACHING AND TEACHING

Scripture: Mark 1:14; 22

Preaching and teaching was the means Jesus used to communicate God's truth and to challenge the people. It was the centerpiece of his three year ministry here on this earth. In his preaching, he called them to follow him and to live a life pleasing to God. In his teaching, he told many parables and taught many things about God's coming kingdom.

We believe Jesus was able to read and write, though we have nothing that he wrote. This is rather strange, as we have books and letters written by people of that same historical period. It does beg the question, "Why?" I believe that Jesus wanted to speak to people directly. He didn't care to risk having his words forever analyzed, twisted, quoted, and possibly even worshiped.

In our second Scriptural reference, we learn there was something different about Jesus' teaching as compared to the teaching of religious leaders of his day. He was teaching with "authority". As Jesus was one with the Father, he had a direct line to God and could speak with great confidence about God's truth and will.

If someone asked me about my father, Nelson Curry, I could speak with authority about him - his nature, his values, and his beliefs. I knew him. I knew him well. I am his son. I knew him so well that I could recognize his walk, if blindfolded. I loved that man, believed in him, and could speak for him, without question.

As me speaking of my father, it was with similar authority that Jesus taught and preached on his father. The other people preached and taught about God in somewhat of an indirect way. Not Jesus. Jesus spoke with first-hand knowledge of his heavenly Father.

Prayer: *Father, I recognize Jesus as the ultimate authority of Your nature, Your thinking, and Your will for all of humankind. Jesus, to You be all honor and glory. In Your name. Amen.*

THURSDAY – MIRACLES

Scripture: Mark 8:22-25

Miracles have a way of attracting attention. If I would see a man walking across Lake Michigan, I would quickly take notice and ask many questions.

Jesus' miracles of healing and casting out demons were not only intended to benefit the people involved but were for the purpose of attracting attention. He wanted every man and woman around him to have some knowledge of this new kingdom that was coming. He could describe it quite well in his teaching and preaching, as he did with many of his parables, but he wanted to demonstrate this kingdom before everyone's eyes. How could they not believe? How could they not understand? It was a good plan. And it worked.

Displaying this kind of power could have easily gotten out-of-hand. The people would have viewed him as the king of magic and would have followed him just for what he could give them, such as when he miraculously fed four thousand people. He was concerned that they not follow him for the loaves and the fishes and thus gave them stern teaching, and they all went away. This didn't seem to bother him. He wanted to do much more than attract a crowd. He wanted them to see and understand God and his coming kingdom.

In India, praying for the sick and casting out demons is the common way to bring people to Christ. Indian missionaries go to a non-Christian village and simply go door to door offering to pray. The sick and those possessed with evil spirits are desperate. Their families have tried everything only to no avail. Missionaries pray with great boldness. God acts. And people are amazed and subsequently repent and believe in Jesus.

Prayer: *Father, thank You that we are not limited to all that we can see and understand with logic. Thank You for all the miraculous works going on around the world in village after village, drawing people into eternal salvation. In Jesus' name. Amen.*

FRIDAY – CRUCIFIXION

Scripture: I Corinthians 2:1-2

The crucifixion of Christ is central to the purpose of his coming. All four Gospels devote more space to Jesus' crucifixion than any other aspect of his life. For example, over 20% of John's Gospel is of Christ's last week. As in our text for today, the Apostle Paul highlights Christ's crucifixion as if to say that he knows of nothing else. In the Apostle's mind, everything else pales in comparison to what happened on that cross.

The one symbol known throughout two thousand years of history to represent Christianity is what? Did you guess the cross? If so, you are correct. The cross is universally recognized. Though at one time, repulsive as a symbol for brutal torture and death, it has grown to be attractive and even fashionable, with Hollywood types wearing crosses of expensive jewelry. Who would have thought?

Like the Passover lamb who was sacrificed for the sins of the people, throughout hundreds of years of Hebrew history, Christ as our Passover lamb, the "*Lamb of God*", is sacrificed for our sins. A healthy, male lamb was used as a symbol of innocence and purity. As sin always brings death in some form, robbing people of life, the shedding of blood was that reminder that a price must be paid for sin. In God's perfect time, he provided the lamb, as he did with Abraham on the mountain with his son, Isaac. He provided a sinless sacrifice once and for all.

The crucifixion is precious in the Believer's mind, because he knows he should have been on that cross, but Christ was there in his place, paying a price that he could never pay. Through the death of Christ, we are pardoned and set free.

Prayer: *Father, the cross is more meaningful to me than a piece of fine jewelry. May I never be ashamed of the cross. May the story of the cross forever be upon my lips. In Jesus' name. Amen.*

SATURDAY – RESURRECTION AND ASCENSION

Scripture: Matthew 28:6-7; I Corinthians 15:12-14

Nothing is more final than death. We were not made to die but to live. God's gift to us is life, not death. Death is so troubling that many people will not allow themselves to think about it. People can successfully avoid the issue until someone close to them dies. No one escapes. Death comes to us all, one at a time.

Humans are the only creatures who contemplate their own death. Neither cows nor dogs nor any other animals show evidence or anxiety over their own mortality. It is a human thing. God knows no death. Since we are created in God's image, we share that aspect of his nature which produces a serious conflict within the soul. Death is a foreign enemy, and every person senses it.

Though the doors of heaven were kicked open for us with the death of Christ on the cross, the deal was sealed with his resurrection. Because death could not hold him in the grave, it cannot hold Believers in the grave, as they are one with him. We identify with his death and therefore with his resurrection. I know of no better news.

Knowing Christ as Savior is better than having a huge inheritance or winning the lottery. It answers life's biggest question, *"What happens next?"* This allows the Believer to make peace with his own death. It gives reassurance and confidence to face life with optimism. When you know how the book ends, you are not too troubled by the events in the middle of the book. Medical test results can be bleak. Careers can be lost. Dreams can be shattered. Abuse and other horrible, painful things can happen, but in Christ, you know how it will all end.

Prayer: *Father, the empty tomb brings joy to my heart today. Bad news is everywhere, but knowing more about You and being reminded again of profound and life-changing truth sends my spirit soaring. Thank you, Father. In Jesus' name. Amen.*

SUNDAY – GOD'S SPECIAL DAY – THE LORD'S DAY

Then David said to all the assembly, "Now bless the Lord your God." And all the assembly blessed the Lord, the God of their fathers, and bowed low and did homage to the Lord and to the king.
I Chronicles 29:20

GOD THE SON – HIS NAME IS JESUS

WEEK #18 – THE NAMES OF CHRIST

MONDAY – PRINCE OF PEACE

Scripture: Isaiah 9:6

This week's readings will be on the many names of Jesus, and there are many. I have chosen a few of the most popular. These names give us hints as to Christ's true nature and role.

Isaiah is the Christmas prophet. He spoke more about the Messiah coming than any other Old Testament prophet. He referred to this coming King as *Wonderful Counselor, Mighty God, Eternal Father*, and *Prince of Peace*.

Years ago, I was on a flight from Kuwait to Bahrain and was seated next to a young man. He was easy to engage in conversation and shared of his Muslim family from Saudi Arabia and of his time in America getting a college education. He was obviously very knowledgeable of world events and quite modern in all ways. In speaking about different religions, I asked how his Muslim faith viewed Jesus. He was quick to say he believed in Jesus and was looking forward to Jesus' coming again. You can imagine my surprise. I asked him to tell me more about his belief in Jesus. He proceeded to explain that when Jesus comes again, all the Jews would be killed in a grand, fierce battle. I then explained that I viewed Jesus as the Prince of Peace, not the Prince of War. On that note, our conversation ended.

Reflecting on the conversation, I realized that my particular view of Jesus was shaped by the Bible, and this young man's view was shaped by the teaching of his religious leaders. I grieved that anyone could have such a skewed view of my Lord and Savior. I remembered the words of the angels to the Shepherds on the day of Christ's birth, *"Peace on earth, goodwill to men"*.

Prayer: *Father, thank You that our ultimate joy and hope in the future is peace, not war. Thank you that someday, all violence and hate will cease, as Your Son reigns. In the name of the Prince of Peace. Amen.*

TUESDAY – SON OF GOD, SON OF MAN

Scripture: Romans 1:1-4

The doctrine of Christ as fully God and fully man is huge, in historic Christian belief. There are many references in the Bible to Jesus as the Son of God and many references to him as the Son of Man. The *"Son of Man"* is a common phrase in the Old Testament and is used repeatedly throughout the four Gospels. The "Son of God" phrase is limited to the New Testament and is also used repeatedly.

It took almost 400 years for the early church to compile the New Testament and agree which letters were to be included. During that time, there was much speculation and disagreement about the actual nature of Christ. A large group of Christians called Arianists believed that Jesus was man only, not God. They concluded that Jesus was the most perfect human ever to live and that God chose Jesus, as an upright and moral man, to reveal himself to the world. In their thinking, Jesus was human, but not God.

Another major group, the Gnostic Christians, believed Jesus to be a spirit, not a human. When people saw Jesus, they saw some type of supernatural mist or spirit. To say Jesus was human, in their eyes, would be to degrade God, as humans were evil. They proclaimed Jesus to be God, not human.

In the year 325, some 318 church leaders from all across the Roman Empire assembled to decide major planks of Christian doctrine, the nature of Christ being one of them. They agreed on a statement, called *The Nicene Creed*, which very plainly describes Jesus as both fully God and fully man. This became the accepted norm for Christian belief as affirmed by all four Gospels – Matthew, Mark, Luke, and John.

Prayer: *Father, again today I marvel at one of the great mysteries of our faith. I do believe Jesus to have been fully human. I do believe Jesus to be fully God. I bow before Him today as Son of God and Son of Man. In His name. Amen.*

WEDNESDAY – BREAD OF LIFE

Scripture: John 6:35, 48

John's Gospel gives several famous statements where Jesus says, "*I am*". Today's statement, "*I am the bread of life*" is one of them.

Jesus says, "*. . . he who believes in Me will never thirst*". He obviously is not speaking of literal water, nor when speaking of bread is he referring to literal bread. He is teaching about spiritual nourishment that is not limited by volume, time, or space.

The God of the Bible is an unseen god and much of the Christian faith is unseen. This makes it quite difficult for some people to accept. When in India, Rhonda and I saw hundreds and thousands of people worshiping gods that could be seen and touched. In some ways, it is easier to worship a god like that. Our god can't be seen or touched yet we argue that he has existed for all of eternity. Spiritual life can't be seen or touched yet we say it can be experienced and nurtured. Talking about things which can't be seen, touched, or heard usually borders on the absurd or irrational. Many people refuse to go there, thinking once that door is opened, there is no shutting it. We like to think we are rational people, believing only that which is logical or proven, but are we really?

For example, love is unseen yet a very powerful force in emotional development. Think of the power of a mother's love, yet it can't be seen or touched. Think of the power of love in romance, yet it can't be seen or touched. Spiritual food is much like that. It is incredibly potent. Jesus provides nourishment for spiritual growth unlike anything one can experience and thus he is the Bread of Life.

Prayer: *Father, thank You that You are far greater than any god that can be manufactured or made with human hands. Thank You for Jesus who is the source of our spiritual food and water. In His name. Amen.*

THURSDAY – LIGHT OF THE WORLD

Scripture: John 8:12

Today's name for Jesus is another of the "*I am*" sayings. Jesus describes himself as a light which beams for everyone in the world. As I wrote a few weeks ago, the Bible begins with darkness and ends with light (Rev. 22:5). Darkness is the natural state of the universe. Light penetrates the darkness.

The sun is the center of our solar system, providing much needed light for all life. Without the sun, our planet would be totally dark, cold, and colorless - void of any life. With the sun or with light, there are trees, plants, flowers, birds, animals, fish, insects, and humans. When you think about the power of light, it is really quite amazing.

Jesus is to be like light to the Christian. Without Jesus, our lives lack hope and purpose. We are colorless. Without Jesus, our hearts tend to be cold to human hurt and need. Without Jesus, there is a darkness in our souls that goes unanswered. Without Jesus, we are restless, feverish creatures desperately trying to be somebody, but we don't know who the somebody is. Without Jesus, we are never satisfied; we are forever wanting more of this and more of that, trying to fill the gnawing emptiness inside.

This reminds me of an old gospel song, *The Lighthouse*. At one point in the song, the words read, "If it wasn't for that lighthouse, where would this ship be?" On the shores of Lake Michigan, there were many lighthouses at one time. They existed for one purpose, to guide the ship safely into harbor, to keep it from crashing into the rocks on a dark, stormy night. Looking to the light of Christ, we will someday reach the harbor, being safe at home.

Prayer: *Father, thank You today for the Light of Jesus Christ. Thank You that we can see the Light and that our ships are guided through a very stormy night. Many other ships are crashing on the rocks, Lord. They refuse to see the Light. Thank You for Jesus, our Light. In His name. Amen.*

FRIDAY — GOOD SHEPHERD

Scripture: John 10:11

Jesus said, "*I am the good shepherd*." The analogy of sheep and shepherds is used repeatedly throughout the Bible.

Sheep are the most insecure of all farm animals. Without a shepherd, they are confused and afraid. They only know herd mentality and find it very difficult to individually go about.

Years ago, I was a livestock hauler, transporting hogs and cattle throughout the Midwest. Occasionally I would haul a load of sheep and would always dread loading and unloading them. Some stockyards keep a "lead sheep" that permanently stays at the stockyards, specifically for the purpose of leading sheep up the loading shutes and into the big trucks. Without a lead sheep, it is almost impossible to get the other sheep up the shute. When one goes, they all want to go at once, but getting the one to go is always the big problem. You guessed it. The lead sheep quickly goes up the loading sheep and all the sheep follow him. Problem solved. A sheep will naturally look for a leader, as if it inherently knows something is missing, if there is no leader or shepherd.

I see a lot of common threads with this analogy. In several ways, we are like sheep. We inherently know something is missing until we find the good Shepherd — Jesus. Jesus said he lays down his life for the sheep. This is the picture of a true shepherd in Jesus' day. Yes, Jesus gave his life for us. He died that we might live, eternally. He is there, like a shepherd, to go before us. He is a "good" shepherd. He doesn't beat the sheep or treat them unkindly. He knows his sheep and his sheep know him.

Prayer: *Father, thank You today for providing a shepherd for me. I get lost easily, Lord. I get confused easily. Thank You again for Jesus, the good, verrrry good Shepherd. In His name. Amen.*

SATURDAY – BEGINNING AND THE END

Scripture: Revelation 1:8; 21:6; 22:13

This title for our Lord is only found in Revelation. In chapter one, it is stated as *"Alpha and Omega"*. *Alpha* is the first letter of the Greek alphabet and *omega* is the last. Since the book was originally written in Greek, the title had obvious meaning as the beginning and the end. It is also used in the last chapter of the Bible. Interestingly, it is used as meaning the first and last and is found in the first and last chapters of Revelation.

In all three instances in Revelation, Jesus speaks first person saying, *"I am . . . "* The message is clear. As the church age winds down and God's kingdom is on the horizon, Jesus is taking ownership of all creation and civilization by using this title. With eternity, there is no beginning and end. Only life, as we know it on this planet, has a beginning and end. It is this that Jesus owns. As the Bible closes, this is the identity Jesus chooses.

The very last time in the Bible Jesus identifies himself is just a few verses down from 13, in verse 16. Here he states, *"I am the root and descendant of David, the bright morning star."* He is the Jewish Messiah, the promised King from the lineage of David. It is truly amazing the number of Jewish churches that have simultaneously popped up in every major, American city. This promised remnant is becoming known in our day. God keeps his promises. Jesus' very last words in the Bible are *"Yes, I am coming quickly."*

The final comment from John, the author of Revelation, in response to Jesus' statement of coming quickly is *"Amen. Come, Lord Jesus."*

Prayer: *Father, it is overwhelming to give serious thought as to the nature of my Lord. No one title can fully describe Jesus. Today, Lord Jesus, I bow to You as the Alpha and Omega, the beginning and the end. In Your name. Amen.*

SUNDAY – GOD'S SPECIAL DAY – THE LORD'S DAY

"Praise the Lord! I will give thanks to the Lord with all my heart, in the company of the upright and in the assembly." Psalms 111:1

GOD THE SON – HIS NAME IS JESUS

WEEK #19 – THE MIRACLES OF CHRIST

MONDAY – PARALYTIC HEALED

Scripture: Luke 5:24-26; Acts 3:6-7

This week we ponder six different miracles performed by our Lord in his three years of ministry. There are 37 recorded miracles with Matthew, Mark, and Luke describing several of the same ones. The Gospel of John records the fewest of the miracles.

Luke gives us the most interesting version of today's miracle. He mentions the power of the Lord being present for Jesus to perform healing. Immediately before this incident, Jesus had gone away to the wilderness to pray. Upon coming back from his prayer summit, Jesus faces a house full of people, some of them religious leaders. Some men carried a paralyzed man to Jesus, on a stretcher. Because the house was so crowded, they lowered the stretcher down from the roof. Jesus sees a teachable moment and surprises everyone with his comment. Instead of saying something like, "You are healed", Jesus says, "your sins are forgiven". This brought the Jewish religious leaders off their seats. Jesus knew it would. He knew that in the Hebrew faith, only through blood sacrifice by the priests could sins be forgiven. After teaching on the subject, in response to the challenge put forth by the religious leaders, he told the man to "pick up your stretcher and go home". The crowd was speechless as the man got up and walked away, glorifying God. Jesus gave them something to think about and then demonstrated the power of God before their very eyes.

The power of the Lord to perform healing is available today. Imagine a church where its leaders spend time seeking the presence of the Holy Spirit a day or two before the service. When the power of God is present, lives are profoundly changed.

Prayer: *Father, thank You for being alive and active for those who really walk in Your presence. Thank you for the many healings that happened just today in different parts of the world. In Jesus' name. Amen.*

TUESDAY – A WOMAN OF FAITH COMES TO JESUS

Scripture: Mark 5:25-26, 34

Though Mark usually gives the shorter version of Jesus' miracles, he gives quite the expanded version of this one. The woman's twelve year hemorrhage problem had been unsuccessfully treated by "many physicians". I can't imagine all she had suffered. She must have heard of Jesus and his miracles. She went to Jesus. In our story, we see Jesus with crowds of people around him, leaving little or no opportunity for a woman to actually meet him.

In most primitive cultures, women would have been pushed to the back of the crowd in such a situation. It would not have been easy for her to get close enough to Jesus to touch his garment. She believed in him so much that she thought, if she could only touch his clothing, she would be healed. This woman is a picture of faith. In her mind, Jesus was the answer. She only touched his garment, but that was enough. She was healed and knew it.

With many of Jesus' miracles of healing, he doesn't mention faith, but this one is different. He told her, ". . . your faith has made you well . . ." We know it was her faith that motivated her to come to Jesus.

I have never been a fan of "faith healers" or "healing crusades". People can be so easily manipulated which is obvious by the behavior of many of these faith healer types. Only God has the power to heal, not man. Where the focus is truly on God, with humble, Godly men and women, miracles still happen today. Many miracles happen through God-gifted doctors and modern medicine. Many lives have been saved by physicians and surgeons. They are our partners in healing.

Prayer: *Father, thank you for healing the woman in today's story. Someday I possibly can meet her when I am home with You. Thank you for all your people who act as your agents of healing. In Jesus' name. Amen.*

WEDNESDAY – BLIND MAN SEES

Scripture: John 9:10-11; Acts 3:16

The entire chapter nine is devoted to this miracle and subsequent events. Being born blind, he was relegated to a life of begging.

When in India, I saw beggars every day. They were in every city, on every major street, in train stations, bus stations, temples, and churches. It is one of India's nasty secrets. Begging is a pitiful life, one not many of us would want. Many beggars are smelly and filthy, not having access to water for bathing or toilets.

This beggar was brought to Jesus' attention by his Disciples who used him to ask a question about the possibility of how sickness is connected to sin, possibly the sin of the parents. We know in some cases there is a connection between sin and sickness, such as when a drunkard suffers from sclerosis of the liver. The Disciples thought maybe this man was born blind because of some secret sin in the life of one or both parents. Jesus responded, putting to rest their suspicion and explaining that this blind man was like this so the works of God could be displayed in him. He then made mud-balls from his spit and applied the mud to the blind man's eyes and told him to go wash. He did and could see, for the first time in his life.

This story tells me that many people with disabilities and diseases are like that through no fault of their own. But the story isn't over. They can be trophies of God's power and grace. The works of God can be displayed in them so others take note. They begin to ask questions, as to how this has happened. God is glorified.

Prayer: *Father, display Your works through my sickened condition, whether it be a physical, emotional, or spiritual sickness. Use even my weaknesses to give You glory. In Jesus' name. Amen.*

THURSDAY – HUNGRY PEOPLE EAT

Scripture: John 6:9-11

Today's story is a picture of 5-10,000 people gathered in a large grassy field to hear Jesus teach and to witness suffering people made whole. Though he knew how he would feed them, he asked the Disciples about this to see them sweat and squirm and then to witness God's power. They found a young boy with five loaves of bread and two fishes. Jesus took the bread and gave thanks, and to everyone's amazement, there was enough bread and fish for everyone to get full and even some leftover fragments.

Again I see the power of Jesus' presence. When Jesus shows up, amazing things happen. Remember Matt. 18:20? "For where two or three are gathered in My name, I am there in their midst." How many church services happen every Sunday in America when Jesus does not show up? Songs are sung about God. A sermon is given. The Bible is read, but is Jesus really there to minister in God's power? Is he desired? Is he invited? Gathering in his name is to adjust the focus to him, not any one person or family or gift or building or even music. Is Jesus truly exalted among the congregation? If he is, then he will show up.

It is good to take note that they did look around to see what food they could come up with on their own. They weren't completely helpless, as they had located some bread and some fish. The miracle didn't happen until the prayer of thanks was offered, and the food was served. Jesus expects us to give thanks and go forth with what we do have, trusting the Lord, praising his name.

Prayer: *Father, I praise You for providing food for that huge crowd of people long ago. Thank You, Jesus, for teaching us how to live and to live by authentic faith. In Your name. Amen.*

FRIDAY – DEMONS DEPART

Scripture: Matthew 17:15, 18

The subject of casting out demons is not the most popular subject in most Christian circles and is often misunderstood. We don't like to think that demon possession could possibly be real. Though most all of Jesus' healing miracles do not mention evil spirits or demons, this one does. The boy in the story was behaving much like we would expect from a person suffering with epilepsy, but the cause of his behavior was a demon. Jesus recognized this and cast out the demon.

Most missionaries in developing countries see demon possession quite often - ten times, maybe one hundred times more than in America. It is very noticeable. Where Christianity has been a strong presence for many years, demon possession is rare.

An interesting part of this healing concerns the Disciples. They had tried to cast the demon out and could not. Jesus had harsh words to say about unbelieving people. Later when the Disciples inquired of Jesus as to why they could not cast out the demon, Jesus pointed out the littleness of their faith.

Though demon possession might be much less in our more Christianized society, the presence of evil is still real. It can be seen more in cases of rape, murder, abuse, corruption, adultery, homosexuality, addictions and greed. All of these sins are rooted in evil and are serious obstacles to Christian growth and development.

Faith starts out small with all of us but should deepen, as we mature in our walk with Christ. A person strong in faith will have great confidence in prayer, will be able to discern the presence of evil, and will act boldly in the name of Jesus when encountering an evil spirit or demon.

Prayer: *Father, there are times that unbelief and lack of faith haunt me. Deepen me, Lord. Mature me, Lord. I praise You that Your power is far greater than anything that could hold me hostage. In Jesus' name. Amen.*

SATURDAY – DEAD MAN LIVES

Scripture: John 11:43-44

Raising a dead man, after dead for four days, is no small matter. This is the only place in the New Testament that mentions Jesus weeping. Mary and Martha were his very close friends, and they were hurting. Lazarus, their brother, had suddenly died of an illness. They were most likely early to middle aged people. Martha protested when Jesus commanded them to remove the stone. She mentioned the four days and the stench. What could Jesus possibly do? He prayed and commanded Lazarus to come forth. . . , and the corpse came to life. After witnessing this spectacle of God's power, the Apostle John records many Jews believing in Jesus.

I can't imagine a corpse which had not been embalmed for four days - the decay and the stench – coming to life. To actually see such a display of supernatural power would stick in my mind a life time.
The implications from this miracle are astounding. Though I have known the Lord for over 45 years, I find myself thinking, "Is this really true?" It is almost more difficult to comprehend than Christ's actual resurrection. I believe it is true, but wow, what a whopper of a miracle.

Though faith and belief are significant factors in many of Christ's miracles, with this one it is somewhat different. Jesus did challenge Martha to believe in God's power to raise the dead, and Mary believed Jesus would have healed Lazarus of his sickness before he died. And, of course, Lazarus couldn't have given evidence of faith, as he was dead. Jesus' bold action caught everyone by surprise. In a sense, every miracle was about faith and belief but some more directly. Without question, death was no obstacle for Jesus.

Prayer: *Father, I look forward to meeting Lazarus some day when I get home. Death did eventually take Lazarus and will eventually take me, but thank You, Lord, that Jesus has conquered death. In His glorious name. Amen.*

SUNDAY – GOD'S SPECIAL DAY – THE LORD'S DAY

"Come and hear, all who fear God, and I will tell of what He has done for my soul" Psalms 66:16

GOD THE SON – HIS NAME IS JESUS

WEEK #20 – THE PARABLES OF CHRIST

MONDAY – THE PHARISEE AND TAX COLLECTOR

Scripture: Luke 18:14

Jesus took transforming truth and clothed it in stories or what is commonly called "parables". Jesus knew that people remember stories much better than bare-boned doctrine. Every important truth he taught was through a parable. In all four gospels, we have a total of fifty-four parables.

The danger of exalting oneself above others is the focus of the parable of the Pharisee and the tax collector. The two Jews go to the Temple to pray, which is a noble act. The Pharisee would have been a very well educated man with high standing in the Jewish religious community. The tax collector would have had very low standing in the Jewish community, being hated by most as a traitor and cheat. The Pharisee had obvious contempt for the one he viewed as a sinner, as he the Pharisee paid much money to the Temple coffers. The proud Pharisee was focused on the sins of the tax collector, not his own. The repentant tax collector was sorrowful for all the areas he fell short and sincerely was seeking God's mercy. The tax collector received mercy and was forgiven. The Pharisee was not forgiven. Jesus concludes this story with a warning to all who exalt themselves, and gives encouragement to all who humble themselves.

Believers should see this as a warning. As those who have been justified and forgiven by the blood of Jesus, we dare not exalt ourselves, regardless of how spiritually mature we think we are, regardless of our education or standing in the community, and regardless of our name or profession. The Believer should never look upon a person of lesser status in arrogance and condescension. This attitude was absolutely repulsive to Jesus.

Prayer: *Father, help me to never think that I am better than anyone else. Help me to see all people through Your eyes. In Jesus' name. Amen.*

TUESDAY – THE TEN YOUNG LADIES

Scripture: Matthew 25:12-13

Many of Jesus' parables are about the "Kingdom of heaven" or "Kingdom of God". This theme was his dominant theme in teaching and preaching; it is mentioned numerous times with his miracles. In the Lord's Prayer, he prays for this kingdom to come.

Five of these ten ladies were "foolish" and five were "prudent" or wise. On the wedding day, apparently an evening wedding, it was customary for the bridesmaids to wait outside with their lamps for the arrival of the bridegroom. All ten were waiting, but five of them came prepared with extra oil in case the groom arrived late, which did happen. The five, whose lamps had gone out for lack of oil, panicked and ran into the village to get oil. While away, the groom arrived. The five with lamps lit accompanied the groom into the wedding hall. When the five foolish ladies arrived back at the wedding site, they were refused entrance. It was too late. The wedding had already begun. Jesus concluded by telling them to be on the alert, for "you do not know the day nor the hour".

Some might think the "day" or the "hour" is the day and hour of one's death. I believe this is a reference to the second coming of Christ and the coming of the kingdom. The analogy of the groom and bride as Jesus being the groom and his church the bride is used also in Revelation.

The point of the story is to be prepared for the second coming of our Lord. Jesus promised to come again, but many Believers are not aware of this promise and are not living their lives in preparation for it. They will be surprised.

Prayer: *Father, thank You for the many parables Jesus gave us. Thank you for today's parable and for the promise of Your kingdom coming. Come, Lord Jesus. Amen.*

WEDNESDAY – THE LOST SON

Scripture: Luke 15:31-32

This chapter in Luke contains three parables which have very similar threads. One parable is about a lost sheep that is found. The second parable is about a lost coin that is found. The third parable is today's parable and is about a lost son who is found.

Two sons are described in the story, one a good and loyal son and one a wayward, reckless, pleasure-seeking son. The prodigal son reaches a low point, returns home, apologizes to his father, and is received with open arms and great fan fare. The good and loyal son sees all this attention given to his wayward brother and expresses his outrage, as he has never received such attention, being such a good son for many years. Jesus ends this powerful story with the father's response to the loyal son, reminding him of the once lost condition of his brother and why there is now occasion for much joy, as he once was lost and dead but now is found and has begun to live.

Thinking of all three stories, one learns that God will go to great effort to search and find lost people. Lost people matter to God. Jesus didn't come to encourage and affirm the righteous people of the earth. Jesus came to seek and save the lost. He came so that the lost could be found and the dead would have life. When that happens, there is occasion for much joy. God's people should have that very same passion. They shouldn't spend most of their time applauding one another for their righteous deeds, but go to the ends of the earth to find those who are spiritually without life and have lost their way.

Prayer: *Father, put within me that same desire and passion for lost people, which is within You. Help me to love them in spite of their sin or sickness and give them the true Living Water. In Jesus' name. Amen.*

THURSDAY – THE MUSTARD SEED

Scripture: Mark 4:30-32

Many of the parables Jesus told were quite short yet exploding with meaning. The parable of the mustard seed is case in point.

Jesus chose this tiny seed to illustrate God's kingdom. The mustard seed is maybe a little bigger than a pinhead. It is one of the smallest seeds known to man but grows to one of the largest plants. Jesus wanted people to understand this important aspect of faith. Though faith starts out very small, it quickly expands into something huge. Faith becomes so large that many others benefit by it.

I am one of those people who has benefitted by knowing someone of great faith. My mother, Reba Thomas, was born with very little sight and subsequently was legally blind all her life. She suffered through numerous surgeries, including the removal of one eye, and the agonizing loss of her first born child. She heard about Jesus as a little girl, placed her faith in Jesus as Lord and Savior, and was baptized. This started out in her young heart as something very small but grew to be the driving force of her life and the hope of her future. My sister and my brother were blessed beyond what could be described by volumes of books. We took shade in the giant faith of this humble, Godly woman.

What about your faith? Is it small? Do you realize what it could become? Have you thought about how many people in future years might benefit by your decision to repent, believe, and be baptized? This is God's plan. It is not about just you. It is about you, granted, but God wants to reach others through you, just as he reached you through others. This is God's kingdom.

Prayer: *Father, sometimes I am embarrassed by just how small my faith is. Grow it, Lord. Fertilize it. Water it. Shine Your Son on it and may many other people be blessed through it. In Jesus' name. Amen.*

FRIDAY – THE RICH FOOL

Scripture: Luke 12:20-21

Today's parable was prompted by a family dispute over an inheritance. Before telling the story, Jesus gives the hearer a clue as to its meaning by issuing a stern warning about greed, which almost always is a problem with settling estates.

The story is about a rich farmer who can think of only one thing – getting more land and more possessions. I would like to have been there when he told this story. I'll bet many people were smiling, eager to hear Jesus' teaching, looking him in the eyes as he began, but then one-by-one were dropping their smiles, staring at the ground.

One of the interesting things about this parable is that God intervenes and speaks. He speaks to the rich man, saying, "You fool!" He then explains that he, the farmer, will die this very night, and asks him about what good will all that land and possessions be then. Jesus concludes by stating that this is the picture for everyone who is not "rich toward God".

Many people don't know that one can be rich toward God. They only understand riches to be money, luxury cars, land, fancy homes and things. If one attends a strong church that teaches the Bible, one can learn about another kind of riches, the kind that can't be taken away from you by death.

An old southern gospel song goes like this. *I'm a poor rich man. Oh, I 'm a poor rich man. Glory be it really happened to me. I'm a millionaire. I know that I'm poor, but I've got a lot more, than many rich friends that I know. I've got a home in the sky that money can't buy. I'm a poor rich man.*

Prayer: *Father, thank you for the true riches. Thank you that these riches are available for everyone. Keep me away from greed, oh Lord. Protect me from such wicked desires. In Jesus' name. Amen.*

SATURDAY – THE VINE AND THE BRANCHES

Scripture: John 15:5

Years ago, when pastoring at my first church in rural Huntington County, Indiana, I had a habit of regularly jogging up the road from our home. Near the road, in the front yard of a newly constructed home, was a pear tree. Growing in the wild, it never had any care. As the new owner finished landscaping, he cut off many branches from the tree, making it look rather bare. I wondered why he did this, as it made the tree look ugly. Over the months, I began to see why. As it grew new leaves, it also sprouted much juicy, appealing fruit. By pruning the tree, this wise man now had a beautiful, productive fruit tree.

This is the image I get when reading today's text. Though it is listed as a parable, it could also be viewed as an analogy. Jesus is the vine, and his followers are the branches. The point of having a vine and branches is to have fruit. If there is no fruit, the branches are useless. Jesus gets quite specific in stating that God is the vinedresser or gardener and that he will take away every branch which does not bear fruit. Jesus also says that if his followers abide in him and he abides in them, they will bear fruit.

It is true that branches cannot bear fruit if they are separated from the vine. Likewise, Christ's followers cannot bear fruit, not any fruit, not the least little bit of fruit, apart from him.

Jesus states that God is glorified by his people who bear much fruit. One bears fruit by taking Christ's words into the heart and mind, opening oneself up to the transforming work of the Holy Spirit.

Prayer: *Father, I want to bear fruit. I want to abide in the words of Jesus. I want His words to abide in me. Help me, Lord. In Jesus' name. Amen.*

SUNDAY – GOD'S SPECIAL DAY – THE LORD'S DAY

"From You comes my praise in the great assembly; I shall pay my vows before those who fear Him."

Psalms 22:25

OLD TESTAMENT GREATS:

WEEK #21 – NOAH AND THE FLOOD

MONDAY – CORRUPTION AND VIOLENCE

Scripture: Genesis 6:5-6

When God gave mankind the freedom to make choices, he took the chance that man would not choose right. Because man's nature was corrupted and poisoned, his heart has always been inclined the wrong direction. For example, one never has to teach a child to say "no". It is one of the first words he learns. One doesn't have to teach a child to do wrong, to lie, to be jealous, or to be selfish. Instead, the parent goes to great effort to teach him right. Wrong comes easily.

I know of no other verse in all of Scripture that saddens me as does verse 6. Here we learn of God's sorrow over his finest act of creation. How could anything so right go so wrong? No other place in the Bible do we read of God saying, "I am sorry". God is sorry that he created man. I am reminded of Jeremiah's words, as to the heart of man being more deceitful than anything else and desperately sick (17:9).

Genesis specifically mentions the appalling sexual behavior of older men, "sons of God", toward young, innocent girls. Later it says the earth was filled with violence and corruption. Adultery, fornication, and sexual perversion are always in the same boat as violence and corruption. What an ugly picture.

A study of ancient and modern history reveals a very similar picture – horrendous and unthinkable brutality by men. I wish it wasn't so, but it is. Only where Christianity is firmly rooted in society do we see anything different. It is no accident that the modern educational system evolved from Christian Western Europe. It is no accident that modern medicine and technology evolved from societies shaped by the teaching of the Bible.

Prayer: *Father, thank You for all those who have gone before who have known You and have chosen to do and to live right. Thank You for righteousness and holiness. Give me a pure heart, oh God. In Jesus' name. Amen.*

TUESDAY – PUSHING THE RESET BUTTON

Scripture: Genesis 6:7

God is far more patient than any man or woman I have ever known. There have been many situations in my life where I would have enjoyed making some people toast, but God saw it differently. When God acts, he does do so with great decisiveness and precision. Though the destruction of all mankind and living things is rather troubling in some ways, it was necessary in God's thinking to preserve mankind and to move forward with his eternal plan.

Many times as a parent, I wished my child had a reset button. If you have parented a child, you know the feeling. There are times when you want to start over with all the default settings in place, but I have yet to see a child with such a button on his forehead or back or any other place on his body. We do see this somewhat, though, in nature. At the end of every day, God presses the reset button for a new day. With the Genesis Flood, God pressed the reset button on mankind. His patience had run out. It was time to act. And he did.

It is interesting that almost every ancient civilization has a flood story. Many archeologists claim there is verifiable evidence of a point in history, thousands of years ago, where water suddenly covered the entire earth. When Allied pilots flew over the mountains of Ararat, during WW II, in what is now Turkey, they sighted something like the hull of a giant, wooden ship stuck in ice. Because of the extreme climate, few people have ever explored the peaks of those mountains. It is amazing that Genesis speaks of those very mountains as being the place where the ark landed.

Prayer: *Father, today I praise You for acting in history to preserve mankind. I would not be here today, without the Genesis Flood. Thank You for Your mercy. In Jesus' name. Amen.*

WEDNESDAY – NOAH THE RIGHTEOUS MAN

Scripture: Genesis 6:9

Noah surfaces as an exceptional man with high moral and ethical standards. His conduct, evidently, was above reproach; though later on in the story we do learn that he was not perfect. The most profound statement about Noah is that he "walked with God". When God came looking for Adam in the Garden of Eden, he came "walking".

My father-in-law, Don Morrison, was one who liked to take walks. Many times when visiting his house or when at family reunions, he would suggest taking a walk. Walking provided the atmosphere for loose, informal conversation about life. The best way to get to know Don Morrison was to walk with him.

Noah "walked" with God. Though there is little or no information about Noah's spiritual life, outside of this simple statement, it is enough to speak volumes. It tells me he enjoyed being with God. It tells me he had conversation with God. It tells me why he had such a high standard of morals and ethics. It tells me why God chose him to do a seismic, special task that would have eternal ramifications.

How would you describe your fellowship with God? Would your spouse or close friend agree, if the comment was made that you "walked with God"? If so, I have a feeling your moral and ethical standards are high. This is precisely the reason why the societies which have little corruption, crime, and violence are the societies with strong churches. Right behavior is rooted in right belief. Right belief is rooted in truth and light, which is God. God is delighted when his children walk with him. He is delighted to laugh, to listen, and to share life with those made in his image.

Prayer: *Father, I want to walk with You. Teach me how. Teach me to trust You enough to pour out my hopes, fears, failures, and dreams to You. In Jesus' name. Amen.*

THURSDAY – AGAIN THE BLESSING

Scripture: Genesis 9:1-3

God gave the same instructions to Noah and his family, as when he created Adam and Eve. He repeated part of his creation discourse but with more detailed instructions about life. He then gave the famous promise with the rainbow in the sky as a reminder of that promise.

I wonder specifically what God did to bless them and why. They obviously had been blessed before. God was with them. God chose them for this mighty task. What was the need of this special blessing now? It had to be an emotional moment for them to exit the ark and see that God's promises were, in fact, true. Noah made an altar and offered burnt offerings to God. God's blessing is, evidently, his response to Noah's offering and an opportunity to impress upon Noah and his family, his love, acceptance, and affirmation of them as his people. God wanted to firm up his relationship with them as they began a new life.

We learn from the story of the Flood that all humans come from one family, though skin tones and other features vary from people to people. The German Nazis, before WW II, put great emphasis on dividing mankind, viewing the German, Aryan race, as a superior master race and other races, such as Jews and Gypsies, as sub-human.

The command to multiply should not be overlooked. It is a key part of God's will for all living creatures. God enjoys life. He authored life. He enjoys multiplication of life. He is pro-life, not just in a political sense as most people think of it, but in a macro-way. Everything about God is life. Jesus is *the way, the truth, and **the life**. God is life!

Prayer: *Father, the picture of Noah and his family beginning a new life is precious. Your word is there. Your blessing is there. We praise You that we are not divided and are of one family. In Jesus' name. Amen.*

FRIDAY – PROMISE WITH A SIGN

Scripture: Genesis 9:12-13

Most of us know the story of the rainbow and God's promise. No it is not a pot of gold, but God's word. He promised to never again destroy the world with a flood. He put his mark in the sky so that on a regular basis, he would remember this moment.

God calls the rainbow a *"sign of the covenant"*. This very same phrase is used throughout the Old Testament in relation to circumcision.

The important thing is not the sign, not the rainbow, but the promise or the covenant God made. In Biblical times, a covenant was a formal agreement between two parties, which was usually accompanied by something visible to remind both parties of the agreement. This is a similar covenant. It is God making a covenant with all living creatures. The sign was to point to the formal agreement and remind everyone involved. The rainbow is to remind God of the promise he made.

Scientists say, a rainbow is an arc of concentric colored bands which become visible when sunlight interacts with raindrops. It is indeed beautiful, being one of the most extraordinary natural wonders. The sun and moon are spoken of to be calendar signs, but the rainbow is the only sign in the sky with a spiritual message. The rainbow's seven colors are red, orange, yellow, green, blue, indigo, and violet. In school we remembered these by the phrase, Roy G. Biv. It is a mystery how every rainbow, in every part of the world, will have the exact same colors, every time.

The rainbow reminds me of God. It also reminds me that God gives his word and plans to keep his word.

Prayer: *Father, thank You for the reminder in the sky. Help me always to remember to look up and never forget Your promises to me. In Jesus' name. Amen.*

SATURDAY – ANOTHER GLOBAL CRISIS

Scripture: Genesis 11:4

Speaking a common language is a powerful unifying force for any society. I am more aware of that after being in India, where the country is sharply divided, mainly because of its many different languages. It is difficult to work together if you can't understand one another.

After the flood, the earth began to populate. Everyone spoke the same language as they were from the same family. This was ok until they started constructing a very large mega city to "make for ourselves a name". It is stated that now nothing they propose to do will be impossible. People coming together to pool their resources and talents makes for unlimited possibilities. Some fear this was similar to the modern day United Nations.

Just a few chapters back, God intervened because of corruption, violence, and immorality. He promised never to destroy life on the earth like that again, and now he sees trouble on the horizon once more. This time, it is man's selfish ego and arrogance running wild with the potential of a one world government with brutal thugs as dictators. God intervenes to prevent it from happening by confusing their language. This divided mankind into language groups, geographically located in different parts of the world, thus laying the groundwork for different races.

In most communities, there are certain names of families that are important, really important. With the right name comes great power and status. Many churches are like that as well. Our sinful nature always moves us in the direction of trying to "make for ourselves a name". The Christian is called to lift up the name of Jesus, not his own name, not to bring glory to self, but to God.

Prayer: *Father, teach me to resist trying to make for myself a name. My name means nothing. I want to use my life to lift up Your name. I want others to lift up Your name. Through Christ. Amen.*

SUNDAY – GOD'S SPECIAL DAY – THE LORD'S DAY

"Praise the Lord! Praise the Lord from the heavens; praise Him in the heights! Praise Him, all His angels, praise Him, all His hosts." Psalms 148:1-2

OLD TESTAMENT GREATS:

WEEK #22 - ABRAHAM

MONDAY – GOD CALLS

Scripture: Genesis 12:1-3

Today's text is one of the most pivotal texts in the entire Bible. From this point on, God is dealing primarily with one family and one lineage group to reveal himself to the world – the Hebrew people. Abraham is the father of the Hebrew (Jewish) people. King David was of this family and all the kings after David were of Abraham's family until the final king was born – Jesus.

There is no evidence that Abraham's family did not participate in the idolatrous practices of their culture. Personal faith begins with Abraham. We don't know the age that he became aware of the one, true, unseen God. We don't know the circumstances. We only know that he believed God, heard God, and obeyed God.

Chapter 12 begins with God speaking to Abraham some very troubling words. He tells him to leave his country, his family, and his relatives and go to a distant land. Our nature is to gravitate to comfort thus we pick out the most comfortable chair in the room and the most comfortable bed. Most people find comfort being with their own family, with their own community or state, and being within their own country. Not too many would welcome the instructions to leave your country and live apart from your relatives and your culture. One might describe Abraham's call as a missionary call.

It would be interesting to know much more of Abraham's past experiences with the Lord. Abraham must have had great confidence in God, enough confidence to risk his life and the life of his immediate family.
To believe God exists is one thing. To believe God speaks to people and has a plan for their lives takes it to a much deeper level.

Prayer: *Father, thank You for Abraham's obedience and faithfulness. I want to hear You, Lord. I know You still are alive; You still speak; and that You have a plan for lives. Praise You. In Jesus' name. Amen.*

TUESDAY – THINKING BIG

Scripture: Genesis 12:3

It is easy to think the Old Testament is all about the Hebrew people and the nation of Israel. Though the bulk of the Old Testament certainly is about the Hebrew people, it is very important that one doesn't miss the global theme that weaves throughout the whole canon. Here in the first book of the Bible, we see that God is thinking of all the peoples of the world, not just Israel. God's purpose in blessing Abraham and Israel is stated in today's verse where he reveals his plan to bless the world.

Many Christians fail to see this. They fail to see that this big picture in God's mind began in Genesis and is the dominant theme of the both the Old and New Testaments, being very evident in the ending book of Revelation. In Revelation, the Apostle John writes of his vision of a great multitude, so great that no one could even count it, standing before God's throne. He sees people from every nation, all tribes, and tongues. John sees the fulfillment of Genesis 12:3.

Most of the Jewish leaders failed to see this as well. They saw God's blessing stopping with the Hebrew people. Rather than seeing their blessing as a means to an end, the end being the world, they saw it as the end. In their mind, God was thinking Jewish, Jewish, Jewish, when in fact, God was thinking world, world, world. Their god was quite small.

It is easy to see Christianity as a pool of privilege for good Christians like ourselves rather than a river of blessing to other peoples of the world. It is easy to focus in rather than out. Remember, God is thinking of the world.

Prayer: *Father, Your will and plan is precious. Thank You for revealing this to us. Thank You for loving the world and for including us in Your plan to bless all the peoples of the world. In Jesus' name. Amen.*

WEDNESDAY – A GLIMPSE AT INTEGRITY

Scripture: Genesis 13:8-9

Today's story gives us precious insights about Abraham and his treatment of other people. When Abraham finally settled in the land of Canaan, his nephew, Lot, is mentioned as coming with him. Abraham had many sheep and goats and was a wealthy man in terms of material wealth. Lot also had much livestock. Both had herdsman who managed their flocks. As their herds had expanded, over time, the land was too small for both, causing problems. There grew to be tension and strife between Abraham's herdsmen and Lot's herdsmen. Abraham takes the initiative to solve this problem. He expressed to Lot his desire for good relations and then suggested they split up and settle in different areas, giving Lot the option of choosing which part of the land he wanted. Lot chose the best land, and that was ok with Abraham. Problem solved.

Abraham could have thought, "Why should Lot get the best land?" If Abraham was greedy, he would have gone to battle with Lot, resulting in a strained relationship and possibly even bloodshed. Abraham valued his relationship with Lot more than he valued his possessions.

In verse 4 of chapter 13, we read that Abraham set up an altar and called on the name of the Lord. I believe Abraham sought God's advice in solving the problem, and God guided him.

Too many families today have strained relationships over money and possessions. Which is more important? If we value our family more than we do our possessions, then doesn't it make sense to "let it go" for the sake of peace? If more people sought the counsel of the Lord, instead of their attorney's counsel, more family problems would get solved with relationships preserved.

Prayer: *Father, keep me from greed. Whether I am rich or poor, keep my mind focused on the right things. Oh Lord, help me to forever be the peacemaker in my family. In Jesus' name. Amen.*

THURSDAY – THE DYNAMIC OF FAITH

Scripture: Genesis 15:6; Romans 4:16

As noted last week in our study of miracles, belief and faith are major factors in our relationship with God. In today's story, God again speaks to Abraham about the future plan for his life. Abraham and Sarah were beyond child-bearing years so all the talk from God about making his family great and having children made no sense. God tells Abraham to look to the heavens and count the stars and then says, *"So shall your descendents be."* Abraham's response was to believe God and because of that belief or faith, God declared him righteous.

The Apostle Paul speaks of Abraham as the Father of all who live by faith. Through Jesus, we have a mighty promise from God, a promise of the coming Kingdom. Paul argues that if we look to Jesus and believe, God will declare us righteous through the shed blood of Jesus. In that sense, we are one with Abraham, the Believer.

Fanny Crosby was such a Believer. Born in 1820 in Brewster, NY, she was blinded at six months of age by a quack surgeon. Saved at an early age, she was captivated by stories of the Bible, memorizing sometimes five chapters a week. She went to music school and started writing Gospel hymns. By the time of death, she had written over 9,000 hymns, many of which are in church hymnals.

The author of the book of Hebrews lists many faith heroes, including Abraham. At the end, he states, *"All these died in faith, without receiving the promises, but having seen them and having welcomed them from a distance . . . Therefore God is not ashamed to be called their God, for He has prepared a city for them. (11:13,16)"*

Prayer: *Father, thank You for great men and women of faith whom I will never meet this side of glory but will meet them around the throne with You. In Jesus' name. Amen.*

FRIDAY – HUMAN SOLUTIONS

Scripture: Genesis 16:2

If I was writing the Bible, I would only include the good stories, but I am not like God. God includes the bad with the good. Included in Genesis is the story of Abraham and Sarah at a weak moment. God had promised them a family but after ten years, no children. Sarah was tired of waiting, as she was old. Where was God? Where were the children? Since God obviously was not doing anything, why not orchestrate a family of her own? Why not? What about Hagar, her young, Egyptian maid? Why not give her to Abraham as his wife? She could be the surrogate mother. Abraham listened to her (Guys, we have to stop doing this!). Jumping in bed with this young maid didn't sound like such a bad idea to him either.

Wellllllll, here is the "rest of the story". A baby boy is born, Ishmael. This became quite a scene for jealousy between Sarah and Hagar. Hagar takes the boy and flees, but God intervenes, speaks to her, and sends her back. Legend has it that Ishmael later fled to the deserts and became the father of the Arab race, which are the Muslims of today. It is interesting that in this same chapter, an angel gives a prophecy about Ishmael – *"He will be a wild donkey of a man, his hand will be against everyone, and everyone's hand will be against him . . . "* Does that shoe fit or what?

When will we ever give up trying to manufacture our own solutions instead of trusting God? Things get very complicated when we don't wait on the Lord. God is still God, and he rescues us, but sometimes the price is quite hefty.

Prayer: *Father, forgive me when Your timetable is not good enough for me. Forgive me when I doubt You. Teach me, Lord, to trust you more and more. In Jesus' name. Amen.*

SATURDAY – SIGN OF THE COVENANT

Scripture: Genesis 17:9-11

The promise (covenant) God was making with Abraham is a really big thing in Genesis, which is repeated over and over. I'm not sure most of us really begin to understand the profound meaning of this covenant. In chapter 17, God restates the covenant and then instructs Abraham and the men of his household to be circumcised as a reminder (sign) of this covenant. Abraham was ninety-nine years old when he was circumcised. Imagine that.

God really, really wanted those men to remember that they were his men, men of the promise, men of faith. I believe there is a connection between what happened to Abraham and Hagar and this sign that God chose. Wasn't there any other part of the body God could have chosen? What about maybe a cut on the ear, or maybe on the top of the hand or arm, where the sailor gets the "Mother" tattoo? Why the man's penis? As no other men of Abraham's time were circumcised, this mark on his body would be very noticeable at a crucial moment.

In thinking of today, could it be that the one area of a man's life, which he is most likely to betray his Lord, is with lust, adultery or fornication? Could it be that God chose that part of the man's body to remind him, in the heat of passion, who he is? I believe that. I believe man easily forgets that he is not an animal; he is not to be taken captive by the lust in his eyes and the testosterone surging through his body. Man has been bought with a price to rise above fleshly desires, not by his own strength, but by the power of God.

Prayer: *Father, give us men in the church who live by Your power, who look to You to rise above fleshly passions, who are faithful to their wives and families. In Jesus' name. Amen.*

SUNDAY – GOD'S SPECIAL DAY – THE LORD'S DAY

"Praise the Lord! Sing to the Lord a new song, and His praise in the congregation of the godly ones." Psalms 149:1

OLD TESTAMENT GREATS:

WEEK #23 - JOSEPH

MONDAY – GOD IN THE MIDST OF FAMILY TENSION

Scripture: Genesis 37:4-5; 18

This week's readings will be from the life of Joseph, which includes a huge chunk of Genesis.

As I have often stated, if I was writing the Bible, I would not be so honest as to give the dirty laundry, as the Biblical authors appear to do. This is just one more reason that I believe God is the superintending author.

Today we look at the nasty little secret of most families – jealousy, envy, favoritism, and hatred. Praise God that for most families there is also the good stuff, but digging below the surface will also reveal some of the shameful things mentioned. With all three, main families of Genesis (Abraham, Isaac, and Jacob), we see some nasty moments which prove they were not exempt from having warts.

Jacob had twelve sons, which became the twelve tribes of Israel (Jacob's name was changed to Israel). Whether he intended to show favoritism or not, he apparently did, which created much tension among the sibling group, even to the point of hatred and plotting to kill. Joseph was the first born of the wife Jacob truly loved, Rachel. As there was tension and rivalry between Jacob and his twin brother, Esau, now we read of tension and rivalry in Jacob's sons.

We make a mistake when we think God can't use imperfect people. A close look at the characters of the Bible reveals people and families who were at times inconsistent, selfish, immoral, dishonest, and deceitful. Sound a little bit like families of today? By seeking the Lord, the possibilities of improved integrity and character are certainly there and should follow those who walk in grace, but that is not to say God's people no longer have a sinful nature.

Prayer: *Father God, thank You for my family, in spite of all the problems which we have faced. Lord I want You to shine through me to my loved ones. In Jesus' name. Amen.*

TUESDAY – GOD WITH HIM

Scripture: Genesis 39:2-3

This chapter is quite eventful and probably could be expanded into a book in and of itself, if one had more details. I call your attention to a phrase which is repeated four times in the chapter – "the Lord was with him". Later on, Pharoah, the grand prince of Egypt, comments about the "divine spirit" in Joseph.

It is truly amazing how Joseph came to Egypt as a slave and rose to such high wealth and status. Egypt was a major world power in that day. For the Pharaoh to even know the name of a Jewish slave is shocking, let alone know the slave well enough to comment on his qualities. The Bible gives God the credit for Joseph's prosperity and advancement.

Why is God "with" some people and not others? Some would argue that it is God's choice as to who he favors with his promises and presence, and some would argue it is man who chooses to walk with God, inviting his favor and blessing. Jesus did say, "You did not choose me, but I choose you . . ." (John 15:16). I see God choosing Joseph for a special task. Though he did not have a clue how God was going to use him, and had every reason to be angry and resentful, he sought the Lord and was aware of God's presence. He successfully resisted fleshly temptations and trusted the Lord to direct his path.

Are you aware of God's presence? By the fact you are reading this devotional says something about your spiritual life. Something stirred in your heart to make you want to know more about the Lord. I believe that "something" is the presence of God, the presence of God's Spirit.

Prayer: *Father, thank You today for such a great example of a Godly man as Joseph. I want to be like him, Father. In spite of all that could make me angry or resentful, I want to rise above it. In Jesus' name. Amen.*

WEDNESDAY – STANDING FIRM

Scripture: Genesis 39:9-10

The story today speaks volumes as to how a man or woman can resist powerful temptation. We learn from the text that Joseph was handsome and was the rising star to a high ranking Egyptian officer named Potiphar. Potiphar saw potential in Joseph and positioned him in a high position of trust and responsibility. When in private, Potiphar's wife seduced Joseph. Joseph resisted, explaining, "How *then could I do this great evil and sin against God*?"

Observe that Joseph recognized this as a "great evil". Satan did not gain an inch with Joseph. It mattered not to Joseph that she might have justified this in her own mind as being possibly ok, because her husband would not find out about it. It was a great evil, and Joseph called it out as such.

Also observe how Joseph viewed this in relation to God. He didn't mention that it might be a sin against her, her husband, or her family. He plainly states it would be a sin against God. First and foremost, God would be offended.

The man or woman who walks with God will have God's power in the heat of the moment when tempted by a situation that may appear anonymous and harmless. The Holy Spirit will give that person sharp discernment to not be deceived by the Deceiver and the Father of Lies. The Holy Spirit will enable the person to see the shameful, despicable act for what it is, allowing the Believer to call it out as such.

The man or woman who walks with God will not try to explain away behavior which is offensive to God but will see it, first and foremost, as a sin against the Father.

Prayer: *Father, thank You for Your Spirit who enlightens my thinking as to right and wrong. Oh Lord, help me to resist the devil in all ways. Keep me on the path to a pure heart and life. In Jesus' name. Amen.*

THURSDAY – SEEKING GOD AMIDST DISAPPOINTMENTS

Scripture: Genesis 39:19-20

Though innocent, Joseph was put in jail because of rape accusations by Potiphar's wife. It appears he was in jail for several years. I could imagine how he might have wondered why God allowed him to be sold by his brothers as a slave and taken to Egypt. I can imagine how he might have wondered why God allowed these unfair things. First slavery. Now prison. *"Where are you God?" "Where are your blessings now?"*

The Bible does say God prospered Joseph, but his prosperity wasn't realized at the moment but after years of bitter hardships and disappointments.

I have officiated many funerals. Several of them were untimely deaths with agonizing grief. The grieving families were haunted by the thought, *"Where are you God?"* They knew God was big enough and powerful enough to have stopped the accident or the disease. But he didn't. Why didn't he stop it? Why didn't he intervene? Does he not care?

Many pastors are teaching and preaching that God will heal you, prosper you, and bless you according to your faith. So what does that say when you aren't healed, prospered, or blessed? Does that mean you have no faith or that you are living in disobedience? Does that mean God is punishing you, when you face hardships? Was God punishing Joseph? I don't think so.

I wish those prosperity preachers would read the story of Joseph and many other Bible stories and not be so quick to take one or two verses here and there to build an entire theology. God does prosper and bless people, but for most cases, it is not instantaneous. Our faith does not exempt us from the tough hits and injustices of this life.

Prayer: *Father, thank You that You are always there with me, as promised, even when things appear to be completely out of control. When evil triumphs, give me the faith and courage to keep looking up. In Jesus' name. Amen.*

FRIDAY – SEEING THE BIGGER PICTURE

Scripture: Genesis 45:8; 50:20

Chapter 50, verse 20, is one of the most profound statements of faith in the Bible. It gives precious insight into the heart and mind of Joseph, who had survived life as a slave and as a prisoner. His theology was solid rock, spot on.

After his time of slavery and imprisonment, through a series of God events, he was raised to a high position of political power and put in charge of all the food supply of Egypt. There was a horrible famine throughout much of the known world. Because of abundant food, people from neighboring nations came to Egypt to buy food. Some of those people were Joseph's brothers. Initially Joseph played tricks on them, causing them to panic and suffer, eventually to bring his father to Egypt as well. Joseph broke down weeping and finally revealed his identity to his brothers. Twice he told them that God had sent him to Egypt to eventually preserve the family. He said this even though they did it. They sold him as a slave. Joseph recognized God's hand in it and refused to exact vengeance on them. When his father died, he reaffirmed his love for his brothers and made that incredible, revealing statement, "... *you meant evil against me, but God meant it for good...* "

This is a clear picture of our sovereign God. He has a plan that gives enough wiggle room for freewill, to take things in different directions. We are called to trust the bigger picture, to know man's injustices are not greater than God. Man may think he is a powerful dude and can do much evil, but he is fool, if he thinks he can thwart God.

Prayer: *Father, Your ways are always higher than my ways. Oh Lord, help me to never lose sight of the bigger picture, when plans are spoiled, when my life situation is in disarray. In Jesus' name. Amen.*

SATURDAY – LETTING GRACE FLOW TO OTHERS

Scripture: Genesis 50:17

After reading of brothers stealing birthrights, deceiving, and plotting to kill one another, it is such a breath of fresh air to end the book of Genesis reading of deep love and affection within this same family, which had previously been severely fractured.

Grown men usually don't cry. But here we see Joseph weeping and assuring his brothers of forgiveness with absolutely no plan of retribution. Take note that the brothers did not weep nor did they ask for forgiveness but only quoted their recently deceased father as requesting Joseph to forgive them. It was unfortunate that they didn't come out and simply ask for forgiveness. Their rather cunning nature is still at play. Joseph takes the high road and with deep emotion, expresses that he is not to judge, as if he was God. He has no plans of a payback. They indeed sold him into slavery, doing it for evil. He didn't sugar coat their dastardly deeds but did give to them the same grace that he himself had received from the Father, an example for people of Christian faith.

All who want to hold on to past grievances, whether in a family setting or church, need to take note. Jesus said (Matt. 6:15), *"But if you do not forgive others, then your Father will not forgive your transgressions."* If one has truly experienced the incredible act of forgiveness from God for numerous offenses, how can he not take that same grace given to him and extend it to others? Jesus even told a parable to further drive this point home. How dare we withhold grace from another person! We do so at the peril of our own forgiveness.

Prayer: *Father, I realize it. I see it. I get it. Your grace and forgiveness is given to me so that I may pass it on to others. Thank You that I do not have any less, when giving it away. How amazing it is, amazing grace. Oh Lord, thank You. In Jesus' name. Amen.*

SUNDAY – GOD'S SPECIAL DAY – THE LORD'S DAY

"Praise the Lord! Praise God in His sanctuary; praise Him in His mighty expanse. Praise Him for His mighty deeds; praise Him according to His excellent greatness." Psalms 150:1-2

OLD TESTAMENT GREATS:

WEEK #24 - MOSES

MONDAY – HOLY GROUND

Scripture: Exodus 3:4-5

Moses is the main character of Exodus, Leviticus, Numbers, and Deuteronomy. He stands very tall in the Bible Hall of Fame. He is the man chosen by God to speak for God and lead his people out of Egyptian bondage to the "Promised Land" or Canaan, or later known as Palestine or Israel.

As the adopted son of Pharoah, Moses was raised in royalty, while maintaining a relationship with his blood mother, who nursed and cared for him. He was thus very aware of his heritage. The Hebrew people in Egypt once enjoyed status but eventually were treated very brutally as slaves. God remembered his covenant with the Hebrew people, saw their suffering, and rescued them.

In defense of a fellow Hebrew, who was beaten by an Egyptian, Moses killed the offender and then fled Egypt. For forty years, he lived in the wilderness. It is there that God appeared to him, in the form of a burning bush, and told him to remove his sandals because he was standing on "holy" ground. This is the first time we get a glimpse of holiness, as it relates to something tangible, set apart for sacred use.

Imagine taking a soil sample of that piece of ground which God called holy? Would it have tested to be of similar substance as the ground surrounding it? I would guess so. Why was it holy? It was not holy because it was better than any other square foot of soil, but because God set it apart for sacred use, making it holy.

In the same way, Christians are humans, not any better than anyone other humans, only set apart by God for a sacred purpose. In that sense, we are holy.

Prayer: *Father, it is awesome to think I have been set apart for something special, something that has a purpose which flows with Your purpose and plan for humanity. Help me to remember that, Lord, each and every day. In Jesus' name. Amen.*

TUESDAY – WHO AM I?

Scripture: Exodus 4:10-11

While standing on the ground designated as "holy", God spoke to Moses. God explained how he would use him to rescue his people. After hearing of this mightily important mission, Moses was not a happy camper. He didn't jump up and down, shouting hallelujah!

Moses didn't see himself as qualified or gifted or positioned to lead a multitude of people anywhere, let alone confront Pharoah, one of the world's most powerful men, the man who wanted him dead. Moses was not a skilled speaker and had some type of speech impediment. One can only imagine Moses' thoughts – "What are you thinking, God? Surely you must have made a mistake. You have the wrong guy."

God knew that Moses had connections to the royal family. God also knew that he would empower Moses to do miraculous deeds to force Pharoah to let the Hebrew people go.

I have always identified with Moses. Having a serious stuttering problem since early childhood, taking speech therapy in school, I was not the most likely candidate for any type of public speaking. When sensing in my heart God calling me to preach a sermon, I resisted, much like Moses, thinking, "Who am I?" God has done miraculous things in my life, as to speaking publicly.

What about you? Have you ever felt God calling you to do something that you didn't think you were qualified to do? Over the years, I have seen many people do incredible things for God, who felt the call but resisted. In fact, I would say that in most cases where God calls, the person he is calling does not feel qualified. Do you know why? Without a miracle, they are not qualified.

Prayer: *Father, it is Your plan that we cannot do great things for You without Your indwelling Holy Spirit, without Your power. With You, all things really are possible. In Jesus' name. Amen.*

WEDNESDAY – I WILL BE WITH YOU

Scripture: Exodus 4:11-12

After hearing Moses' excuse of a speech problem, God reminds Moses that God is the one who made man's mouth, eyes and ears. He then commands Moses to "go".

Here we find that little word "go" once again. This is an action verb. One cannot stay sitting and go at the same time. He must leave his seat, leave the bed or couch, leave a stationary position, and become mobile. This is the word God used when calling Abraham to leave his village and relatives, and to "go". This is also the word that is used by Jesus, when he told his followers to "go" make disciples of all nations.

The church of Jesus Christ is not to be stationary. She is to be active. She is to be mobile. The famous pastor, John Wesley, once said, "*all the world is my parish*". God has a big plan, and it involves people going to gossip the Gospel, going to communities, going to workplaces, and going to the ends of the earth. There will come a time when God's people will rest. It is not now.

God told Moses that he would be with his "mouth", getting specific about how God would empower him. Many times, God uses us and empowers us precisely in our area weakness. The Apostle Paul said (II Cor. 12:10), "When I am weak, then I am strong."

Today, are you willing to go for God? It is tempting to keep our Christianity inside a stained glass building, to reserve our Christian witness for our comfortable, Christian bubble . . ., but that is not God's plan. Our marching orders carry a sense of urgency. Lives matter to God. The eternal destiny of people is at stake.

Prayer: *Father, I confess that too many times, when you have given me the opportunity, I have not been willing to go. Lord, I am sorry. I want to go. I want to go to my family, to my community, and to wherever You lead. In Jesus' name. Amen.*

THURSDAY – WHITE KNUCKLE RIDE

Scripture: Exodus 4:2-4

What would have happened if Moses would have initially agreed with God, not resisted, and willingly gone forth? We will never know. We only know what happened when he did resist. God wanted to convince him so he told him to throw his shepherd's staff on the ground, and Moses did. It instantly turned into a snake. Being afraid of snakes, like many people, Moses ran for his life. He didn't want to get bit. Snakes can be very dangerous. In India, there are cobras and vipers. People die when they get bit.

Then God told him to grasp its tail. Yikes! "Are you kidding God? Go back to that snake and get close to that awful creature. Grab its tail? Pick it up? No! God, anything but that!" Things are getting quite exciting at this moment. Moses goes back to the snake. How long did it take him to go back? When he went back, did he go inch by inch? Was he sweating? Was he shaking? Oh, if someone would have had a video camera!

When he grabbed its tail, boom, it didn't bite him. It turned back into a staff. If that wasn't enough of a demonstration of God's power, he did another miracle involving Moses' hand turning leprous. I have a feeling when Moses left that mountain, his determination and faith in the power of God was refreshed.

Almost always, following the Lord will lead to something like the snake and the leprous hand. Do you question whether God can really empower you to do what he is telling you to do? Do you really? Be prepared for a roller coaster ride, white knuckles and all. He will show you.

Prayer: *Father, I don't know how you do it. I only know that you do it. You call ordinary people, who doubt you and resist You. You patiently work with my inconsistent and even rebellious moments. Thank You Lord. In Jesus' name. Amen.*

FRIDAY – TEN PLAGUES

Scripture: Exodus 10:1-2

The story of God hardening Pharoah's heart and subsequently God inflicting ten plagues on the Egyptian people is quite the display of God's judgment upon nations who ruthlessly persecute, and exploit God's covenant people. It is also a story of God's patience, as he tolerated much pain and suffering inflicted on his people for many years, before acting, but then acted in a dramatic and decisive way.

Many people wonder why God would harden anyone's heart. Years ago I heard one Bible teacher say that, as with Pharoah, God will grease the tracks for anyone who blatantly refuses his invitation to change and who insists on going their own way. In other words, he will even help you get there, if that is the direction you want go. Thus, he hardened Pharoah's heart.

I think today's text gives some light to the subject. I see God giving Pharoah and the Egyptian people many chances to back the train up, as to their treatment of his people. I see him being overly patient, but then drawing a line and creating drama. He wanted the drama of the ten plagues and the destruction of the entire Egyptian Army in the Red Sea so the world would forever take note and never forget, and more especially so his covenant people would never forget.

Abusing and exploiting innocent people may be convenient and profitable, and even permissible in some parts of the world, but the end of it all is not pretty. It is interesting that Jesus describes the suffering of the wicked as "weeping and gnashing of teeth". He does this seven times in the four Gospels. Death is preferable to pain being so severe that one involuntarily gnashes his teeth.

Prayer: *Father, the death of the wicked is troubling. It is hard to understand why people resist You. Oh Lord, keep my heart tender. Purify it day after day. Keep my mind clean and rid my soul of any dark spots. In Jesus' name. Amen.*

SATURDAY – SHOW ME THY GLORY

Scripture: Exodus 33:17-18

Moses had this intimate relationship with God that most of us would envy. As Moses was up on the mountain, God gave him the Ten Commandments and all the many regulations involving religious practices and laws. At one point, the Bible says (33:11) that "the *Lord used to speak to Moses face to face, just as a man speaks to his friend.*"

After the people came through the Red Sea and were at the foot of the mountain, while Moses was receiving all this wonderful instruction from God, they slipped back into idolatry, worshipping a golden calf. When Moses saw this, he was very angry and broke the stone tablets of the Ten Commandments. God was also very angry and told Moses that he would no longer go with them, but would send his angel in his place. Moses argued with God and refused to go forward, unless God would go with them. God gave in to Moses' pleas and change his mind. After all this, Moses was very humbled and finally said, "*Show me Your glory*". God responded that no man could see his face and live, but that if he would hide behind this big rock, God would cover him with his hand, as his glory passed by. And he did.

The longer I walk with the Lord, the more I desire him, the more I want to see his glory. This should be the ultimate goal of every service of worship – to see his glory - the sparkling, dazzling, pure white glory that surrounds the Lord day and night. It is good to enjoy fellowship, meet people, and hear prayer requests, but the focus of every worship time should be the Lord and his glory.

Prayer: *Father, show me thy glory. Take me to the mountain and put me in the cleft of the rock. Cover me with Your hand, Lord, and show me thy glory. In Jesus' name. Amen.*

SUNDAY – GOD'S SPECIAL DAY – THE LORD'S DAY

"I will proclaim Your name to my brethren, in the midst of the congregation, I will sing Your praise."

Ps. 22:22

OLD TESTAMENT GREATS

WEEK #25 – JOB

MONDAY – SATAN TESTS MANKIND

Scripture: Job 1:6-8

All this week, we will take a closer look at this great man, Job, who was tested by Satan. We believe Job lived sometime in the era of Abraham.

Job begins with God's blessing upon his life being described as really big – many children and much wealth. He is referred to as the "greatest of all the men of the east". Was he from India? China? Persia? We are not sure.

In the story, Satan is said to have come from "roaming about on the earth". Satan appears with the sons of God and challenges God concerning Job. He accuses Job of serving God only for the wealth God has given Job. Satan tells God that Job will curse God to his face, if it were not for all the goodies God gave him. The test is on. God gives Satan permission to harm Job's fortune, but not Job himself.

The picture of Satan roaming about the earth fits with the description in Revelation 12 of Satan being thrown out of heaven, down to earth. In Revelation, Satan is called the "accuser of our brethren". This is precisely the scene we see when reading Job chapter one.

We dare not forget this Biblical truth. The "accuser" is stunningly real. He is there to accuse you, always there accusing you, saying things like, "You are no good". "You cannot do anything." To the young teen-age girl in the infancy of her fragile faith, Satan is there to tell her, "You are not pretty. You are ugly." To the church members, Satan is there sewing seeds of suspicion, envy and hunger for control. During this life, we face many times of testing, which are directly rooted in darkness.

Prayer: *Father, keep me from the grip of Satan. Keep my life free from any dark moment, free from any and all accusations Satan can throw in my face. By Your power, give me life in its fullness. In Jesus' name. Amen.*

TUESDAY – LOVING GOD UNCONDITIONALLY

Scripture: Job 1:11

The challenge put before God by Satan deserves some further thought. Does Job serve God because of Job's love for God? Or does he serve God because of what God has given him? Would Job serve God, if he were poor? Would he fear God if he suddenly lost everything?

The narrative before us is that Job did suddenly lose everything - all ten children, and all seven thousand sheep and three thousand camels in one day. Satan was probably thinking to himself, "Ha. Ha. Now we will see the real Job."

In my Bible is an old cross-stitch book mark. Knowing this verse meant so much to me, in my struggle with grief over the loss of our little Joni, Sandy (my sister) made it for me, some thirty-five years ago. It has Job 13:15 stitched in the material. It reads, "Though He slay me, yet I will I trust in Him." This verse captures the heart of Job. He did not fear God and love God because of the good times. He could serve God in the bad times, when every star in his heaven came down. No, God didn't have to do certain things for Job to win him over. God didn't have to buy Job's allegiance. Job simply loved God for who He was – the author of all life.

I made a big decision back in 1978. I decided that I could be like Job. I decided that God didn't have to do a certain number of things to make my life easy and comfortable to buy my allegiance. I decided to love and serve God for the rest of my life, based on what he had done in creation and in sending his Son.

Prayer: *Father, today I am reminded that Your greatness is not determined by my possessions, what I have or don't have. You don't owe me anything. I praise You, today, not because of my blessings, but because of who You are. In Jesus' name. Amen.*

WEDNESDAY – HOLDING FAST INTEGRITY

Scripture: Job 2:3; 27:5-6

Job refused to curse God, upon the loss of his children and possessions. As a response, Satan put forth plan B. Satan challenged God to inflict Job with disease and pain and then to watch him curse God to his face.

God gave Satan permission, and Satan struck Job with very painful boils throughout his body. Back then, not too many Wal-Greens and CVS stores were around. Ask any nurse or doctor, excruciating pain, 24-7, will break the spirit of the toughest man. Even Job's wife, encouraged him to end it all – "curse God and die" – but he didn't. He held his integrity.

It is worth noting that in almost all Bible translations, the English word "integrity" is used more than once to describe Job's character. According to the dictionary, "integrity" is the undivided or unbroken completeness of a man or woman's moral life. At one point in today's story, God is even quoted as using the word, "integrity", to describe Job's character. His character was obviously of an unusually high nature. In chapter two and then in chapter twenty-seven, the comment is made that through all his suffering, Job still held fast to his integrity. The pain of his outward circumstances did not trump, sway, or influence his character.

Sometimes the painful circumstances of life are indeed a test. Though the infliction comes from the devil, not God, the approval or permission comes from God, and there is a reason for it. God does not delight in seeing his people suffer. Many times it is a test. It causes us to question our faith and analyze our lives. Often, it is a reality check of who we are and who we serve.

Prayer: *Father, give me the character of Job. Through all of life's circumstances, help me, Lord, to always hold fast to my integrity. It is valuable in Your sight. In Jesus' name. Amen.*

THURSDAY – ARGUING WITH GOD

Scripture: Job 13:3; 15-16; 30:26-30

Severe depression would be a phrase to describe Job's condition. One expects this when there is chronic pain day after day and night after night. Job is not a happy camper. He is not shouting hallelujah and praising the Lord. He was not pretending to be super spiritual, but instead was angry with God and was quite forward about expressing his dissatisfaction to God.

The prevailing theology of his day was quite similar to the prevailing theology in many Christian circles today. It is called "prosperity theology". It espouses the belief that if you do certain things then God will bless you and make you healthy and rich. If you attend church regularly, you will not get sick. If you give 10% of your salary to the church, you will get back many times more. If you are honest and good, life will go well, and you will prosper in all ways. Though it is not a Biblical theology, it is preached from many pulpits. People who know their Bibles will always bristle at such nonsense.

The story of Job flies in the face of prosperity theology. Job was a righteousness man, a man of high integrity, yet he lost all his children, his possessions and his wealth. Where was God? How could this happen? It made no sense to him. Fortunately, his relationship with God was healthy enough that he was not afraid to disagree with God and question God. This surprised his friends. How dare anyone question God? Job feared God, indeed, but his knowledge of God was great enough for him to know that God valued honesty far above pious superficiality. He knew that God would listen if he sincerely questioned Him.

Prayer: *Father, it is good to know that we are always welcome in Your presence. It is good to know that we can openly express our deepest fears and doubts, and most embarrassing failures. Thank You, Lord. In Jesus' name. Amen.*

FRIDAY – WELL MEANING FRIENDS

Scripture: Job 5:17-19

Over the years, I have officiated many funerals. People who come to comfort the bereaved are at a loss of words so, many times, they speak before giving their words much thought. They repeat glib, pious phrases like, "God wanted another flower in heaven" or "God's will is always best". Some of these things said may very well be true, but usually, the person grieving does not find those responses to be helpful.

With Job's four friends, they had the answers, or so they thought. Most of the book is devoted to the dialogue between Job and his friends. All their explanations are generally the same. God punished and disciplined Job for selfishness, insensitivity, and greed. In other words, Job got what he deserved.

In pastoral counseling there is the "theology of presence". Basically, it is the wisdom of simply being present with someone without feeling the necessity of saying words or explaining why the tragic event happened. It is a hug. It is putting your arm around the person grieving or holding their hand. It is simply "being there" or "being present". Job's friends did not understand that too well. At times of intense grief, actions speak much louder than words.

The same is true when someone is seriously ill. The person visiting should resist the temptation to give an explanation for the illness. Let the doctor do that. Most of us know what it is like to be around someone who has an answer for everything. Don't be that way. Don't hesitate to say, "I don't know why . . ." Though as Christians, we have the answers to some basic life questions, but certainly not the answers to everything. Be real.

Prayer: *Father, all around us are people struggling with disappointment, injustice, and sometimes grief and serious illness. Help us, Lord, to be there for our friends, without thinking we have to answer every question. Help us to truly be a blessing. In Jesus' name. Amen.*

SATURDAY – ALL IS WELL

Scripture: Job 42:1-6; 10

The book of Job ends with God speaking directly to Job, reminding him of his insignificance as compared to all of God's creation and nature. Job was humbled. He repented with a renewed appreciation of God's greatness. God's final response is to restore all that Job had lost. Job went on to have ten more children and more possessions than ever before, was respected by the entire community as a righteous man, and lived to a ripe old age. God was indeed correct about Job. Satan was clearly wrong.

The end of the story for everyone who has cancer and honors the Lord through it is a new body that will never get sick and die. The end of the story to everyone who has lost loved ones and persevered in faith is "welcome home my son/daughter". The end of the story to everyone who has lost businesses, jobs, and dreams but has refused to let the disappointing circumstances of life poison their belief in God is "well done thou good and faithful servant".

When the wheels come off of one's life, faith is suddenly on display for everyone to see. There may have been previous attempts to share the story of Jesus with family and friends, but how the Believer responds in adversity and difficulty will speak a message ten times louder than the most polished and rehearsed Gospel presentation. I have seen this played out in numerous people's lives.

The last chapter of Job reminds me of Revelation chapter 22, the last chapter of the Bible - a chapter every Believer should know quite well. It is the end of the story. It is God's final triumph over evil. It is our hope.

Prayer: *Father, Your ways are way above my ways. Forgive me for failing to see the larger picture at times. Instill in my mind, throughout my entire life, the fresh hope of Your Kingdom, as in the final chapter of Your Holy Word. In Jesus' name. Amen.*

SUNDAY – GOD'S SPECIAL DAY – THE LORD'S DAY

"They were continually devoting themselves to the apostles' teaching and to fellowship, to the breaking of bread and to prayer. Everyone kept feeling a sense of awe; and many wonders and signs were taking place through the apostles." Acts 2:42-43

OLD TESTAMENT GREATS

WEEK #26 – SAMUEL

MONDAY – WORD FROM THE LORD

Scripture: I Samuel 2:35; 3:1

In Samuel, we see the political structure of Israel in transition from being ruled by prophets to kings. Samuel is known as both a priest and prophet. He was born at a time in Israel's history known as the period of Judges (as in the book of Judges) where Israel was spiritually at a very low point.

The statement in today's reading is quite chilling. It reads, "And word from the Lord was rare in those days . . ." Rather than say God wasn't speaking, I would prefer to think there weren't men or women who were listening to God. As they did not have the Bible, as God's word, they received God's word through visions, visitations of angels, and direct revelation. This just was not happening, and as a result, the people were spiritually suffering and had resorted to many cultural perversions.

Young Samuel's ministry began with God's word. Samuel heard God speak during the night hours, though he had difficulty discerning the voice of God. He thought it was his priest, Eli. After knowing it was God, he received God's word, which transformed his life.

I have attended many "clergy meetings" over thirty plus years of ministry. At most of those meetings, if someone would ask the question, "Anyone have a fresh word from the Lord?", heads would drop with eyes hitting the floor. Does anyone wonder why many churches in America are weak?

The power of God's word is amazing. God is still looking for men and women who will spend time in his word and hear his voice. In India, I have seen thousands of people bowing down to dead gods. We serve a living god, one that speaks and one that has spoken.

Prayer: *Father, thank You again for giving me the Bible as Your recorded word. Help me to know it and put it deep in my mind, to hear You speak in and through it. In Jesus' name. Amen.*

157

TUESDAY – KNOWING THE LORD

Scripture: I Samuel 3:6-7

If one is raised in church, it is easy to know a lot about the Lord but not truly "know the Lord". This is a very real danger. Such was the case for the young boy Samuel. He had been dedicated to the Lord by his parents, while a baby. He spent most of his childhood as an assistant to Eli the priest. Even as a boy, it is stated that he wore the "linen ephod", which was a specific kind of vest, only for those serving in Jewish religious services. In today's story, we read of God calling Samuel four times in the night. After the second time, it became known that Samuel did not yet know the Lord. How tragic. This explains why Samuel did not recognize God's voice calling to him.

In the previous chapter, we read that Eli's sons also did not "know the Lord", though they functioned as priests. In many ancient cultures, the trade of the father is passed down to the sons so if the father is a priest, so is the son. This is very evident in Hebrew culture as the tribe of Levi was to be a priestly tribe. All the males were to be Jewish priests.

When Jesus was confronted by some Jewish priests, he called them "white-washed tombs". In other words, they knew how to present themselves on the outside as being spiritual and holy but were void or empty of any spiritual life. They were seen as representing the living God but were themselves dead.

Every Christian should "know the Lord". If they do not, they are a hypocrite. Being a Christian is making the claim to know God, through Jesus Christ.

Prayer: *Father, I want to do much more than learn many things about You. I want to know You and to learn to know You more intimately throughout my whole life. In Jesus' name. Amen.*

WEDNESDAY – THE VALUE OF GODLY COUNSEL

Scripture: I Samuel 3:8-9

We live in a world of competing voices. Add to that the voice of evil and the voice of God and who can tell for sure if the voice one is hearing is truly God? People who struggle with some forms of mental illness hear voices so the whole idea of hearing God's voice is viewed as suspect by many. It is easier to dismiss the possibility altogether and go about life as if God doesn't speak.

If God doesn't speak, then don't bother reading the Bible or you really will be confused. The Bible is full of instances where God speaks. Samuel is one of the big ones. Through interacting with God, Samuel did come to "know the Lord" and to actually know him quite well. The process for Samuel discerning the Lord's voice is worth noting.

Eli the priest was a major player in this process. Samuel heard God's voice, but he didn't know it was God. He repeatedly thought it was Eli. Eli quickly picked up on what was going on and gave young Samuel very wise counsel. He informed him that it was God speaking and gave him direction as to how to respond when God spoke again. The rest is history. Samuel made the connection when God spoke. His life was never the same again. He went forth as a mighty prophet and priest.

Young people following the Lord would do well to take the counsel of older, wiser Godly men and women. Doing so would help them a lot in sorting through all the competing voices of our day. This can take the form of assistance in a disciplined Bible study and as a partner in prayer when seeking specific direction.

Prayer: *Father, thank You for the counsel of women and men who have followed You and known You for many years. They have seen You work in many situations. Help me to appreciate their counsel more and more. In Jesus' name. Amen.*

THURSDAY – THE CHALLENGE OF PARENTAL DISCIPLINE

Scripture: I Samuel 2:22,29; 8:1-3

Samuel's sons were a sad disappointment, just as Eli's sons were. In chapter two, we read of God questioning Eli as to why he would honor his sons above him – God. His sons didn't know the Lord, and it was obvious they were not walking with the Lord but were fornicating, sleeping with women outside the covenant of marriage. Evidently Eli refused to discipline them, but instead, allowed them to continue as priests. This was anything but pleasing to God.

Later on with Samuel, we see the same unfortunate picture. Samuel had appointed his sons as judges, but instead of administering justice, they were perverting justice and taking bribes. The people saw this blatant inconsistency and protested to Samuel.

This story casts light on a truth all parents and church leaders should see. Christian faith is not automatically transferred from one generation to another, without intentional teaching and modeling. In the book of Psalms, we are assured that if a child is raised in the ways of God, he will return to those ways when he is old. When a child is dedicated or baptized, those promises are usually highlighted. The key is to truly raise a child in the way of the Lord.

I have seen the son or daughter of a prominent member of a church given preference for a church position over a person who didn't have any relatives in the church. This is unfortunate. It is a set-up for a spiritual train wreck. This will bring a response from God that won't be pleasant. Though the church may have a Godly pastor and have sound, Biblical doctrine, God does not honor this way of doing church. This is evident in the book of Samuel.

Prayer: *Father, it is troubling to see children of Christian parents failing to enjoy You and the fruit of knowing You. Oh Lord, give us men and women in the church who are truly humble like Jesus, whose love for You trumps all else. In Jesus' name. Amen.*

FRIDAY – ADMONITION TO PRAY

Scripture: I Samuel 12:23; Colossians 1:9

God used Samuel to anoint Israel's first king, Saul, and to be a prophet to him. Upon King Saul's coronation, Samuel spoke a stern message to the people. He warned them of the price they would pay if they refused to serve the Lord with their whole heart. In the midst of such a strong admonition, he makes a very revealing statement about his own prayer life. He said that it would be a "*sin against the Lord*" if he ceased to pray for the people.

Churches place huge expectations on their pastors. One of the most overlooked but most important tasks of any pastor or church leader is to pray for his people. It is easy to get so busy doing good things in ministry but be weak in this most basic area. John Wesley, a great figure in church history, once said when facing a very busy day, "I am so busy today that I dare not neglect to spend much time in prayer."

Praying for others is called "intercession". When one intercedes for another, he stands between heaven and earth to make the connection for them, on their behalf. The Apostle Paul understood the importance of intercession. He wrote, ". . . *we have not ceased to pray for you* . . ." He was writing to the church of Colosse, people he had grown to care for and love.

Serving two churches over the course of twenty-seven years gives one the occasion to know and love many people. Though I have not been at my first church, St. Paul's Church near Huntington, Indiana, for over sixteen years, I still pray for most of those people by name, regularly. It is my privilege.

Prayer: *Father, thank You for the ministry of intercessory prayer. Thank You for brothers and sisters in the faith that we can support and agree with in prayer. It is our privilege. In Jesus' name. Amen.*

SATURDAY – SEEING AS GOD SEES

Scripture: I Samuel 16:6-7

The account of Samuel anointing David to replace Saul as King is another incredible story. Today's verse takes us to Bethlehem, to the home of Jesse, David's father. David was the youngest of eight brothers. In ancient cultures, the first born son carried special status. Samuel was about to make a huge mistake by anointing the eldest son of Jesse, and God stopped him and spoke to him. We have the famous statement, " . . . *for man looks at the outward appearance, but the Lord looks at the heart . . ."*

As the story goes, Jesse paraded each of his seven sons before Samuel, and God stopped Samuel from choosing any of them. It was only after Samuel inquired about the possibility of more sons that Jesse finally mentioned young David, out in the pasture, tending sheep. Samuel instructed them to bring David, and God gave Samuel the green light to anoint David, who would go on to be the greatest King of Israel.

It is true that we put too much emphasis on outward appearances. Many of the world's greatest leaders throughout history were not handsome. Their integrity was proven through difficult times and agonizing situations. Abraham Lincoln is a good example.

One of the weaknesses of the congregational system of church government is that the pastoral selection process can be greatly influenced by outward appearance rather than a history of proven leadership.

The average Christian spends much more time on Sunday morning preparing the outside of the body than the inner spirit. Think of the time taken to bath, do hair, make-up, etc. We can be easily fooled, if not guided by the Lord. Remember, the Lord looks at the heart.

Prayer: *Thank You, Lord, that we don't have to measure everyone's character by how pretty or handsome they are. Thank You, God, that You see through our silly attempts to make ourselves righteous by perfume and fancy clothes. In Jesus' name. Amen.*

SUNDAY – GOD'S SPECIAL DAY – THE LORD'S DAY

"On the first day of the week, when we were gathered together to break bread, Paul began talking to them, intending to leave the next day, and he prolonged his message until midnight." Acts 20:7

WEEK #27 – DAVID

MONDAY – FACING THE GIANTS

Scripture: I Samuel 17:36-37, 45

David, the greatest King of Israel, is certainly one of the most colorful figures in the Bible. Described as "ruddy" yet handsome, this young man spent much of his youth tending sheep and protecting the sheep from dangerous animals, such as lions and bears. Because he was the youngest of eight boys, he got the short end of the stick most of the time. Tending sheep was dirty work with little status. Indeed it was surprising that God chose him to replace Saul as King. Immediately after Samuel anointed David, we read that the Spirit of the Lord came mightily upon him.

The story of David and Goliath is quite famous. It is a picture of a small, but tough, young man defeating and killing one of the biggest and most dangerous military soldiers ever to live. It is the story of a person with a great faith and trust in God, going head to head with the brute force of evil.

The 23rd Psalm gives us a picture of David the shepherd boy, realizing the power and presence of Almighty God. David's firm belief in God's existence and willingness to miraculously intervene on behalf of God's people is on display. He made it known publicly where his strength and might was rooted, not in sword or spear, but in the name of the Lord of hosts.

Everyone who pursues a relationship with God will face giants. They may come in the form of a physical illness, loss of a marriage, a job or career, or of family problems, but there will be giants. There will be something the devil has put in your path that stands between where you are and where God wants you to be.

Prayer: *Father, You are greater than the giant I am facing today. You are more powerful. My trust is not in any other force in this world but You. Praise Your name. Through Christ, our Lord. Amen.*

TUESDAY – AN INCREDIBLE REALITY

Scripture: I Sam 18: 12, 14; II Sam 5:10

Like Joseph, David excelled and prospered in everything he did, whether it was tending sheep, fighting battles as an Israelite soldier, writing songs and poetry, or leading a nation. People who knew him were quick to observe something very special. God was "with him". God was on his side. His faith in God molded his worldview and shaped his character. David delighted in knowing the God of Abraham, Isaac, and Jacob.

David had his share of human moments, when he proved that he was not perfect. He was not exempt from personal, moral failures and the sins of his culture. But in spite of all that was bad, David had a very tender heart for God, repented when he messed up, and maintained the joy of the Lord most of his life. Jerusalem was named the "City of David". Jesus, our Lord, is spoken of as being the "Son of David".

One of the Biblical names for Jesus is "Immanuel", meaning God with us. Matthew records Jesus giving his final instructions to the Disciples telling them to make disciples of all the nations, ending it by saying he is with them always, even to the end of the age.

The incredible truth that God can actually be with someone is absolutely mind boggling. All Christians have that promise, if they truly follow in Christ's footsteps and live in obedience to his word. Hindus in India go to Temples to be with their gods. Sometimes this means riding trains for one or two days. Christians don't have to go to a church building to experience God's presence. Through the Holy Spirit's filling and anointing, God is with them at the office or workplace, at home, and everywhere they go.

Prayer: *Father, I long for You to be so present in my life that others would notice something special. In spite of my failures, when I repent, You forgive and pick me up. Oh Lord, thank You. In Jesus' name. Amen.*

WEDNESDAY - RESPECT FOR THE ANOINTED

Scripture: I Samuel 24:5-6, 16-17

Throughout the history of the church there have been Believers who carry a special anointing of God for a specific task. The Apostle Paul was one such man, along with Martin Luther, John Wesley and Billy Graham. In some ways, it doesn't appear they deserve such anointing, as they are people who have a flawed nature and are at times inconsistent and disobedient. Some are more humble and Godly than others, being only mere men.

The first king of Israel, Saul, began his ministry seeking and honoring the Lord but pride and arrogance slowly took over. God removed his Spirit from Saul and placed his Spirit upon young David, who was to take Saul's place. Saul was jealous and tried numerous times to kill David.

Today's story was one of those times. Saul had three thousand of his soldiers in pursuit of David. While taking a nap in a cave, David just happens to come along. David's men believe the Lord put Saul into David's hand and gave David an opportunity to do away with Saul. David refused. He didn't listen to his men but listened to his conscience. David's respect for the King of Israel would not allow him to harm King Saul. When King Saul realized this, he wept. He realized the greatness of this young man, David.

Many times in church situations, people with control tendencies will ignore the anointing of the Holy Spirit upon a pastor and openly criticize him. It reveals their lack of respect for the office of pastor. It reveals their lust for power and disregard for the anointing of God. The Lord never honors such behavior. It will always bring harm to the advance of God's kingdom.

Prayer: *Father, thank You that You anoint people with Your Spirit to teach, to guide, and to shepherd Your people. Lord, help me to recognize that anointing and to always respect it. In Jesus' name. Amen.*

THURSDAY – STRENGTH IN TIMES OF CRISIS

Scripture: I Samuel 30:4-6

Reading the Bible, with its crude stories of wars, can be somewhat disturbing for Americans, as America is such a soft and compassionate society, as compared to much of the world and much of history. Such is the story of the city of Ziklag, where David and his family, and his men and their families resided. While David and his men were gone doing battle, the Amalekites raided the city, burned it, and took all the women and children captive. Can you imagine being taken hostage under those circumstances? Can you imagine the scene when David and his men returned? We read that they *". . . wept until there was not strength in them to weep."*

The comment at the end of verse six gives us another glimpse into the spiritual life of David. Here we read that David *". . . strengthened himself in the Lord his God."* How did David strengthen himself in the Lord? His men were blaming him and threatening to stone him for this tragedy. Possibly he went off to himself and spent the night in prayer. We're not sure. We only know that he connected with God in such a way that he was energized and renewed to lead his men in pursuit of the enemy and bring back the wives and children, which did happen.

Have you ever wept until you have no more strength to weep? Many people going through rejection and abandonment with divorce know how David felt. Many women suffering abuse, can identify with David. Many who have experienced the sudden and tragic loss of spouses and children understand. Though we live in a soft and compassionate society, it does not exempt us from life's tragedies.

Prayer: *Father, today I remember those who weep until they have no more strength to weep. Oh Lord, comfort them and strengthen them in ways beyond human understanding. In Jesus' name. Amen.*

FRIDAY – LUST, PRIDE AND POWER

Scripture: II Samuel 11:26-27

God's truth and his moral standards are unchanging. We can easily see that when reading the Bible. Men and women in Biblical times struggled with the same issues as we see today.

Though David was a great and Godly king, the King of Israel after God's own heart, the Bible does not ignore David's time of gross moral failure. David sees a beautiful woman bathing, lusts after her, orders her to be brought to him, and commits adultery. The woman, Bathsheba, became pregnant. David ordered her husband, who was intensely loyal to David, to be put on the front line of battle, knowing that he would be killed, which he was.

David was King. He could do or have anything he wanted. Who would hold him accountable? What court would he answer to? Though he had, at one time, a tender heart for the Lord and great faith and trust in the Lord, power and pride appears to have ruled the day. He had, most likely, justified this behavior in his own mind. I am reminded of the verse in Proverbs 21:2, *"Every man's way is right in his own eyes, but the Lord weighs the heart."* David might have been able to manipulate and control others, but God was still God. God called David's behavior "evil".

Societies can become so arrogant that they see themselves being above God. America is a case in point. At one time in its history, America fully recognized God's sovereign power as being a higher power than any human institution. Today that doesn't seem to be true. Whether it is the taking of life in abortion or rewriting the definition of marriage, America has put its own laws above God's law.

Prayer: *Father, forgive us as a nation. Forgive us when we flaunt Your standards of conduct. Help me never to rationalize my own behavior, as if You don't exist. In Jesus' name. Amen.*

SATURDAY – SPEAKING THE TRUTH

Scripture: II Samuel 12:7-9

David is viewed as the greatest king of Israel, but would David be viewed today as that great had it not been for his trusted friend, Nathan? Would David have realized the error of his way without someone to get in his face? Would David have even heard the word of the Lord without the help of a friend? Would David have sought the Lord's forgiveness and restoration without a raw moment of confrontation?

Nathan saw David's behavior with Bathsheba and Uriah as "evil". Adultery and murder are serious offenses to God. Going to the King to confront him with sin was risky business. The King, though a close friend, could have Nathan's head cut off. No doubt, Nathan pondered this for many days, before he came forth with a strategy. II Samuel 12 gives us details.

Stories catch people's attention and such was with Nathan and David, as Nathan told the King about this rich, greedy, selfish man who took advantage of a poor, humble man. When David ordered this man to be found and punished, Nathan responded, "You are the man!" Oh, if only I could have been there. I'll bet you could have heard a pin drop. Nathan went on to tell him why, and then spoke God's word to him.

We lack men and women with Nathan's kind of courage. Many of us live in fear of offending others or looking judgmental so we keep quiet in the face of evil, when we should speak up. We lack the depth of friendships which give us the right to be heard. We fear punishment if the person we confront has power over us. And the kingdom suffers.

Prayer: *Father, thank You for men like Nathan. Lord, put people in our lives who love us deeply and love us enough to confront us, when we rationalize our sin and close our ears to You. In Jesus' name. Amen.*

SUNDAY – GOD'S SPECIAL DAY – THE LORD'S DAY

"I will tell of Your name to my brethren; in the midst of the assembly I will praise You." Ps. 22:22

168

OLD TESTAMENT GREATS

WEEK #28 – DAVID, SOLOMON

MONDAY – TRUE REPENTANCE

Scripture: Psalm 51:4, 10-12

The picture we get of David in Psalm 51 is that of a broken man, seeking forgiveness and restoration. I have often compared David to his son, Solomon, who followed David as King. Both had a heart for God. Both had enormous wealth and power yet both had a weakness with women, which led to major moral failure. David died as a respected, Godly leader and wrote almost all of the book of Psalms, which became the Hebrew songbook for worship and subsequently influenced Christian worship for some 2,000 years. Solomon died a depressed, cynical, and defeated man. What did David have that Solomon did not have? The only difference is reflected in Psalm 51. To our knowledge, Solomon never had that time of remorse and repentance in his life. He never recognized his multiple relationships with women as evil, crying out to God for a clean heart, crying out to God to restore to him the joy of his salvation.

In David's prayer, he says, "Against You, only, I have sinned . . ." We know that David's offense was also to Bathsheba, her family, and her husband's family. In his prayer to God, it is as though that David's offense to God was so big that nothing else compared.

Christians today should remember that when they disobey God and subsequently disappoint and injure other people, they primarily have offended God. They need to do serious reflection as to how their sin has damaged their relationship with God, first and foremost. They need to get brutally honest before God and cry out like David, putting into words the remorse they feel, asking him to give them a clean heart and to restore the joy of their salvation.

Prayer: *Father, thank You for extending Your compassion and forgiveness to David and for restoring him. Help me, Lord, to see the sin which stands between where I am and where You want me to be. Create in me a clean heart, oh God. In Jesus' name. Amen.*

TUESDAY – POWER OF PRAYER

Scripture: II Samuel 21:1; 14

Today's text speaks of a severe famine in the land of Israel, caused by the evil deeds of its former king, Saul. It appears God was angry with Israel for trying to exterminate a neighboring people (Gibeonites) and thus God withheld rain as punishment. In today's text we read, *". . . and David sought the presence of the Lord."*

This horrendous plot by King Saul was atoned for by the surrendering of seven of the king's sons to the Gibeonites. They hung them as an act of justice. After David brought their bones back for proper burial, it is stated that *"God was moved by prayer for the land"*. It is assumed the famine ended as God again blessed the land with rain.

Again, this is one of the Old Testament stories which appears quite brutal to most of us. Rather than being distracted by the crude methods of justice employed by ancient cultures, let's take note of David's attempt to seek God's presence in the midst of wars and bloodshed, and the fact that prayer played a huge role in solving this crisis. We don't get the details of how David sought the presence of the Lord but only that he did. This most likely was by an extended period of time alone with God in reflection, meditation, fasting, and intercession.

The world doesn't understand the power of prayer, the act of time alone with God. The Believer finds a quiet place where he seeks to look at himself as God sees him, where he repents of attitudes or actions that have brought shame to the Lord, where he voluntarily participates in a season of fasting for the purpose of seeking God and hearing God's voice.

Prayer: *Father, today I praise You for all the men and women around the world who seek Your presence, whether it be in China, Europe, Russia, India, Africa, South America or North America. Praise Your holy name. Through Christ, our Lord. Amen.*

WEDNESDAY – MIGHTY PRAISE

Scripture: I Chronicles 23:5, Psalms 150

I get so pumped when reading about Hebrew worship in David's day. When Solomon (David's son), was to be consecrated as king, David planned a huge service of praise to God. Remember, this was before the Jerusalem Temple was built, when they worshiped in a massive tent. We read of a four thousand member choir. Imagine that.

Years ago, Rhonda and I attended a large Billy Graham crusade in Cincinnati. The choir was huge, maybe one to two hundred people. We were impressed.

For the past few months, while I have been writing these devotional readings, we have been going to the First Christian Church, here in Crawfordsville, just a block away from where we are staying. We sing in their thirty member choir, which sounds quite beautiful. To think of a four thousand member choir is like trying to imagine living in a house the size of Chicago. It is mind boggling. Oh how majestic that must have been!

The Hebrew word for "praise the Lord" is "hallelujah". I have heard that word proclaimed in many different types of worship services, in many different languages around the world. It is special. The last five chapters of Psalms begins with "Praise the Lord". Though many of the Psalms speak of depressing struggles and cries for justice, the final note for this large songbook, written by David, is praise. It was the theme of King David's life.

Think of the role music has played in Christian worship. It would be inconceivable to plan a service of worship without music, without praise. The older I get, in the Lord, the more I agree with Martin Luther, the 16th century Protestant Reformer, "Music drives the devil away".

Prayer: *Oh Father, praise Your holy name. Thank You for blessing the church throughout the world with song writers and musicians who take us to heights of majestic worship. Oh Lord, thank You. In Jesus' name. Amen.*

THURSDAY – SOLOMON'S PRAYER FOR WISDOM

Scripture: I Kings 3:10-12

Whenever a great leader steps down, there almost always is a power struggle and thus the struggle when King David died. Solomon was the son, out of all David's sons, who emerged as the succeeding king. Like David, he reigned forty years.

It was God's direction that David not build the Jerusalem Temple, but that it would be constructed during Solomon's reign, and it was. Solomon was known for unusual wisdom and incredible riches. Kings and Queens from other nations came to hear his wisdom and observe the glittering gold and silver on display in the Temple of Jerusalem. It must have been a sight to behold.

Upon inauguration as King, Solomon expressed to God his anxiety and feelings of inadequacy about leading/governing the great nation of Israel. Later on we learn that it was God's observation that Solomon could have asked for riches or other things for himself, but he didn't. He asked for discernment and wisdom in judging the people. This was pleasing in God's sight. God granted him his request and thus his worldwide fame for wisdom followed him. The books of Proverbs and Ecclesiastes are attributed to him.

In the book of James (1:5), we read, "*But if any of you lacks wisdom, let him ask of God . . .*" When I first came to Christ, in the seventh grade, I began to read the New Testament, daily reading one chapter. When reading this verse, I camped on it and began to pray for wisdom. Over the years, people have commented that I am far beyond my age in wisdom. Though I don't consider myself a super smart person or anything like that, I do believe the Lord answered the regular plea of my young heart.

Prayer: *Father, thank You for the many promises You have given us in the Bible. In facing all of life's challenges, oh Lord, I need wisdom and discernment beyond my own. Give me wisdom, precious Father. In Jesus' name. Amen.*

FRIDAY – SOLOMON – ISRAEL'S HIGH MOMENT

Scripture: I Kings 8:10-11; 9:22-24

When the Jerusalem Temple was finished and the ark of the covenant was brought into the Temple by the Jewish Priests, it was a high and holy day, maybe it was Israel in her finest hour. With several thousand people singing in the choir, with the actual Ten Commandments in the ark of the covenant, with King Solomon praying such a profound and powerful prayer, it must have been unbelievable. At that moment in history, the whole known world was looking to Israel, possibly much like it is today with the whole world watching the United States.

The most striking aspect of this day is the glory of the Lord being visibly present. Remember Moses on the mountain receiving the Ten Commandments and instructions for Jewish worship? Remember how the glory of the Lord would surround Moses? Remember when Moses led the people of Israel through the wilderness for forty years? Remember the Tabernacle, a portable Temple, a massive tent? There would be a pillar of fire by night, above the Tabernacle, and a cloud which would be in the Tabernacle and above it. When the cloud descended upon the Tabernacle, we read the "glory of the Lord" filled it, like with Moses on the mountain. Now many years later, we see the same picture as the Jerusalem Temple is dedicated, the glory of the Lord fills it in the form of a cloud. Wow.

This should be the goal of every worship service today. With the songs, with the preaching, with the praying, the glory of the Lord descends. Men, women, boys and girls know something special is happening. God is here. God is moving in hearts. God is speaking. God is healing and making people whole. Wow.

Prayer: *Oh Father, we long to see Your glory. We praise You for all You have done in human history and are doing today. Shine Your glory on us and everywhere Your people gather. Lord Jesus, You are the King of glory. In Your name. Amen.*

SATURDAY – THE DEMISE OF A GREAT MAN

Scripture: I Kings 11:1-4

We go from the mountain top, with yesterday's reading, to the valley. It didn't take long for wealth, power, and lust to spiritually destroy Solomon. Because of uncontrolled passion, which turned Solomon's heart to other gods, the Lord took the Kingdom from Solomon's house. The book of Ecclesiastes shows him as a very sad and pitiful old man, questioning the purpose of life. It is so unfortunate that he started out in the will and favor of God but ended up an embarrassment to his family and to the entire nation.

Years ago, I heard an ex-devil worshiper share how Satanists would recruit men. He told how most young men on college campuses could be easily recruited using one of three things – money, drugs, or sex. If one didn't work, they would try another. By the time they tried all three, they would have another recruit in their group. Few young men could resist. How tragic.

Did you know that a 90% Christian is 10% short, a 60% Christian is 40% short? In God's kingdom, there are only 100% Christians. We read in I Kings that Solomon's heart was not fully devoted to the Lord. I think of him as a 90% Christian. It was the 10% that took him down.

Many people go forth in life being 60%, 80%, or 90% Christian. They compare themselves to someone else who may go to some church and tell themselves, *"Well I am better than this person or that person."* They use the moral life of another person to define their Christian faith, rather than the Bible.

Jesus said, *"If anyone wishes to come after Me, he must deny himself and take up his cross and follow Me (Mark 8:34)."*

Prayer: *Father, show me where I am weak, show me where my heart is not fully given over to You. Keep me away from half-hearted commitment. I surrender every ounce of my being to You today. In Jesus' name. Amen.*

SUNDAY – GOD'S SPECIAL DAY – THE LORD'S DAY

"I have proclaimed glad tidings of righteousness in the great congregation; behold, I will not restrain my lips." Psalms 40:9-10

OLD TESTAMENT GREATS

WEEK #29 – ELIJAH, JOSIAH, ESTHER

MONDAY – PRAYERS THAT MAKE A DIFFERENCE

Scripture: I Kings 17:21-22

One of the most dynamic prophets of the Old Testament is Elijah. He lived after Israel had been divided by a civil war, with the north being called Israel and the south, Judah. He spoke the word of the Lord boldly to Ahab the King of Israel. Because of Ahab's blatant disobedience, the Lord withheld rain from Israel, according to Elijah's word. God used a widow and her son to hide Elijah for a period of time, while King Ahab was searching to kill him. Her son became sick and died, and she appealed to Elijah for help. Elijah went to the young boy's dead body and stretched himself out on the corpse, literally crying out to God for the child's life to return to him. The boy miraculously came back to life.

I was at a small Bible College in Lalitpur, Utter Pradesh, India. At the end of a day's teaching, while in bed, our host came to the door and explained that a small baby was very sick and needed prayer. His mother had been in my class that day. My friend and I went to the room of that young couple only to find the mother sitting on the bed, in a candle lit, dark room, uncontrollably weeping and wailing, with her naked baby lying in front of her. I had never touched a human body so hot. His temp must have been dangerously high. I held the baby and started to pray and was overcome with emotion. I literally cried out to God for the life of that little boy. In going to bed, I feared what we might hear come morning. To my surprise, the baby's temp was normal.

Prayer: *Father, why are we too composed and too afraid to release our spirits and emotions in fervent prayer for others? Your word says that Jesus prayed with "loud crying and tears". Forgive us, Lord, when we are timid in our prayers. Give me a holy boldness to pray in the powerful name of Jesus. Amen.*

TUESDAY – ELIJAH: WHEN SAINTS GET DEPRESSED

Scripture: I Kings 19:4, 9-10

We normally think of Elijah as being this very bold, confident, aggressive prophet, which he was. But he had his difficult moments and today's text is one of those moments. After an amazing display of God's power in the sight of all Israel, four hundred-fifty false prophets were killed, and rain finally came upon the land. King Ahab's evil wife, Jezebel, vowed to kill Elijah as an act of revenge. Elijah ran and hid under a juniper tree.

The Bible says Elijah prayed to God to take his life. I think most of us would agree that Elijah was depressed. When he regained composure, he went to the mountain to seek the Lord. The Lord spoke to him and said, *"What are you doing here, Elijah?"*

Elijah revealed his sad state of mind when he replied to God that he was the only one left who was zealous for the Lord. Elijah told God this three times. God finally reminded him there were seven thousand who had not bowed their knees to Baal.

Though the Christian might have done amazing things for God at different times in his life, he still can be vulnerable to weak moments when he thinks he is the only one facing such difficulties, and others are out to get him. He can get so depressed that he asks God to take his life. Ever been there?

It is easy to become battle weary when the evil one appears to be winning on every front. It is then that Satan, the father of lies, feeds us another big lie by making us think we are the only one, when we are not. Hearing from God and knowing the truth is always the key.

Prayer: *Father, we are such weak creatures. Oh Lord, pick us up and straighten out our thinking when we fall down and think bad thoughts. Keep Your joy pumping through my veins today. In Jesus' name. Amen.*

WEDNESDAY – JOSIAH FINDS THE BOOK

Scripture: II Kings 23:1-3

About 350 years passed from the time of King David to the time when Jerusalem was destroyed. During that time, there were many kings of Judah and Israel. Josiah is spoken of as being the greatest.

Over the course of several bad kings, the "book of the law" (most likely the first five books of the Old Testament) had been misplaced in the Temple, and had not been read for many years. While remodeling the Temple, they discovered these scrolls. They were promptly taken to the King and read. Upon hearing the word of the Lord, King Josiah was convicted over the blatant disobedience of his people. He tore his clothes and wept, quite the moving scene.

The story in our text is King Josiah publicly committing to the Lord to keep his commandments and lead the nation by God's word. After this he brought about huge reforms and because of his leadership, God withheld his judgment from the land.

The discovery of God's word has changed millions of lives over the years and is still changing lives today. Being the number one bestseller of all time, it is translated into more languages than any other book in the history of civilization. Entire nations have been civilized by the teachings of the Bible.

Dan Buttafuoca, an attorney in New York City, writes, *"The Bible is the single most important book ever written. It is an eyewitness account of historical events of such magnitude that they have literally shaped the world in which we live. Without this book, the Western world and a good deal of the Eastern world would be completely different today than if the events of this book had never occurred."*

Prayer: *Father, again today, I am reminded of the power of Your holy word. I thank You for preserving the Bible throughout hundreds and thousands of years. In Jesus' name. Amen.*

THURSDAY – JOSIAH: REINSTATING REALLY IMPORTANT THINGS

Scripture: II Kings 23:21-23

One of the most significant reforms under King Josiah is the reinstatement of the Passover. Remember how the angel of death "passed over" the houses of Jewish people when God struck the first born of Egypt, in bringing his people out of bondage? Remember how Moses instructed the people to celebrate this once yearly? It is amazing to me that this was not done for over 300 years, not since the time of Samuel.

Also, remember how the Passover was a foreshadow of the Lord's Supper? Remember how we eat a meal remembering Jesus as the unblemished lamb through which his body is broken and blood shed, for the sins of the world? It is easy for Christians today to be slack in the celebration of this event. The early Christians did it every week. Even today, most who call themselves Christian in the world, celebrate communion every week, but many, trendy type churches put much more emphasis on entertainment than the Lord's Supper.

I have taken communion to older people in nursing facilities many times. In the sharing of the bread and cup in such a setting, where a person's mind has weakened, the presence of the Lord has been truly powerful. Jesus said, *"this is my body and this is my blood"*. Like many things about my faith, I have never truly understood how the bread and cup could actually be his body and blood, but I have always sensed a special presence of the Lord, where the elements are properly shared. Many times, after taking communion, the person will begin to speak quite clearly about things in their past or about their present spiritual life. They will do this when previously either unwilling or unable.

Prayer: *Father, thank You for many churches and believers who have rediscovered the mystery of Your presence in Holy Communion. Thank You for all those who truly love Your word and are serious about doing the things instructed by Jesus. In His name. Amen.*

FRIDAY – ESTHER: TAKING A STAND AT A KEY MOMENT

Scripture: Esther 3:12-13

It really is quite the story how, during the time of Christ, colonies of Jews were existent in most of the known world. For example, Jews existed in what is now Bombay for over two thousand years. Today's story explains in part, at least, how this happened.

After Babylon destroyed Jerusalem and took the Jewish people captive, Persia conquered Babylon, replacing Babylon as the world's dominant power. Persian rule extended all the way East into India, as mentioned in the first verse of the book of Esther.

Esther was a very beautiful Jewish young lady who found favor with the King of Persia and who became his wife. Most of us would question the morals of how this came about, but it is indicative of the world back then. Since the Jews were not well liked, she kept her nationality a secret. Because of jealousy among some high level government officials, the King of Persia issued an edict giving permission for the people to exterminate and completely annihilate the Jews on a certain day and to take their possessions.

Coming out of the closet with her Jewish identity, risking her own safety, she used her position as the King's wife to appeal to the King for the sake of her people. As the result, the edict was cancelled and many people converted to Judaism throughout the entire empire.

When Paul and the early missionaries went forth, they first went to Jewish synagogues and immediately had a platform to proclaim the Gospel of Christ. This greased the tracks for the spreading of the Gospel, as these synagogues were in all the known world. Young Esther is one of the reasons this was possible. Isn't it amazing how God works?

Prayer: *Father, I thank You for Esther. Thank You for every person who has risked their life for the sake of Your people. I believe she is alive today with You in heaven. In Jesus' name. Amen.*

SATURDAY – ESTHER: GOD'S PLAN AND PURPOSE

Scripture: Esther 4:13-14

In the story of Esther, her uncle, Mordecai, plays a major role. Her parents had died. Mordecai raised her and promoted her into the royal palace. She made the decision to go before the King to plead for her people, after Mordecai appealed to her and suggested that *"who knows whether you have not attained royalty for such a time as this?"*

In challenging her, Mordecai also stated that *"if you remain silent at this time, relief and deliverance will arise for the Jews from another place . . ."* That comment is quite revealing. It highlights again the tension between God's sovereignty and man's freewill. It was important that Esther speak up, very important, but yet God is powerful enough to use someone else, if she didn't. God's sovereign plan and work cannot be stopped by human flesh.

This is good to know as the world around appears to be uncertain at best. Nations rise and fall. At no time in human history has there been complete safety and stability. More times than not, there has been utter chaos as great societies have come and gone. America is different in many ways, as it is the only nation ever founded on Biblical principles, but the future looks somewhat frightening.

God has a plan for human civilization. This we know. He has a plan and will accomplish his plan in spite of disobedient and selfish church leaders, cruel dictators, and corrupt government officials. Our decision to speak up and stand strong is important, very important. Your "karma" does not determine your destiny; God does. The stakes are high. This is not a practice run or a game. We only get one life, regardless of what Buddhist monks say.

Prayer: *Oh Father, thank You for giving me life, for giving me an opportunity to use my life to take a stand and to make a difference in the world. In Jesus' name. Amen.*

SUNDAY – GOD'S SPECIAL DAY – THE LORD'S DAY

"They have seen Your procession, O God, the procession of my God, my King, into the sanctuary. The singers went on, the musicians after them, in the midst of the maidens beating tambourines. Bless God in the congregations, even the Lord, you who are of the fountain of Israel." Psalms. 68:24-26

WEEK #30 – ISAIAH

MONDAY – REAL AND LIVING HOPE

Scripture: Isaiah 2:4-5; 11:6

Years ago when faced with hopelessness through the unfortunate loss of our daughter, I began to see the value of hope. Never before had I given it any thought. It was only as I stared hopelessness in the face, day after day, did hope become real and living. With hope, one believes the future will be better. With hope, one can see a ray of light, though surrounded by the demons of darkness.

Isaiah is the prophet of hope in the Old Testament. He was the first to present a picture of the coming King who would reign with absolute righteousness, ushering in a new era.

Hatred, violence, and war had ruled the day for human civilization. It was the norm rather than the exception. Isaiah proclaimed a new day where this would not be so, where men would not hate and fight and rape and kill, where men would *"hammer their swords into plowshares and spears into pruning hooks"*. Swords and spears were the primary instruments of war. A modern paraphrase might read, *"melt their machine guns, tanks, bombers and drones into cars and commercial airplanes"*. He boldly states, *"Never again will they learn war"*. Later on in chapter 11, he describes even the animals, which normally feed on eating one another, being at peace, enjoying one another's presence. This was the hope for God's people and was their hope for centuries leading up to the birth of Jesus, the "Prince of Peace".

It really is hard to imagine a world with no violence, no hatred, and no killing. As the story of the Bible unfolds, this picture of hope gets much more vivid, reaching its climax in the Bible's final chapters.

Prayer: *Father, the world around us can be so depressing, as the wheels appear to be coming off of many aspects of our society. Father, thank You for hope. Thank You for giving us a reason to believe in the future and to believe it truly will be better. Through Jesus. Amen.*

TUESDAY – GOD COMES KNOCKING

Scripture: Isaiah 6:4-5

One of the classic stories of the Bible is Isaiah's calling. It is the beautiful picture of Isaiah in the Jerusalem Temple. He experiences the awesome presence of the Lord God. He describes it saying, "I saw the Lord". This experience was quite shaking and life-changing.

When confronted with such purity, holiness, and righteousness, he saw the picture so much clearer as to how he was not so pure, not so holy, and not so righteous. He was overwhelmed by a feeling of shame and inadequacy. It reminds me when God came looking for Adam in the garden only to find him hiding, ashamed of himself.

We find the same reaction by Peter when Jesus told Peter to put out his nets on the other side of the boat, after Peter and his friends had been fishing all night with little to show. Peter initially protested but then obeyed, only to get such a large catch that they could not haul them all in. Peter said to Jesus, "*Go away from me Lord, for I am a sinful man*"(Lk. 5:8).

A flashlight shining across the floor of a room will reveal dirt and dust balls not seen before. God's presence has this same effect on his people, laying the ground work for complete honesty and transparency with no more need of pretense. Once this has happened, a person's heart is usually ready to receive a word from the Lord.

This picture should be the goal for every worship service. Having inspirational music is not the bottom line. Having a good sermon is not the bottom line. Creating an atmosphere for God to show up is the bottom line - the goal. Everything else is window-dressing; everything else pales.

Prayer: *Thank You, Lord, for worship services all around the world where these kind of God moments are happening today. Thank You for Isaiah, another one of Your great witnesses. In Jesus' name. Amen.*

WEDNESDAY – HERE I AM. SEND ME.

Scripture: Isaiah 6:6-8

The title of today's devotional is one of the most famous of Biblical quotes. It is a quote all missionaries know and keep close to their hearts. After Isaiah's sin problem is dealt with, his unworthiness removed, Isaiah is confronted with God's piercing question, *"Whom shall I send, and who will go for Us?"*

It has always been interesting to me that God's first interaction with Isaiah, after his sins were forgiven, was in the form of a question, not a command. In Genesis 12, God commanded Abraham to leave his family and "go", and all the peoples of the world would be blessed. Jesus commanded his followers to "go", make disciples of all nations (Matthew 28:19). It would appear to be more consistent for God to have simply instructed Isaiah to "go", rather than to ask him a question.

God choosing to ask Isaiah this probing question puts the emphasis on Isaiah's burning passion to step up to the plate, and without any coercion, to volunteer. This eager spirit should be displayed by all who are sent to represent God the Father and Jesus the Son. Our act of service, surrender, and submission should not be an act of half-hearted obedience, fearing God's wrath if we don't go. It should not be a scene whereby we say, "Send my brother. Send my friend. Send my pastor. Send my Sunday School teacher, or send someone else, please Lord!"

I believe God asks that very same question today to everyone who truly comes into his presence. Yes, the sin issue must be addressed first. It is addressed for every one of us through the cross, but then comes the question, *"Whom shall I send, and who will go for Us?"*

Prayer: *Father, thank You for removing the obstacle of my sin so that I may lift up my head and heart to You and voluntarily say to You, the very words Isaiah said, "Here am I, Lord, send me." In Jesus' name. Amen.*

THURSDAY – THE CHRISTMAS PROPHET

Scripture: Isaiah 9:2, 6-7

Isaiah is referred to as "the Christmas prophet" by many scholars. He is the first prophet to so graphically describe a "child" being born, who would be a "great light" for those who walk in darkness. It is Isaiah who even names this child as Wonderful Counselor, Mighty God, Eternal Father, Prince of Peace. Every Christmas season, Isaiah is quoted time and time again, all around the world.

John, the Gospel writer, picks up on using "light" as a metaphor for Christ. In his introduction, in chapter one, John refers to Jesus as "light" in stating (vs. 5), *"The Light shines in the darkness, and the darkness did not comprehend it."* Later he writes (vs. 9), *"There was the true Light which, coming into the world, enlightens every man."*

Biblical inspiration is such a mystery. Think of it. Isaiah lived maybe 600 to 700 years before Jesus. During his years, neighboring armies were capturing different sections of Israel and Judah. It was hard to be optimistic about the future of God's people, the Hebrew people. After being ruled by idolatrous and immoral kings, the demise of the great kingdom, once a world power, was seemingly inevitable. With such a depressing and uncertain future, Isaiah begins to vision a king like the world had never seen before, a king who would usher in justice and righteousness far beyond anything in the past, even when David was king. This king or messiah would rescue and ransom God's people. This king or messiah would not be a prince of war, but a prince of peace, and his government would never, ever end. No other Biblical prophet presents this theme so colorfully and strong as Isaiah.

Prayer: *Father, thank You for ancient prophecy, recorded in print for all to read. Thank You for this grand and glorious story of revelation and redemption. In Jesus' name. Amen.*

FRIDAY – THE GLOBAL PROPHET

Scripture: Isaiah 49:6; 52:10

Isaiah also is distinguished in the sense that his vision for Israel went far beyond the Hebrew people. Most Jewish leaders in Old Testament times lost sight of their role in the world. They saw the Jewish people as the one race favored by God and blessed by God. They failed to understand God's message way back in Genesis 12, where God very clearly states to Abraham, that through the Hebrew race (the Jews), all the peoples of the world would be blessed. They failed to grasp the truth that God loved all races and peoples and included them in his plans and purposes. This inward focus is evident in most all Old Testament writings and even at the time of Christ. It was almost impossible for the Jews to see or think beyond their own race.

This global theme surfaces repeatedly throughout the book of Isaiah. Statements found in today's readings, where Isaiah quotes God as saying, ". . . *My salvation may reach to the end of the earth*", are quite unusual in Jewish writings of Isaiah's era. Just three chapters later another similar verse is found, "*That all the ends of the earth may see the salvation of our God.*" Where did Isaiah get this understanding of God? It is amazing. It is further proof that Isaiah was a truly inspired prophet, speaking words that are not plagiarized or popularized sayings.

Today, Christians face a similar challenge. Do they see God's favor and blessing as something for them and their own race or do they feel God's heart for all the peoples of the world? Are churches and pastors preoccupied with their own survival and favored status or are their heads lifted up?

Prayer: *Father, help us to see the world as You see the world. Keep our heads lifted up, Lord, to see the gospel fields that are ripe for the harvest. In Jesus' name. Amen.*

SATURDAY – THE EASTER PROPHET

Scripture: Isaiah 53:2-7

By now you have probably guessed my favorite prophet. Isaiah stands so tall among the other prophets. Jesus must have spent much time reading Isaiah.

Today's Scripture reading is much longer than usual. I hope you have the time to read it. It is unbelievable how accurately Isaiah describes the crucifixion of the Messiah. It is almost as if he was there when Jesus was crucified, that he witnessed the actual horror of the event. To think this prophecy was given more than five hundred years before it happened is stunning.

I have described Isaiah as the "Christmas Prophet", the "Global Prophet", and the "Easter Prophet". All of these descriptions point to Jesus. Isaiah's book wreaks of Jesus. Yes, there are prophecies concerning the judgment of Israel and several neighboring nations, but every other chapter is a reminder of Jesus.

Someday, I hope to meet Isaiah. Is that such a bizarre thought? Imagine his response when he entered the Paradise of God and beheld the Lamb of God. What would it be like to shake Isaiah's hand, to engage him in conversation over a cup of coffee? What joy!

The writer of Hebrews speaks of a great cloud of witnesses who are our cheerleaders, observing us going through life. Each day in my morning prayer time, when giving thanks to God for my parents, Nelson and Reba Curry, Rhonda's parents, and all my grandparents, I think of this grand cloud of witnesses mentioned in the book of Hebrews. I thank God for them, for their staunch faith, and unflinching resolve to walk in the way of Christ. I think of the early church leaders who were martyred, some of the greatest men and women to ever live.

Prayer: *Father, I am so humbled by the greatness of men and women who have gone before me. Am I worthy to be counted among them? Oh Lord, make me worthy. Purify my heart and take away the impurities in my soul. In Jesus' name. Amen.*

SUNDAY – GOD'S SPECIAL DAY – THE LORD'S DAY

"From You comes my praise in the great assembly; I shall pay my vows before those who fear Him."

Psalms 22:25

WEEK #31 – JONAH

MONDAY – THE CALL

Scripture: Jonah 1:1-2

Most Biblical scholars, throughout history, have viewed Jonah as an actual prophet. Mentioned in II Kings 14:25, he lived and prophesied during the reign of Jeroboam, King of Israel, not long before Israel was conquered by Assyria. Though some might think of this story as a type of parable, I agree that it was an actual, historical event.

Nineveh is the oldest and most populated city of the ancient Assyrian Empire, a hated enemy of Israel. It was located on the east bank of the Tigris River, opposite of what is modern day Mosul, Iraq.

A call from God to go to Nineveh in Jonah's day, would be like a call to go to Adolf Hitler's, Berlin, Germany, in the thick of WWII. Most of us would have run the other way, about as fast as we could run. This was not the typical "missionary call".

We know from the text that it was not just a troubling dream for Jonah, but was, in fact, God speaking to Jonah, telling him to go to Nineveh and preach to the Assyrian people. Because these people were enemies and not of the "chosen race", to think that God would have cared for these Gentiles would have been completely outside the realm of Jewish belief. Jewish people believed that God only cared about the Jews. They were God's people, not the Gentiles. They were the focus of God's attention. They, only, were to be blessed and favored.

In the final chapter of the book, it is interesting that God is described as "gracious and compassionate". With the story of Jonah, we see again the theme of a global God, who loves and cares for all the peoples of the world.

Prayer: *Oh Father, it is so amazing to see the theme of Your love and grace all throughout the Bible. Thank You again for this wonderful book, full of stories that teach us so much about You. In Jesus' name. Amen.*

TUESDAY – THE FLIGHT

Scripture: Jonah 1:3-4

When one runs from God, it is never good. It always turns out rather embarrassing and painful. Thus it was with Jonah.

Instead of going to Nineveh, as he had been told, Jonah went in the opposite direction. He purchased a ticket on a big ship. A huge storm came upon them. The other men concluded that because Jonah's God was the God of the wind and sea, Jonah had offended his God and thus the storm came as punishment. Jonah told the men to throw him overboard, and they did. Not the comfortable cruise first envisioned.

The Biblical story would seem to say that life on this planet is not to be our heaven. It is not to be the time to pursue personal pleasure and self gratification. That time is coming, but it is not now. As God has sacrificed for us, we are to sacrifice for him.

Jesus could have lived a life of royalty and status, but for our sake, he chose the way of the cross. We are to pick up our cross and follow him. To truly follow the Lord in this life is to forsake the call of entertainment and cheap thrills. It is to go wherever he leads, knowing that being in God's will, even if it be in the most unthinkable place, is where one will be the happiest.

When we heard the call of God to go to India, we knew it would involve sacrifice and suffering. Relatives opposed us and all but disowned us. Financially, we took a huge cut in pay. The experience of having dengue fever twice was not pleasant, but the joy in our hearts and the fruit of obedience far outweighed the inconveniences.

Prayer: *Father, I know that running from You will never make me happy, though it might look to be a better life doing this or that. Oh Lord, keep me in the center of Your will my entire life. In Jesus' name. Amen.*

WEDNESDAY – THE PRAYER

Scripture: Jonah 2:1-2, 7

When Jonah was thrashing about in the water, gasping for air, a big fish swallowed him. His pursuit of personal pleasure was not working too well. In today's text, we learn that, while in the belly of the whale, Jonah's approach to the situation radically changed. Rather than avoiding the Lord, he turned to him. He cried out to God in prayer.

It is quite amazing that we have Jonah's prayer, word for word. He speaks of the weeds wrapped around his head and almost drowning in water. How much more graphic can it get?

God heard his prayer and commanded the fish to vomit Jonah up on the shore. What a scene. Imagine what Jonah must have looked like, stumbling about on the beach. Though he may not have looked too much like someone emerging from a prayer closet, his attitude was significantly altered. His state of mind was much more conducive to seeing the wisdom of obeying the Lord. Jonah got a second chance.

Most of us should identify with Jonah. Most of us have heard the call to discipleship many times and have ignored it or gone the opposite direction. Our selfish plans got in the way of God's plan, and we chose several other roads to walk, and they all ended up as dead-end roads, not near what we thought they would be. But this was not the end of the story. We cried out to God. God heard our prayer and gave us a second chance.

Regardless of where you are at today - in the whale, maybe on the beach, maybe on your way to Nineveh - know that heart obedience to the Lord is key to a life of blessing.

Prayer: *Father, thank You for second chances, and third chances, and fourth chances. Thank You for Your patience in my life. Show me the path to obedience, and help me to trust You, regardless of the circumstances. In Jesus' name. Amen.*

THURSDAY – THE CRUSADE

Scripture: Jonah 3:1-4

In ancient times, it was not uncommon for cities to be overthrown by neighboring armies with masses of people murdered or taken captive. A foreigner proclaiming, that in 40 days a city will be overthrown, would have gotten the attention of the city fathers.

The nations bordering Israel had heard mighty stories of the God of Israel and how he had done miraculous things in battle. Jonah had their ear and preached to them a message of turning from evil in fasting and repentance, crying out to God to spare them. He must have challenged their belief system, as it is stated, ". . . *the people believed in God*." Even the King of Nineveh repented. He called for a fast so widespread that even the animals were not to be given food while the fast was in force.

Billy Graham has done many city-wide evangelistic crusades but none of them compare to what we read about in the book of Jonah. The people responded to Jonah's preaching in huge numbers. It may be the most successful city-wide evangelistic campaign in the history of the world.

I wish I could have heard Jonah preach. I'll bet he wasn't dry and boring! I'll bet he spoke like God meant business. I'll bet the passion in his heart and the fervency of his spirit was obvious. God's anointing was upon him.

Because of God's tender heart for people and his compassion for men, women, boys and girls, who were not even within the circle of his covenant people, he saw their sorrow was genuine and heard their cries for help. The Bible says that God relented and withheld his hand of judgment, and the city of Nineveh was spared.

Prayer: *Father, someday I may meet some of those people from Nineveh who heard Jonah's preaching, repented, and believed in You. What a treat that would be. Oh Lord, thank You for compassion and mercy. In Jesus' name. Amen.*

FRIDAY – THE PROPHET

Scripture: Jonah 4: 1-4

Jonah ends with a beautiful picture of God and a not-so-beautiful picture of Jonah. Let's look at the not-so-beautiful picture of Jonah first.

With the most successful evangelistic campaign in all of history, one would think Jonah would be singing praises to God all the way back to Jerusalem. But remember how the Jews viewed Gentiles, especially their enemies the Assyrians. Jonah would have been happy if God would have made them toast, those mongrels who knew nothing of Judaic priesthood and all the laws and rituals of God's people. The Assyrians posed a serious, military threat to Israel. Why should God do anything but destroy them?

Jonah would not be hailed as a famous evangelist back in Israel. He would not be received with great fanfare and pomp. If anything, his conduct would be under suspicion, raising many questions about his true motives.

So the picture we get of Jonah is one where he goes off to himself, pouting. He is so disgusted, so angry, and so depressed that he asks God to take his life. Imagine! God uses a plant to illustrate how he loves the Ninevite people. This doesn't appear to change Jonah's view of the situation.

God didn't choose the Jews to be his covenant people because they were morally any better than any other group of people. Like the ground where Moses stood, which God called "holy", because God had selected it for a sacred purpose, God selected the Hebrew people for a sacred purpose - to bless all the peoples of the world.

Christians today are chosen by God for the exact same purpose. If we think of ourselves as better than any other people in the world, we have made a serious error.

Prayer: *Father, all around us we see groups of people who view themselves as a little better than other groups of people. Forgive me, Lord, when I fail to see people as You see them. In Jesus' name. Amen.*

SATURDAY – THE GOD OF COMPASSION

Scripture: Jonah 4:10-11

These verses give profound insight into the goodness of God. Many people can't imagine God's compassion being highlighted in the Old Testament, but here it is, full blown and beautiful.

Jonah had compassion on a plant, something that he (Jonah) had not invested any of himself to bring it to life or sustain it. God asks Jonah why he (God) thinks he (God) should not have compassion on this city with some 120,000 children. The implication is that God was highly invested in bringing these people to life and sustaining them, possibly 2-300,000 people total. How could God not have compassion on them? They bear his image. They are his children too!!

I recognize there are incidents in the Old Testament where God commands the armies of Israel to go forward in battle where much blood is shed and where many innocent women and children are killed. This appears quite contradictory to the God we see in Jonah and the New Testament. I am at peace that it is not contradictory, but at times in the course of human affairs in a broken, sin-infested world, tough choices must be made that fall short of God's ideal. When this happens, it is good to remember that God grieves even more than we do, wherever there is human suffering and pain.

It is so important to have an accurate picture of God. No, he is not a celestial policeman waiting for people to make a mistake so he can display his wrath. No, he is not a detached, doting grandfather who really is not quite with it as to current events or life. He very much is active, alive, caring, compassionate, engaged and knowledgeable.

Prayer: *Father, thank for this powerful story whereby real aspects of Your character are on display. Thank You for loving the least, the lost, and the lonely. I praise Your name today. Through Jesus. Amen.*

SUNDAY – GOD'S SPECIAL DAY – THE LORD'S DAY

"I will proclaim Your name to My brethren, in the midst of the congregation I will sing Your praise."

Hebrews 2:12

192

OLD TESTAMENT GREATS

WEEK #32 – DANIEL

MONDAY - KINGS, DREAMS, AND GOD

Scripture: Daniel 2:19-23

Daniel lived and prophesied long after Jerusalem had been destroyed. The Hebrew people had been taken captive, resettled in a foreign land (Babylon) and greatly humbled by God's discipline. Much like Joseph rising to power in Egypt, young Daniel came up through the ranks of political power, without compromising his faith and character. Also like Joseph, Daniel is presented to us as interpreting a dream for a king, but for Daniel it was the King of Babylon and maybe a thousand or more years later.

In our story today, the King was troubled by "dreams", possibly a recurring dream. None of the King's top cabinet people could interpret the dream, without first hearing the dream. The King refused to tell them the dream and insisted they discern the dream or be killed, which would include Daniel and his three friends, who had risen to power with Daniel. They all cried out to God, seeking a word from the Lord, as to this dream. God answered by revealing to Daniel in a dream, during the night, the King's dream and interpretation. The King is impressed and raises them all to even higher positions of responsibility.

The actual dream was a picture of the rise and fall of world powers, ending with a clear reference to the coming of God's kingdom.

I have been surprised by the number of times really important decisions have come to me in the night, when unable to sleep. It is true that one's problems appear to be magnified at night. When daylight comes, after worrying about this or that, tossing and turning for hours, problems seem to be much less of a concern. It is as if something mystical happens when the sun rises.

Prayer: *Father, thank You for Daniel, for his desire to seek You above all else. Thank You, Lord, for speaking to us in different ways and especially when You speak to us at night. In Jesus' name. Amen.*

TUESDAY – SERVICE TO GOD WITH NO IFS

Scripture: Daniel 3:16-17

Daniel was appointed by the King as ruler over the entire province of Babylon, He succeeded in getting his three Jewish friends appointed over its administration. The story of how Daniel and his friends maintained their health is quite interesting. They surpassed the other select youth by eating only vegetables and water instead of the "King's food" with the finest of wines. It may be that because of religious commitments, they refrained from pork and wine.

All of this was fine and dandy until his three friends, Shadrach, Meshach and Abed-nego, refused to bow down and worship the King's gigantic, golden idol. The penalty for this refusal was death by a fiery furnace. Since they were such high ranking officials, this was a major insult to the King so he ordered the heat of the furnace to be increased seven times. After stating their belief in God's ability to rescue them from the fire, they also stated their firm commitment to God, even if he didn't rescue them.

Their loyalty to the unseen God of the universe (the God of Abraham, Isaac, and Jacob) was much greater than life itself. Their service to God was not conditional. It was not "if" God blessed them or "if" God gave them health and wealth. In their minds, God had already done enough for them to serve him to their last breath.

After tasting of God's rich grace and experiencing Christ's resurrection power, his promise and presence, why does one think God owes them anything more? The least one can do is to give back to God a life of service with no conditions. This means serving God in spite of disappointment, tragedies, illnesses and injustices.

Prayer: *Father, you owe me nothing more. I owe You, Lord. I owe a debt to You that I can never in this lifetime repay. I can, though, serve You with my whole heart. Father, thank You for such an incredible opportunity. In Jesus' name. Amen.*

WEDNESDAY – AMAZING PROPHECY

Scripture: Isaiah 43:1-2; Daniel 3:24-25

Daniel speaks of this great "king" or "messiah" to come in future times, who will reign eternally. His words line up very closely to Isaiah's prophecies. One of the greatest prophecies in the book of Daniel is revealed through the story of Daniel's three friends in the fiery furnace.

After being tied up and thrown into the blazing fire of the furnace, we learn that the King (Nebuchadnezzar) was stunned as he looked into the furnace only to see, not just three men walking around, but four men. The fourth is different from the other three. He is described as being "like a son of the gods".

The King called the three men out of the fire only to see that their clothes were not burnt nor their skin or hair singed, nor was even the smell of smoke found on them. The King got the message, was humbled, and gave official recognition to the God of Israel.

I believe the "fourth man" in the furnace was Jesus. The numerous prophecies of Jesus in the Old Testament laid the groundwork for the birth of Jesus Christ. It is not surprising that much of the known world, such as the "wise men from the East", was expecting this king to be born when Mary gave birth to Jesus in Bethlehem.

At the end of Luke's gospel, we read of Jesus appearing to two men walking on the road to Emmaus. While walking, Jesus spoke of numerous places in the Old Testament prophets that spoke of him. Most likely, he reminded them of today's story in Daniel 3 and the mention of the "fourth man" in the furnace. They later commented that their hearts were "burning" as Jesus explained the Scriptures.

Prayer: *Father, my heart burns when You walk with me through the Bible and show me things I have never seen before. May that fire always consume me for Your glory, throughout eternity. In Jesus' name. Amen.*

THURSDAY – THE LIVING GOD

Scripture: Daniel 6:19-22; 25-26

The story of Daniel in the lions' den is one of the Bible's great stories. It puts on display the God of Israel as not being like the other gods worshiped by peoples of the earth. It portrays the God of Israel as not dead, but alive. He is not passive but active. He intervenes in the affairs of man on behalf of his covenant people.

As the nation of Babylon was conquered by the Medes and the Persians, a new king enters on the scene, King Darius. He is impressed with Daniel and gives Daniel great responsibility in his political cabinet. This was met with envy and jealousy by two of his rivals, who plotted and tricked the King into a situation where he had no choice but to have Daniel thrown into the feared "lions' den".

It is amazing that as Daniel was being thrown into the den, the King showed belief that Daniel's God would rescue him, which God did. An angel of the Lord is described as shutting the mouths of the lions. The King was so moved by this phenomenal display of divine power that he spoke in honor of the God of Israel to his entire kingdom. King Darius refers to Daniel's God as the "living God".

It is so easy to allow the hum-drum of everyday life to reduce one's view of God to a Sunday morning, spiritual moment God. It is easy to forget that the same God who split the Red Sea, who provided manna in the wilderness for a million people, and who shut the mouths of lions in rescuing Daniel, is the very same God who has adopted us into his family and is with us today.

Prayer: *Father, thank You for being with Daniel in that lions' den of long ago. Thank You for being with me every time I find myself facing lions. Thank You, oh Lord, for caring and for acting. In Jesus' name. Amen.*

FRIDAY – THE REVELATION PROPHET

Scripture: Daniel 7:13-14; Revelation 7:9-12

One should read and study the book of Daniel before reading and studying the book of Revelation. These two books of the Bible are very closely connected with similar analogies and symbols.

Since the text from Revelation 7 is a text that is close to my heart, the Scripture in Daniel 7 jumps out at me every time I read it. It captures the plan of God as revealed to Abraham, back in Genesis 12, where God speaks of his vision to bless all the peoples of the earth. Daniel expands this description, stating that all peoples, nations and men of every language will serve God. This is the global theme of the Great Commission of Christ found in Matthew 28:19 and is the final picture of Revelation 7 where this great crowd of people, so great that no one can count the number, are gathered around God's throne. Here we see people from every tribe, tongue and nation dressed in white robes with palm branches in their hands.

At this point, world missions is finished. Not that all the people in the world will be Christian, but that all peoples of the world have had the chance to become Christian. Some from every tribe, tongue and nation will have said "yes" to the Gospel. They are now within the fold of those redeemed by the blood of the Lamb.

Some describe this global theme as the golden thread of the Bible, weaving its way from Genesis to Revelation. Certainly in the book of Daniel, it is quite pronounced.

God's gradual revelation of this theme is not seen by all who study the Bible, but it is there when you look at the Bible as a whole.

Prayer: *Father, thank You for showing us Your big and wonderful plan for the human race. It is beyond my mind how Your love and compassion can be so great and reach to so many people. In Jesus' name. Amen.*

SATURDAY – SCRIPTURE MEMORIZATION

Scripture: Deuteronomy 11:18-20; II Peter 3:1-2

People commit to memory the really important things in life, such as social security numbers, birthdays, addresses, names and capitals of states, the alphabet and definitions to thousands of words. Many Christians live their entire life without memorizing much Scripture. The memorization of Scripture is not any different than the memorization of word definitions. It involves repetition and regular effort.

God's people in the Old Testament were admonished to keep God's words afresh in their lives by keeping tiny scrolls of Scripture rolled up as bracelets and headbands, by writing God's words on their doorposts and walls. They didn't have access to thousands of books like we do. They would not have had one book, as we know a book. Peter in today's Scripture teaches Believers to *"remember the words spoken beforehand by the holy prophets and the commandment of the Lord and Savior spoken by the apostles."*

An older German couple in my first church, John and Frieda Stephan, come to mind. John was a hard-working farmer. Frieda was a staunch mother and worker in the church. Frieda memorized many Bible verses. John did not. In their elder years, both lost their sight. Frieda would quote from the Bible several times daily, though she couldn't see to read it. She had put God's word in her mind and no one could take that from her. One time when visiting John, after Frieda was gone, he told me he deeply regretted not memorizing Scripture. He had such fond memories of hearing Frieda quoting from the Bible. John's spoken regrets, motivated me, as a young pastor, to get serious about Scripture memorization. Today I see Scripture memorization as one way God has richly blessed me.

Prayer: *Father, thank You for giving us good minds that are capable of remembering many things, including Your holy word. Oh Lord, increase my desire to memorize Bible verses. In Jesus' name. Amen.*

SUNDAY – GOD'S SPECIAL DAY – THE LORD'S DAY
"Praise the Lord! Sing to the Lord a new song, and His praise in the congregation of the godly ones."

Psalm 149:1

WEEK #33

MONDAY - HEZEKIAH – THE VALUE OF GOD'S PRESENCE

Scripture: II Kings 18:5-7

In thinking of the history of the Hebrew people, two kings surface in our minds – King David and King Solomon. There are two other kings who were truly great – Hezekiah and Josiah.

Much like other great Biblical characters, the Bible clearly states that the presence of the Lord was with Hezekiah, and he prospered.

It is good to ponder often the phenomena of God's presence. Why does God's presence go with some people and other people it does not?

With King Hezekiah, we know that he *"did right in the sight of the Lord"* and that he *"trusted in the Lord"*. This is in contrast to most of the kings of Israel. Hezekiah is one rare duck in that light. As it is with all rare ducks who truly pull out all the stops to obey the Lord, God honored the faith of this man in two ways – with his presence and with prosperity.

When giving his final marching orders to his followers, as to making disciples of all the nations, Jesus promised his presence in stating, *"and lo I am with you always, even to the end of the age (Matt. 28:20)."* Jesus' disciples obeyed him by taking his message to other cultures and other lands. God blessed them with his presence and prospered their lives with an abundant harvest of souls.

Let me ask you the question. How would you grade yourself in *"doing right in the sight of the Lord"*? Would anyone who observed your life conclude that you *"trusted the Lord"*? If you have done well in both of the above areas then you know the presence of the Lord and you can be assured that God is, indeed, prospering your life.

Prayer: *Father, thank You for being with thousands and thousands of men and women gone before me who trusted You and obeyed You. Lord, I want to be one of them. I want my life to count for You. Help me Jesus. In Your name. Amen.*

TUESDAY - THE VALUE OF GODLY COUNSEL

Scripture: II Kings 19:5 & 6

Before the end of summer months, I will highlight the popular prophet, Isaiah, who authored the book of Isaiah, found in the later part of the Old Testament. Long before we get to this book of Isaiah, we read of Isaiah the prophet in II Kings.

King Hezekiah was facing the crisis of his life. The King of Assyria with his ruthless army had brutally crushed one nation after another and now was at the doorstep of Jerusalem making serious threats. King Hezekiah and his army was no match. The impending doom of Jerusalem was most evident. Would King Hezekiah seek assistance from other aligned nations? Would he seek divine favor from idols? What would he do? What did he do?

The Bible tells us that he sought counsel from Isaiah, a prophet of the unseen God, the God of Abraham, Isaac, and Jacob - the Father of our Lord Jesus Christ. Later in the story, we learn that Isaiah gave counsel to King Hezekiah on a regular basis. Here we find one of the secrets to Hezekiah's spiritual success and of the spiritual success of people throughout the ages – seeking true, Godly counsel.

Just a few moments ago, a man knocked at the door of our house, inviting me to a conference to learn of future world events. I inquired as to who was sponsoring this conference. He responded, *"The Jehovah's Witnesses"*. I immediately ordered him to *"repent for you are doing much damage to God's Kingdom"*. The man turned and very quickly exited the porch and briskly walked down the sidewalk. The counsel coming from that conference was not the kind of true, Godly counsel that would help me in following the Lord.

Prayer: *Oh Lord, every day I face an enemy who wants to deceive me and rob me of Your peace and joy. Voices all around me tell me to think this way or think that way. Oh Lord, put people in my life who are the real thing, people who are truly Your people. In Jesus' name. Amen.*

Scripture: II Kings 20:3-5

One's response to life events usually displays one's character . . . and so with King Hezekiah. After God had miraculously intervened, destroying 185,000 Assyrian soldiers, by means of an epidemic, preventing the fall of Jerusalem, Hezekiah became very ill and was on his deathbed. Isaiah the prophet told him to *"set your house in order, for you shall die . . ."*

Hezekiah's response is worth noting. He cried out to the Lord in prayer and *"wept bitterly"*. The Lord spoke to Isaiah and Isaiah forwarded God's message. God said, *". . . I have heard your prayer. I have seen your tears. I will heal you. . . "* As the result of Hezekiah's plea, bathed in tears, God gave Hezekiah fifteen more years.

I am reminded of the time when the Disciples asked Jesus to teach them to pray. They already knew how to pray, but there was something different about Jesus' prayers. The author of Hebrews describes Jesus' prayers as *". . . supplications with loud crying and tears . . . (Hebrews 4:7)."*

You will visit many churches today before hearing anyone praying with loud crying and tears. I wonder, at times, if this is part of the reason why it appears so many prayers go unanswered.

Unless it is for show or pretense, tears come only after the heart is hurting. It is easy to pray prayers without the heart hurting. When one identifies with the pain of the person suffering, the heart hurts and the tears come.

I am challenged by this kind of intense, unrestrained prayer. Jesus modeled for us the same kind of prayer that King Hezekiah prayed. God hears the prayers of the weeping heart.

Prayer: *Father, break my heart with the things that break Your heart. Let my heart hurt until the tears flow down my cheeks. Hear my prayers Lord. Hear my prayers. In Jesus' name. Amen.*

THURSDAY - THE SIMPLE TEACHING OF HUMILITY

Scripture: Luke 14:11

Humility is one of those qualities admired the world over. Jesus was not only humble but told stories to illustrate the value of humility. He recognized that humility is contrary to the natural tendency to exalt oneself.

The parable in today's story is about the seating arrangement at a wedding feast. Jesus instructs the one invited to the feast to not take the seat of honor, only to be later embarrassed by the host who seats someone else in your place, asking you to move. Jesus said to take the seat of less honor, allowing your host to move you up, if he so desired. Taking the seat of honor on your own would be exalting yourself. Taking the seat of honor, after the host insists, is letting others exalt you.

Jesus sums up this teaching by cautioning his followers to not exalt themselves but instead to humble themselves.

We live in a world where people do desperate things to exalt themselves. They fantasize being movie stars, famous singers, or sports figures. In some ways, we are forced to promote ourselves in seeking a job or position. It is difficult to find a balance.

God promises to exalt you, if you humble yourself before him. This is a promise that is repeated many times throughout the Bible. Yes, we naturally desire to be first, but the way of God is to be satisfied being last and to trust God to make you first, in his timing and in his way.

James, the brother of Jesus, says, "*Humble yourself in the sight of the Lord and he will lift you up.* (James 4:10)" It is our job to humble ourselves. It is God's job to lift us up.

Prayer: *Father, help me to learn Your way of life. Help me, today, to learn ways to humble myself, as Jesus did. In His name. Amen.*

FRIDAY - THE WORD OF GOD AND PEOPLE

Scripture: Luke 8:15

The parable of the sower and the seed is one of the few parables where Jesus explained the meaning of the parable to his disciples. The picture given is that of a farmer scattering seed in a field with some falling beside the road, some falling among rocky soil, some falling in soil overgrown with thorns, and some falling on good soil. The good soil produced a large crop while the seed in the other three types of soil died and thus produced no crop.

Jesus did specifically say that the seed is the word of God. We know the word of God has great power yet because of Satanic activity, hardened hearts, and busyness, the word of God can tragically die out. Though somewhat troubling, this truth can be seen by observation. When the Bible is preached, taught, put forth through song, or given in personal testimony, it will not always result in authentic, disciples of Christ. This should not surprise us.

The good soil is described as being a good heart which holds fast to God's word and bears fruit in spite of difficulties and disappointments. We should ask God to give us this kind of heart - a soft and good heart, one that is a nurturing environment for the word of God to take root, grow, and produce a hundred fold.

Over the years doing youth camps each summer, I have seen many young people bow to their knees to receive Jesus Christ as Lord. Some of them are indeed like good soil. Their lives were transformed by the power of God. The light of Christ shone through them to bring many others to the Savior.

Prayer: *Father, make my heart good soil. By Your Holy Spirit, work in my life in such a way that I will grow in the grace and knowledge of Jesus Christ and produce much fruit. In His name. Amen.*

SATURDAY - THE PEARL OF GREAT VALUE

Scripture: Matthew 13:44

This chapter gives us three parables on the same subject – the kingdom of heaven. Two out of the three are very similar and quite short. One of the two compares the kingdom of heaven to hidden treasure. The other one compares the kingdom of heaven to a pearl of great worth. In both cases, that which was found was of such great value that the person sacrifices all he has to possess or own it.

Imagine someone selling house, business, or farm just to purchase something of great value. The item of great value would have to be really great and thus the point of these parables. This kingdom of heaven is just that – really great. Remember in The Lord's Prayer, Jesus prays *"thy kingdom come"*. Remember when Jesus cast out the devil and said, *"the kingdom of God has come upon you"*? The realm of God came when Jesus came to earth, and does come today when people repent and believe, and will come in its fullness when Jesus comes again.

It is this new way of life, new way of thinking, new way of treating one another, and new way of looking at the world that is transforming entire societies, bringing civility and kindness into communities where selfishness, envy, arrogance, and hatred ruled for generations. The light of Jesus Christ is truly the Light of the world.

I look forward to the final coming of this kingdom in its entirety. I pray for it every day. It is my hope, and it is a living hope. It gives me reason to think things will be better in the future. It is described in detail in the last few chapters of Revelation.

Prayer: *Father, thank You for the Bible which tells about this pearl of great worth and about this incredible hidden treasure. Oh Father, it has worth much greater than houses, land, or cars. Through Jesus, You bring me into Your kingdom. Thank You, Lord. In Jesus' name. Amen.*

SUNDAY – GOD'S SPECIAL DAY – THE LORD'S DAY
"Praise the Lord! Sing to the Lord a new song, and His praise in the congregation of the godly ones."
                    Psalm 149:1

WEEK #34: THE HOLY SPIRIT

MONDAY - THE OLD TESTAMENT AND THE "SPIRIT"

Scripture: Numbers 11:16-17, 25, 28-29; Joel 2:28

Some Biblical scholars over the years have described the Old Testament as being primarily about God, the New Testament about Jesus, and the church age about the Holy Spirit. Such a description does appear to fit Trinitarian thinking, but one would certainly be in error to overlook the many times the Holy Spirit is mentioned in the Old Testament.

The Holy Spirit is mentioned in the second verse of the Bible, as hovering over God's creation. All three persons of the Trinity (Father, Son, and Holy Spirit) are thought to be present and active in creation.

In our text from Numbers, we learn that the Holy Spirit was vibrantly upon Moses and that God anointed the seventy elders of Israel with the Holy Spirit, and they spoke God's word. They must have suddenly spoke God's word with an unusual boldness, as their ability to prophesy was noticeable. Later we learn that Moses desired and yearned for God to put his Spirit upon all the people, not just the seventy.

Then many years later, after the rise and fall of Israel, the prophet Joel uttered a famous prophecy which was quoted when Peter preached the first Christian sermon on the Day of Pentecost. Joel looks forward in time and proclaims that what Moses desired would in fact happen, when God established his eternal kingdom. God would pour forth his Spirit upon all mankind.

Every true, Gospel preacher will desire that same anointing when standing before a congregation or a gathered assembly. It is historic in our circle. When God grips a person (man or woman), shakes him, and sets his heart aflame, he cannot keep quiet. The words which are uttered are anointed of the Lord.

Prayer: *Father, Your word continues to amaze me. Your Spirit is mighty and powerful. Thank You, Lord, for anointing Your servants over the years to speak Your holy Word. In Jesus' name. Amen.*

TUESDAY - DRY BONES COME ALIVE

Scripture: Ezekiel 2:1-2; 37:1

Isaiah and Ezekiel mention the Holy Spirit more than any of the other prophets. In several references, Ezekiel speaks of the Spirit picking him up and carrying him to this place or that and giving him visions. Some of these visions are quite dramatic, making some of us to question maybe what he was smoking, but to him it was the Holy Spirit coming upon him mightily.

One of the more famous of Ezekiel's Spirit inspired visions is the valley of dry bones in chapter 37. These bones represented the house of Israel. The Holy Spirit asks Ezekiel, "Can these bones live?" Ezekiel hesitates, responding with a rather ambiguous answer. The Spirit tells him to prophesy over the bones. God gives him the very words to say, "*Now hear the word of the Lord . . .*" God tells him to speak to the wind to fill these beings with breath. Ezekiel cries out, "Breathe on these slain, that they come to life." Flesh and tendons came upon the bones, and breath came into them; they became an "exceedingly great army".

If you would picture the church of Jesus Christ throughout the world, without the Holy Spirit, you would see a valley of dry bones. It is only by the Spirit that we in the church have life. God's Holy Spirit gives us life. God breathes on our dry bones through prophesy, through the words of men like Ezekiel who stand before us and say, "Now hear the word of the Lord. . ."

Protestant churches have this incredibly rich history of fiery sermons. We don't want to be dry bones! We want God to breathe on us through his Holy Spirit and give us life.

Prayer: *Father, thank You for this mental picture of the valley of dry bones. Before You filled me with Your Spirit and gave me the hope of eternal life, though I had a pulse, and my heart was beating, I was dead as dead could be and pitifully lost. Oh Lord, thank You. In Jesus' name. Amen.*

WEDNESDAY - CONCEIVED OF THE HOLY SPIRIT

Scripture: Matthew 1:18; 3:16-17

I know of no other Scripture verse so power-packed full of meaning than verse 18 of Matthew chapter one. The content of this verse is repeated when the "angel of the Lord" speaks to Joseph, explaining that this *"Child who has been conceived in her is of the Holy Spirit."* To try to comprehend a baby conceived of the Holy Spirit is to engage in mental gymnastics far beyond the limits of my imagination. This is mixing the physiological world with the spiritual world. It is miracle of all miracles.

When pregnant with Jesus, Mary visits her cousin, Elizabeth. Upon hearing Mary's greeting, the baby in Elizabeth's womb (John the Baptist) leaped and Elizabeth was *"filled with the Holy Spirit"*. When John the Baptist was born, his father, Zacharias was *"filled with the Holy Spirit"*.

At the proper time, the baby Jesus was brought to the Jerusalem Temple. Here was an old man, Simeon, who took the baby Jesus and offered an incredible prophecy. Simeon is described as having the Holy Spirit upon him and the message given was revealed to him by the Holy Spirit.

Then at Jesus' baptism, people actually saw the Spirit of God descending upon Jesus as a dove.

It would be difficult to avoid mention of the Holy Spirit when studying Jesus' birth. God's Spirit was obviously a major player in the birth of God's Son. With Jesus, we see another picture of the Trinity – Father, Son, and Holy Spirit.

The reality of spiritual truths is breathtaking. Atheists are quick to dismiss it all as utter folly and unenlightened nonsense. I do believe. I believe God breaks through our black and white world, putting color into otherwise meaningless existence.

Prayer: *Father, this day I praise You for putting Your Spirit all over every aspect of Jesus' birth. You, through Your Spirit, fathered a child. You came to be with us. Praise Your name forever. Through Jesus. Amen.*

THURSDAY - JESUS: GUIDED BY THE SPIRIT

Scripture: Luke 4:1; 17-18

Between Jesus' baptism and the beginning of his public ministry was a forty day period of intense prayer, fasting and spiritual warfare. The Holy Spirit is described as leading Jesus into this so-called ministry boot camp. Emerging from the wilderness in the *"power of the Spirit"*, Jesus immediately went to his hometown synagogue and stood before the people to read from the book of Isaiah, chapter 61, the words, *"The Spirit of the Lord is upon Me . . ."*

Should it surprise us that the first words out of Jesus' mouth, when he spoke publicly the very first time, called attention to the anointing of God's Spirit upon him? The very Spirit who had conceived him, now gripped him, inspired him, motivated him and filled him. Don't you wish you could have been there?

It is interesting to note the content of Jesus' first message. Jesus announced that his coming would bring God's favor and blessing to a certain audience – the poor, those in prison, the blind, and the oppressed - not the typical health and wealth, prosperity gospel we hear on the TV. We are reminded that Jesus didn't come to give the rich more riches, to give more comfort to the comfortable, to give more education to the highly educated, or to give more power to the powerful. The people on his radar screen were not the people most of us would like to identify with.

The Holy Spirit was clearly the driving force of Jesus' life and ministry, his teaching and preaching, his healing and casting out demons, and his obedience to the Father in the sacrifice of his life on the cross. This is the picture we get of a truly Spirit-filled life.

Prayer: *Father, help me to be like Jesus in my speech and in my actions. Put that very same Spirit upon me that inspired and empower Jesus, my Lord. In his name. Amen.*

FRIDAY - JESUS: EMPOWERED BY THE SPIRIT

Scripture: Luke 4:14; 6:12; Matthew 12:28

The anointing of the Holy Spirit on Jesus was truly the key to his power in healing and in casting out demons. Jesus was intent on destroying one kingdom (the Devil's kingdom) to replace it with another kingdom (God's kingdom).

We don't know the details of that night, recorded by Luke, where Jesus went off by himself for a whole night of prayer. We do know the events of the next day in that he chose his twelve disciples and healed many people. The crowd who gathered around Jesus was described as a "great throng" of people. It is said of Jesus that *"power was coming from Him to heal them all."*

Jesus' prayer time was probably not boring, not repetitive, but alive and full of intimacy and spontaneity. Jesus must have been energized and mesmerized by the presence of God, through the Holy Spirit, which therefore empowered him for ministry and gave him great discernment.

I haven't had many times like that in my prayer life. One time, though, was when I was deported from India. After being taken into custody by the Immigration Department for suspicion of missionary activity, I was put on a jet for the 15 hour flight from Delhi to Chicago. All the rest of the some 300 passengers were asleep. I couldn't sleep for obvious reasons. My mind was swirling with various thoughts. I turned on my reading light and opened my Bible to the book of John, chapter one. I began to read, ponder, and pray. When I looked at my watch, five hours had passed, and I had finished the book of John. It was as if, the Holy Spirit took me captive, and for five hours, time did not exist.

Prayer: *Father, when I pray, take me captive by Your Holy Spirit. Take me into Your presence, that I may truly sit at Your feet, and go forth into the world filled with Your light and love. In Jesus' name. Amen.*

SATURDAY - HOLY SPIRIT: THIRD PERSON

Scripture: Matthew 28:18-19

The word "Trinity" is not found in the Bible, as it evolved long after the Bible was written. Three people considered as one unit would be appropriately described as a "trinity". This word is not necessarily a theological term but was picked by theologians to describe these three divine beings we see moving across the stage, in the Biblical drama which unfolds.

We see God the Father on stage in creation and throughout the Old Testament. We see Jesus on stage, in the background at creation, prophesied in the Old Testament, and the main actor in the New Testament, and from that point on throughout eternity. We see God the Spirit on stage in creation and sporadically throughout the Old Testament, playing a much larger role in the New Testament, and then the leading role in the birth and subsequent life of the Church. These three actors are separate persons yet they are one. Each one is God.

Think of water or H20. It has three forms: liquid, vapor, and solid. Each form is water yet each form is its own entity. God is like that.

When Jesus gave his grand marching orders to the Church (today's Scripture), he told the Apostles to ". . . *make disciples of all the nations, baptizing them in the name of the Father, Son, and Holy Spirit. . .*" Do you see the Trinity in the statement? That famous command is known as "The Great Commission". It is the backbone of Christ's Church, the appropriate, main theme of most churches and Christian organizations.

One true test of a church that is faithful to the Bible and historical Christianity is its view of God the Father, God the Son, and God the Spirit.

Prayer: *Father, thank You today for acting throughout history and giving me insights as to Your being, Your character, and Your will. In Jesus' name. Amen.*

SUNDAY – GOD'S SPECIAL DAY – THE LORD'S DAY

". . . and let us consider how to stimulate one another to love and good deeds, not forsaking our own assembling together, as is the habit of some, but encouraging one another; and all the more as you see the day drawing near." Hebrews 10:24-25

WEEK #35

MONDAY - SPIRIT PREDICTIONS AND SPIRIT HAPPENINGS

Scripture: John 7:37-39

John added commentary to Jesus' teaching on this "living water" bubbling up inside of those who believed in him. John explained that this was the Holy Spirit whom had not yet come but would come later when Jesus would be glorified, obviously referring to his resurrection and ascension. Earlier, John records Jesus speaking to the Samaritan woman about "living water" which would spring up in her to eternal life.

Jesus spoke to Nicodemas in John 3, as he told the religious leader it was necessary for him to be born again, which he later described as being born of the Spirit. Nicodemus struggled in understanding this new kind of Spirit birth.

Jesus raised people's expectations in teaching that God would move in a special way in each of their lives, individually, which would be a once-in-a-life-time experience lasting forever. John the Baptist said he baptized with water, but Jesus would baptize with the Holy Spirit.

Jesus was well aware of God's plan to pour out his Holy Spirit on the Church, as was prophesied by Old Testament prophets. He instructed his disciples to stay in Jerusalem and wait for this dynamic event. They didn't fully understand what would happen or how it would happen but could understand enough to wait and pray. This they did. All his disciples were gathered together in one place when the Holy Spirit came like a rush of wind and rested upon each of them like "tongues of fire".

This outpouring of God's Spirit shook Jerusalem to the core, as these Believers could not keep quiet about God's good news of salvation. As a result, three thousand people became Believers and were baptized. The Church of Jesus Christ was born.

Prayer: *Father, that outpouring of Your Holy Spirit upon the disciples was incredible. Thank You, Lord. Thank You for pouring forth Your Spirit upon all who have received Your Son throughout the ages, including me. In His name. Amen.*

TUESDAY - THE HELPER, THE HOLY SPIRIT

Scripture: John 14:16-17; 26

The Holy Spirit also is referred to as the "Helper" and the "Spirit of truth". In today's account, Jesus informs his disciples that he will specifically ask God to send the "Helper". He further states that this Helper will be with them forever and will dwell in them. Keep in mind, this is the same being that conceived the baby Jesus in the womb of Mary, the same divine being that empowered Jesus for his preaching, teaching and miracles.

The disciples were not clueless when the Holy Spirit came upon them. Jesus had put forth intentional teaching on the Holy Spirit so they would have some level of understanding when this outpouring happened.

Later in chapter 14, Jesus explains that the Helper's presence in them would have a teaching effect and would actually work also in their minds, helping them remember the things Jesus taught. If they were going to launch a global movement, they would need to have a good knowledge of all that Jesus taught. They would need to know how to respond and what to say when persecuted, prosecuted, and accused of causing trouble. They would need to know how to respond to relatives and family members who would not understand why they were going away to take this so-called message to the world.

While in India, I visited the place where the Apostle Thomas was martyred and then visited his supposed burial place. Stories are still told of the handful of churches Thomas started. At the time I wondered, "What was India like back then?" "What would it have been like to travel from the Middle East to India?" "What were his fears?" "What did his family think?"

Prayer: *Father, thank You for each one of the Apostles who went to different parts of the world many years ago. I may not be a Believer today without their sacrifice. Thank You Father. In Jesus' name. Amen.*

WEDNESDAY - THE HOLY SPIRIT GLORIFIES JESUS

Scripture: John 15:26-27; 16:13-15

Many churches today put great emphasis upon the baptism of the Holy Spirit, praying for the Holy Spirit, and receiving the Holy Spirit. They point to ecstatic utterances or gibberish as proof that the Holy Spirit is in them. Many of these people cry out to God to speak in tongues, prophesy, and do miracles. People jump up and down uncontrollably, claiming to have been touched by the Holy Spirit. Some people fall over backwards, claiming the Holy Spirit knocked them down, while others bark like dogs or laugh like hyenas, claiming the Holy Spirit has come upon them.

The leaders of those churches need to study what Jesus taught about the Holy Spirit. Jesus said the Holy Spirit would testify about him, Jesus. He also said the Holy Spirit will glorify him, Jesus. In other words, the Holy Spirit will not call attention to himself, but will point to Jesus. People who are truly filled with the Holy Spirit will not take pride in their ability to do this or that, exalting themselves, but will instead, exalt Jesus and glorify him.

Possibly the analogy of a frame to a picture would describe the relationship of the Holy Spirit to Jesus. A good frame will not be noticed by the admirer. At best, the frame enhances the picture. So it is with the Holy Spirit. When the Holy Spirit is hitting on all cylinders in the Believer's life, one notices Jesus, not the Holy Spirit.

In our study of the Holy Spirit, we need to be careful not to lose focus of Jesus. Jesus is our Savior, our Lord. Jesus is the King of Kings, the Prince of Peace, the Light of the world.

Prayer: *Father, thank You that Jesus taught us what to believe about Your Spirit. It can be confusing with so many "Bible teachers" teaching different things. Oh Father, keep me at the feet of Jesus. In His name. Amen.*

THURSDAY - THE HOLY SPIRIT CONVICTS

Scripture: John 16:7-11

Jesus not only said that he would ask the Father to send the Holy Spirit, but in today's text, he said that when he goes, he will send the Holy Spirit. I think we can conclude that the Holy Spirit will be sent to us whether it be by the Father or by Jesus. The Spirit will come.

Convicting the world of sin, righteousness, and judgment is a huge task. Jesus explains that the Holy Spirit will do this. The disciples may have worried about how the people would react when they went to towns and villages to share Christ's story. Would they believe? Would anyone believe?

Have you ever worried as to how your friend or relative or coworker would react if you shared the gospel with them? Jesus gave us insights into the work of the Holy Spirit so we would have confidence in going forth, encountering opposition, and facing struggles.

Jesus didn't want the disciples to think it was their responsibility to persuade people with savy presentations and slick words. Jesus wanted them to simply speak the message, and the Holy Spirit would do the rest. The Holy Spirit would convince and convict them, not human ability and talent.

Churches today desperately need reminded of this. Too many times, church leaders think it is the quality of their sound system, or the quality of their music, or the comfort level of the people in the pew, that persuade people. They think people are convicted because the preacher can tell a few jokes and make them laugh, read a poem and throw in a few words about God. We need church leaders who truly understand how the Holy Spirit works in the hearts and lives of people.

Prayer: *Father, thank You for convicting me by Your Holy Spirit. I needed that. I needed to realize how foolish and how stupid it was for me to try to be my own god. Your Spirit made me realize that. Thank You, Lord. In Jesus' name. Amen.*

FRIDAY - THE HOLY SPIRIT COMES

Scripture: Acts 1:4-5, 8; 2:1-4

Jesus' final word to his disciples, as recorded in the book of Acts, was to wait in Jerusalem for the Holy Spirit to come upon them like a baptism. They had been baptized with water and had heard John the Baptist prophesy that he baptized with water, but Jesus would baptize with the Holy Spirit and fire. Jesus was now telling them this baptism will happen in a few days. Jesus explained the Holy Spirit would empower them to be his witnesses to the ends of the earth. About 120 of his disciples gathered in an upper room for prayer and to wait.

Acts chapter two is the big story of the coming of the Holy Spirit. The Spirit suddenly came upon them as a rushing wind. Little flames of fire appear above their heads. Remember John the Baptist telling of Jesus baptizing with the Holy Spirit and fire? They began to speak in other languages, as people had come to Jerusalem from many different countries, speaking many different languages. This was the Jewish Day of Pentecost, a celebration for all Jews in all parts of the world to come to the Holy City. The Disciples began telling the story of Jesus in languages they had never spoken before, an incredible miracle. Some even accused them of being drunk.

As mentioned in Monday's readings of this week, three thousand people responded to Peter's message, repented, and were baptized. These people were the very first people to hear the Gospel message about the death and resurrection of Jesus Christ and the need for repentance, with the call to be baptized. When this happened, the Church of Jesus Christ was born. Halleluyah! Praise His name!

Prayer: *Father, it is really hard to begin to wrap my mind around such an event so many years ago. Since then, the world has never been the same. Thank You for Your Church spread all around the world. In Jesus' name. Amen.*

SATURDAY - THE HOLY SPIRIT DRAWS PEOPLE TOGETHER

Scripture: Genesis 11:8-9; Acts 2:43-44

There is a mystery surrounding the coming of the Holy Spirit, the birth of the Church, and the coming together of people. The birth of the church is quite the contrast with the Genesis story of the tower of Babel. One story is people dividing and separating because they could not understand one another. The other story is people, once divided, now coming together because they can understand one another. With Jesus and the power of the Holy Spirit, there is understanding of one another, love of one another, and mutual respect, making it possible for people to put aside differences of culture, nationality, socio-economic status, and race.

The growth of Christianity has been the greatest force in the history of civilization for reconciliation and peace. It has as its core teaching that all men are equal in God's eyes. Jesus commanded his followers to love one another as he loved them. As men are by nature, selfish, egotistical, and proud, this teaching goes against the grain of unrestrained human behavior. Men by nature don't love one another; they fight, like male dogs fight. Coming together with mutual respect and appreciation for one another has only come about through the outpouring of God's Holy Spirit. It has only come about when the love of God has burst forth in human hearts.

Every church who claims to be born of the Spirit should be very aware that the "proof of the pudding" is not tongues or erratic behavior. It is God's redemptive love on display in the lives of ordinary people who otherwise would be out and about doing "their own thing". The Apostle Paul does an excellent job of stating this in I Corinthians 13 - the "love chapter".

Prayer: *Father, I am hungry for true fellowship of men and women whose lives give testimony to changed hearts, transformed by the fire of Your holy love. Praise You for bringing me into Your body, the Church. In Jesus' name. Amen.*

SUNDAY – GOD'S SPECIAL DAY – THE LORD'S DAY

"Let the peace of Christ rule in your hearts, to which indeed you were called in one body; and be thankful. Let the word of Christ richly dwell within you, with all wisdom teaching and admonishing one another with psalms and hymns and spiritual songs, singing with thankfulness in your hearts to God." Colossians 3:15-16

WEEK #36

MONDAY - THE SPIRIT BLOWS AGAIN AND AGAIN

Scripture: Acts 8:14-17; 11:12-15

As the Holy Spirit came upon the Believers in Jerusalem, similar events are recorded in Acts at two very critical moments in the growth of the Church.

God wanted the gospel message to go far beyond any Jewish ghetto, out into the far reaches of the world. How would this happen? The Jews viewed other peoples, Gentiles, as inferior races. Though Samaritans were half Jewish, the Jews could not associate with them, because they were not pure Jewish. This elitist, condescending attitude would be a major obstacle to the future expansion of the kingdom.

God's answer was persecution and two more Pentecost moments, one involving Samaritans and one involving people who were not Jewish in any way (Gentiles). Because Christians were persecuted in Jerusalem, the Believers spread out and fled to different regions, and you guessed it, they took the Gospel with them. Our first text today tells of Philip going to Samaria and later the Apostles, with God's Holy Spirit coming upon these half-Jews, Samaritans. The gospel crossed its first ethnic/racial barrier.

Acts 10 through part of chapter eleven tells the story of the gospel crossing another ethnic/racial barrier, a very big one. This is a pivotal story in the book of Acts. Through a vision and other events involving Peter, the Holy Spirit forces the church out of its Jewish bubble, fully into the Gentile world, with a Gentile, Roman soldier and his relatives receiving the Holy Spirit, just as happened on the Day of Pentecost.

God, through the Holy Spirit, is forever taking us beyond our comfort zones, beyond our wildest imaginations. The Holy Spirit is relentless in challenging elitist attitudes, forcing God's people to see beyond stained glass ghettos, out into a messy, chaotic world of hurt.

Prayer: *Oh Father, what stories! The growth and expansion of Your kingdom has shaken planet earth and continues to do so in the most unexpected places. Thank You Father. Thank You Lord. In Jesus' name. Amen.*

TUESDAY - THE SPIRIT BLOWS AND BLOWS

Scripture: Acts 19:1-2,5-7

The last time in the book of Acts we read of the Holy Spirit coming upon people, like he did in Jerusalem, is at the strategic city of Ephesus. Those times of outpouring seemed to be perfectly timed of the Lord.

Ephesus was a gateway city to Asia, a famous port city of about 200,000 people, with the very famous Temple of Artemis. Paul visited there in his third missionary journey and encountered great opposition but had fruitful ministry in the city and region for some two to three years. In verse 10 we learn an incredible fact – all of Asia heard the gospel during Paul's time there.

When Paul arrived in Ephesus he found a small Christian community who were in desperate need of his teaching. They had heard nothing of the Holy Spirit and had never had Christian baptism. Paul baptized them in the name of the Lord Jesus, and the Holy Spirit came upon them in such a way that they did speak in other unknown languages and prophesy.

The modern day Pentecostal movement has put a huge emphasis upon what they call "speaking in tongues". This appears to most people as unrestrained gibberish, not what one reads about in the book of Acts when God pours forth his Spirit. Paul cautions against this, as many women in the church at Corinth were making a sideshow out of ecstatic utterances. This has caused many church splits and much confusion, not what you would expect from a genuine move of the Spirit.

When the Spirit of God blew across the hearts of Jesus' followers in dramatic ways, it did so at times and places which would significantly alter the landscape as to the spread of the gospel.

Prayer: *Father, the birth and spread of the gospel message thrills my heart today. May You use my life today in such a way that kingdom results would come forth. In Jesus' name. Amen.*

WEDNESDAY - THE SPIRIT EMPOWERS & SENDS

Scripture: Acts 4:31; 13:2-4; 20:28

If you don't have a spark plug to ignite the fuel in the piston chamber of a gas engine, the engine will not run. The spark is necessary. Thus the Holy Spirit was to the early Church, igniting her and setting her aflame. Slick marketing programs were not responsible for the growth of the first century Church. There were no fancy buildings and no seminaries, yet the early Church was a powerhouse for God, transforming lives and societies.

When persecution came, the Believers fasted and cried out to God and were continually filled with the Holy Spirit. Wherever one reads of the Holy Spirit, there is confidence and boldness to proclaim God's message, even amidst cruel threats and harsh circumstances.

In the first Gentile church, there were humble, Godly leaders who knew how to minister in Jesus name, fast and pray. The Holy Spirit is actually quoted, speaking to them, telling them specifically who to set apart for a mission project to other nations. The Holy Spirit is given the credit for sending them out.

The third reading today portrays the Holy Spirit as selecting overseers or senior pastors who would be capable of supervising networks of churches. Church leaders should not rise to power on the magnetism of personality or charisma but under the direction and leading of the Holy Spirit.

The Church of Jesus Christ has taken many different shapes throughout history. Not one denomination or church system is perfect, because man is involved. Flawed as she is, the Church is triumphant throughout history. No other institution with so many problems could have survived some two thousand years. She is born of the Spirit and empowered by the Spirit.

Prayer: *Father, today I praise You for the work of Your Spirit, through Your people gathering in congregations and churches. Oh precious Spirit, continue to fill Your people with contagious joy and boldness to expand Your kingdom. In Jesus' name. Amen.*

THURSDAY - THE SPIRIT BLESSES

Scripture: Acts 2:42, 46-47; 20:7

When the Spirit came and thousands of new Believers were blessed with Christian fellowship, something really special happened. Peter, James, John and the other Apostles were regularly teaching the people. In sharing meals together, there was "gladness and sincerity of heart". Together they were praying, praising God, which most likely meant they were singing songs and sharing testimonies with one another. When non-Christians witnessed this level of love and compassion, and heard the gospel story, they reached out to God in repentance and faith in large numbers.

The last text illustrates just how much the early church hungered for teaching about God's grace and faith. We read of the Apostle Paul preaching in a service where he *"prolonged his message until midnight"*.

I have been in church services in Africa and India where this could have happened. Where there is extreme poverty and persecution, people are not so easily consumed with mindless entertainment. When tasting of the kingdom, many are incredibly hungry and eager to hear more about God and Jesus.

Christian fellowship which is authentic and real is contagious. It is a blessing. When this type of fellowship happens, growth is the natural by-product. The warmth of true Christian fellowship goes beyond what can be described in words. This doesn't happen just because people gather in a church building and sing a few songs. It does happen when Jesus is the honored guest, when God shows up, when the Holy Spirit is present. Christian fellowship should be far superior to anything experienced in the Lion's Club, the Library Club, or the Chamber of Commerce. The divine aspect puts it in a completely different class of enjoyment and blessing than anything experienced anywhere else in this life.

Prayer: *Father, thank You for the love and compassion shown to one another in Jesus name. Thank You where Biblical teaching is regularly shared and Your presence is the main thing. Through Christ my Lord. Amen.*

FRIDAY - THE SPIRIT INSPIRES

Scripture: Acts 5:40-42; 13:52

God's Spirit did many amazing things in and through the New Testament church. One of those things is to continually give God's people joy in the midst of stiff opposition and persecution.

Flogging was an excruciating and brutal punishment inflicted by local government authorities in response to criminal activity. It is quite the stretch of imagination for any one of Jesus' apostles to do anything that would warrant flogging, yet it happened to most, if not all apostles.

We read of the apostles, after the flogging, going on their way "... *rejoicing that they had been considered worthy to suffer shame for his name.*" Later we read that the disciples were "*continually filled with joy and with the Holy Spirit.*" God had truly become known to them in a dynamic and personal way. It was much more than reciting doctrinal beliefs in a stained glass building and listening to a sermon. It was a lifestyle, a radical lifestyle that reeked of God's love and compassion and hope.

The Holy Spirit was a daily reality to the early Christians. They sought the Holy Spirit's presence and prayed for others to receive the Holy Spirit. They were not focused on increasing bank accounts, the latest digital gadgets, and moving up corporate ladders. They shared life with other Believers, challenged and admonished one another, laughed with one another, wept with one another, and encouraged one another. The indwelling of the Holy Spirit inspired them to live like this.

I am so challenged every time I read the book of Acts. I long for a church like the church in Acts. I want fellowship that has depth and authenticity. I want to experience daily the Spirit's joy and power and presence.

Prayer: *Father, forgive me when I have pity party moments, thinking of myself and not others. Oh Lord, mold me and shape me by Your Spirit. Give me Your holy joy this day. In Jesus' name. Amen.*

SATURDAY - THE SPIRIT MULTIPLIES

Scripture: Acts 2:41; 4:4; 6:7

There has never been such an exponential church growth story like the one we read about in Acts. Three thousand repented and responded in faith the first day God poured out his Spirit. Within a day or two, an additional five thousand were converted. The word of the Lord spread rapidly in Jerusalem and then in the subsequent regions around Jerusalem until all of Asia had heard the gospel. Acts ends with Paul in Rome, the epicenter of the known world of that period of history.

Today in America, if one has a degree in marketing, one can grow a church. It has nothing to do with God, nothing to do with the Holy Spirit, and nothing to with Believers loving and caring for one another. Provide good entertainment in a well-lit and newly furnished building with the latest sound and video technology. Provide amusement center-like fun for children and youth. Never mention redemption, sin, hell, or judgment. Do all these things, and presto, one can have a big church. With thousands of people coming every Sunday, people will be amazed at how "God is blessing." But is he really?

God truly blesses church growth that is guided and directed by the Holy Spirit, not by the snake-oil salesmen wearing crosses and living in million dollar mansions. When the Spirit comes, discouraged, weary people find hope, grace, peace, and joy. Peoples' lives are transformed by God.

This is the picture we see in the book of Acts. When getting a good feel for the state of mind and heart of the early Believers, does anyone not understand why so many received Christ when exposed to those Christians and their contagious joy and peace and message of hope?

Prayer: *Father, my heart wants the real thing - wants You, wants Jesus, wants Your Spirit. America needs You, oh Lord, not cheap tricks. Oh Lord, purify Your Church in our land. In Jesus' name. Amen.*

SUNDAY – GOD'S SPECIAL DAY – THE LORD'S DAY

"Remember the sabbath day to keep it holy. Six days you shall labor and do all your work, but on the seventh day is a sabbath of the Lord your God . . ." Exodus 20:8-10

MONDAY - THE SPIRIT INDWELLS

Scripture: Luke 11:13; Acts 9:17

Some Christian leaders today have questioned the wisdom of asking God to fill you with the Holy Spirit. They see the error in the teaching of the Pentecostals and therefore resist much talk about the Holy Spirit or praying for the Holy Spirit. I don't deny the error in Pentecostal teaching, but I think we ignore obvious Biblical teaching if we don't emphasize the indwelling of the Holy Spirit.

Luke gives us this parable of Jesus whereby Jesus teaches persistence in prayer, saying, "*. . . ask, and it will be given to you; seek, and you will find, knock, and it will be opened to you.* (11:9)" At the end of the story Jesus makes a surprising promise saying, "*. . . . how much more will your heavenly Father give the Holy Spirit to those who ask Him.*" With this statement, it is clear that Jesus gave particular instructions to pray for the Holy Spirit.

In our Acts reference, the Apostle Paul had just been blinded by a vision of Jesus. He was stunned, knowing that this new teaching about this man, Jesus, which he had so vigorously opposed, was actually true. Jesus sent Ananias to him to pray for two specific things for Paul – to receive his sight and be filled with the Holy Spirit. He received his sight and was baptized. Speaking in tongues is not mentioned. The implication is that he repented, received Christ, received the Holy Spirit, and was water baptized.

I want to encourage everyone who receives Christ to not only be baptized with water but to receive and be filled with the Holy Spirit. I want all to be empowered and blessed with God's Holy Spirit.

Prayer: *Oh Father, I see it now much clearer than ever before. I want to be like Paul and the early Christians. I want Your Holy Spirit. Fill me, Father, today and every day, with Your breath, Your Spirit. In Jesus' name. Amen.*

TUESDAY - THE SPIRIT LEADS

Scripture: Romans 8:1-2; 14

Life in the Spirit was the goal of Christian discipleship in the New Testament. Rather than being under the law of sin and death, as forgiven and set free, the Believers were to be alive to God, alive in the Spirit. They were to be no longer living "*in the flesh*" but instead "*in the Spirit*".

Later in chapter 8, the Apostle describes those being led by the Spirit as those who are truly sons of God. The implication being that if you are not being led by the Spirit, you are not a real child of God. This puts great importance on being led by the Holy Spirit.

The Christian is to be led of the Spirit daily. Seeking God's specific leading as to a ministry or occupation or mate is not so much on Paul's mind with this text. Living a Spirit led life is having the awareness each day of the Spirit's presence and being in communion with the Spirit as the day goes forth.

In my early morning prayer-time, I ask God to fill me with his Spirit for this new day - the morning, the afternoon, and the evening. Intentionally opening one's mind to the voice of the Spirit is key to following him throughout the day. If your mind is not open, how do you expect to hear him when he speaks?

Though not too many of us go through our day "hearing voices", we do sense in our spirit that subtle nudging or quiet voice of God's Spirit, as the day unfolds. Our God is not only there to rescue us from this crisis or that but is there to guide our every step.

Prayer: *Father, fill me again today with Your Spirit. Be there throughout my day as my best friend and guide. In Jesus' name. Amen.*

WEDNESDAY - THE SPIRIT COUNSELS

Scripture: Acts 8:29; 15:28; 16:6-7

Receiving direct counsel and direction from the Holy Spirit is not always easy. Since being deported from India last September, Rhonda and I have spent huge amounts of time seeking the Spirit's guidance. I have been doing a "Daniel fast" for almost two months along with praying for the Lord's leading. There are many doors open, but doors that fit God's leading are the only ones we want.

Hearing from God as to specifics was not always easy for the New Testament church. In the book of Acts there were those times when the Spirit promptly gave verbal direction, such as when Philip went up into the chariot to share the gospel with a man from Ethiopia. Later we read about the gathering of church leaders in Jerusalem who concluded that it *"seemed good to the Holy Spirit and to us"*. This kind of leading was not quite as definitive. They most likely spent much time in prayer without the Holy Spirit speaking words to anyone and then came to a reasonable conclusion.

When Paul first tried to bring the gospel to Asia, he was *"forbidden by the Holy Spirit"* to go forward. In the next verse the *"Spirit of Jesus"* did not permit them to enter another region. How did this happen? Did Paul misunderstand the Holy Spirit when he first tried to go into Asia? How did the Holy Spirit forbid him to enter? We don't know the answer to these questions, but it seems obvious that Paul didn't have a clear understanding of the Spirit's leading at every step of the way.

As the Holy Spirit gives us counsel, the path is many times fraught with obstacles and challenges.

Prayer: *Father, thank You for Your wise counsel throughout life. You see down the road a long way. My sight is so very short. Guide my every step. In Jesus' name. Amen.*

THURSDAY - THE SPIRIT COMFORTS

Scripture: Acts 6:5; 7:55

My mother, Reba Curry, was good at motherly comfort. Many times in my childhood, life didn't make sense. I would question mom as to "Why? Why? Why?" She would listen and say, *"Tommy your little mind cannot understand everything now, but later on, you will. Trust me, Tommy."* Then she would take me in her arms and hold me. Like a warm blanket on a cold night were my mother's arms. The world could seem quite frightening, but mom's arms would change everything. She was my *"comforter"*.

Jesus referred to the Holy Spirit as a *"comforter"*. When I read the tragic story of Stephen being stoned, and read how during the stoning he *"being full of the Holy Spirit gazed intently into heaven and saw the glory of God. . .",* I realize that, at that moment, the Holy Spirit was comforting him in ways no human mind can grasp. Jesus was not there in physical form with his arms around Stephen, but the Holy Spirit was very much present.

Life for the Apostle Paul was certainly not giddy and fun. He wrote the church at Ephesus, ". . . *remembering that night and day for a period of three years I did not cease to admonish each one with tears."*

I wish I could tell every boy and girl that life in this world is fair and good. It is not. I have done the funerals, witnessed the tears and wailing, seen the suffering and heard many vain apologies. Yes, there is good in this world, and yes, sometimes the average person gets justice, but for many people in most of the world, life is quite brutal, and hope beyond this life is very attractive.

Prayer: *Father, thank You for the Comforter, for Your Spirit, especially when life doesn't make much sense. Thank You, oh Lord, for taking me in Your arms often and holding me. In Jesus' name. Amen.*

FRIDAY - THE SPIRIT TEACHES

Scripture: John 14:25-26; 15:18

Jesus was constantly in a teaching mode with his Disciples. He would teach the large crowds and then pull the Disciples aside and offer additional insights, question them, and challenge them. He knew the importance of learning a new way of viewing the world, a new way of seeing people and engaging people. He wanted them to "get it".

When Jesus talked about leaving, the Disciples panicked. What would they do? Jesus was their leader. Jesus did the miracles, not them. How would they carry on? One can imagine how any talk of Jesus going away would cause them to sweat bullets. Jesus said, "*I will not leave you as orphans. I will come to you.*"
He promised them the Holy Spirit would "*teach you all things*".

Luke, in his Gospel, records Jesus preparing them for the opposition to come. Jesus spoke to the Disciples about being brought before authorities and rulers because of their gospel efforts. In describing the Holy Spirit, he said, "*. . . for the Holy Spirit will teach you that very hour what you ought to say. (12:12)*"

Each day in my prayer time, I ask the Holy Spirit to "*teach me*". I realize that I am but a child, in great need of learning more and more about God and life. Having a Master's Degree and an Honorary Doctorate of Divinity degree doesn't mean that I have "*arrived*" and have all knowledge. I know only a small, teeny, tiny drop in comparison to God my Father.

Every day brings new opportunities to carry forth God's kingdom work. Sometimes this puts us in embarrassing and awkward situations. The Holy Spirit is there to help us respond to situations in such a way that God is truly glorified.

Prayer: *Father, keep me on the learning curve with Your Holy Spirit. Help me to lean on You more and more. Teach me, oh Lord, teach me. In Jesus' name. Amen.*

SATURDAY - THE SPIRIT INTERCEEDS

Scripture: Romans 8:26-27

Many times we don't know how to pray as we should. Life situations come, and it is difficult to know and understand the specific will of God and how he is using this adversity or that adversity. Sometimes the devil is attacking, and we, like Job, speak as if God is punishing us. Sometimes it is God, and sometimes it isn't. How are we to know?

Most of us are weak in this area, as mentioned in our text today. The Apostle Paul tells us that God helps us in our weakness and then explains how. Isn't that neat? He tells that the Holy Spirit intercedes (prays) for us with ". . . *groaning too deep for words*"

We all have been in situations where we were speechless. We didn't know what to say. The pain is way too deep to even begin to explain. When my friend's fifteen-year-old son was killed in a car wreck, I immediately went to the hospital to see him. What could I say? What words could possibly change anything? It is in precisely those moments that the Holy Spirit is intensely praying, interceding before the very throne of God for us.

Paul explains that the Holy Spirit intercedes for us according to the will of God. The Holy Spirit sees the bigger picture where we only see a small piece. The Holy Spirit is not weak in this area like we are. He knows what to pray for and how to pray for us. This is an incredible truth.

> Holy Spirit, all divine,
> Dwell within this heart of mine;
> Cast down every idol throne,
> Reign supreme and reign alone.
> - Reed (Our Daily Bread 2014)

Prayer: *Precious Father, take my life and let it be, consecrated Lord to Thee. Take my heart. It is Thine own. It shall be Thy royal throne. In Jesus' name. Amen.*

SUNDAY – GOD'S SPECIAL DAY – THE LORD'S DAY

"Let them give thanks to the Lord for His lovingkindness, and for His wonders to the sons of men! Let them extol Him also in the congregation of the people, and praise Him at the seat of the elders."

Ps. 107:31-32

THE INFANT CHURCH

WEEK #38: THE INFANT CHURCH – AWESOME

MONDAY - A FLAMING CHURCH

Scripture: Exodus 3:1-3; Acts 2:1-3

The book of Acts gives a picture of all those who repented and were baptized on the Day of Pentecost, as receiving the gift of the Holy Spirit. This gift and anointing was the key for living the Christian life and for ministry – teaching, preaching, casting out demons, serving the poor, healing, etc. This is the picture of the birth of Christ's Church.

In last month's readings, I cast light on the coming of the Holy Spirit. I mentioned how the Spirit rested on each of the Disciples like a tongue of fire and that John the Baptist had foretold of Jesus baptizing with the Holy Spirit and fire. When God appeared to Moses on the mountain, for the very first time, God provided something visible, a bush that was burning but not being consumed. It burned and burned and kept on burning. This caught Moses' attention in a big way.

The first century church was much like that bush. It was quite visible, burning brightly, but not being consumed by the fire. With desperate attempts by government officials to silence them, Peter and John, and Paul were jailed. The other Apostles were threatened with jail. Stephen was stoned because of his Christian testimony and many more were martyred. They sacrificed their possessions and even their lives, but the Church was not silenced.

Within the first hundred years of the church, the people of the Roman Empire took notice of this flaming group of people. The followers of Jesus valued their faith in Christ more than they valued life. This got the attention of the masses. They were attracted to what appeared to be a strange phenomenon, like a bush on fire but not being consumed.

Prayer: Thank You, Father, for passion that changes lives, for passion You give Your people. The burning sensation in my heart today, through Your Holy Spirit, will never die. Thank You, Father. In Jesus' name. Amen.

TUESDAY - A GENEROUS CHURCH

Scripture: Acts 2:43-45; 4:34-35

It is difficult to fully comprehend the commitment of the early Believers. I have heard it said that if you want to know what is really important to a person, look at his checkbook, or maybe in this day and age, it would be look at his credit card/ATM statement. The lives of the first century Christians were turned topsy-turvy by the power of God. They were so deeply touched by the love of God that their love for one another moved them to share all things, even property ownership.

The early church in Acts experimented with communal living, where the church owned everything and everyone's assets and funds were put into one pot and shared equally. This apparently didn't last long, as evidenced by Paul's writings, as most attempts at communal living are usually short-lived. Their generosity was certainly impressive and contagious.

In Acts 5 we read of a man and wife who promised God a portion of the sale of their land and then kept it for themselves. God responded by taking their lives, both of them. Understandably, the response of the people was panic and fear.

It shouldn't surprise anyone that God is serious and that he means business. Lives are at stake. I am mindful of the story Jesus told of the "widow's mite". Though she gave little, it was all that she had. Jesus said she gave more than the rich people who actually gave more but gave out of their surplus. People who are faithful to God in their generosity as to the work of God's Kingdom will experience a blessing in profound ways. This has been true throughout the history of the church and is true today.

Prayer: *Father, when we come to You, we surrender all to You, and that means all. We give you 10% as our tithe, and You give us 90% back to cover our practical needs. Thank You, Father, for honoring the gifts and sacrifices of Your people. In Jesus' name. Amen.*

WEDNESDAY - A RECONCILING CHURCH

Scripture: Acts 2:46; Colossians 3:12-14

When there is understanding and love, people don't thrive in a cloud of suspicion and division. So it was with the first century church. They gathered together in one another's homes because they liked one another. They could see Jesus in one another, and they loved Jesus. The Jesus in each of them wanted to serve the Jesus in one another.

In describing the atmosphere prevalent in their circles, Luke uses the phrase, "gladness *and sincerity of heart*". This was contagious. We should also take note that they were "praising God", which put a strong spiritual spin on their meetings. They invited others in their midst who were amazed at the love these people showed to one another. They were taken back as to how they cared for one another, shared with one another, and gave thanks to God.

Choose any period of history and any culture, when you find Christians coming together out of love of God, love and concern for one another, doing so in gladness and sincerity of heart, you will find the dark cloud of suspicion, which divides people, dissipating. When these ingredients are present, people come together in harmony and God is glorified. People are made whole and marriages and families strengthened.

Doctrine is very important, but even when a congregation's doctrine is not completely orthodox, but they love and care for one another, you find the same result – lives changes, families and marriages made whole. Good, solid Biblical doctrine should make it easier for people to know God, praise God, and embrace the love of God and therefore extend it to one another. When God's people are hitting on all cylinders, the world stands in awe.

Prayer: *Father, praise You for driving away the dark clouds of suspicion and fear. Thank You for teaching us to love and care for one another. Thank You, Lord. In Jesus' name.*

THURSDAY - A COMMUNING CHURCH

Scripture: Acts 2:46; I Corinthians 11:23-26

There is abundant evidence that the early church shared the Lord's Supper on a regular basis. They remembered the Last Supper with Jesus and his Disciples and the connection it made to the Passover Meal, with the Angel of Death passing over them, through the blood of the lamb painted on the doorposts of the house. Jesus, to them, was that Lamb of God.

The story of the two men walking to Emmaus the day after Jesus was crucified is quite interesting. Jesus walked with them and explained the Scriptures to them, without them knowing it was Jesus. When they got to their home, they invited him in for a meal. It was in the "breaking of the bread" that their eyes were "opened", and they recognized him.

Not all Christian groups agree on whether the literal body of Christ is in the bread and cup, but they all agree that it is a sacred moment when Holy Communion is shared in a proper way, according to the Scriptures. The Apostle Paul teaches that a Believer should "*examine himself*" before taking of the bread and cup. This is why there is usually a unison prayer confessing sins immediately before the elements are served. Paul warns harsh judgment to come upon those that misuse this simple meal. It is the Lord's Table, the Lord's meal. We are the invited guests.

I appreciate Holy Communion much more now than I did years ago. I want to celebrate it every Sunday in worship. It is so powerful when people approach the Lord's Table with great reverence and sincerity. Yes, it is a meal of remembrance, but more than that, it is a meal with Christ present.

Prayer: *Father, again I am in awe when pondering the things You have given us. Thank You for calling me to Your Table. Thank You for reserving a place for me at that Table every time it is set. In Jesus' name. Amen.*

FRIDAY - A LEARNING CHURCH

Scripture: Acts 4:2; 5:42

After the manner of their Lord, who went about teaching and preaching, the early church had a very strong aspect of teaching God's word. When the thousands were converted on the Day of Pentecost, they were ". . . *continually devoting themselves to the apostles teaching . . .*" Later on and throughout the book of Acts we read of how the church was regularly feeding on the teaching given by its leaders. The assumption is that the people were of a mind to learn. They were eager. They desired more knowledge of God and his word.

The authorities knew if they could keep these flaming Christians from teaching and preaching, they could put out the fire and stop it from spreading. God's word is powerful when it is shared.

In the first century, they did not have the New Testament, but only the Old Testament and first hand stories of Jesus. As time went forth, the apostles began to write letters to the churches. They were read to the people and viewed as Scripture. This is how the New Testament came into being, which is a collection of these letters.

If a person is not genuinely converted to Christ, he will never desire to know more about God. When the heart is open, God puts that desire in the Christian. It then becomes a natural hunger, much like hungering for food.

It is easy to tell if people have a hunger to know God. One of the best indicators is the adult Sunday School or the small group program of any church. If there is little interest in learning more and more of God's word, there is reason to be concerned.

Prayer: *Father, praise You for blessing Your church with gifted and Holy Spirit anointed teachers and preachers. Oh Lord, keep the fire going. Put a deep hunger in me to learn more of Your holy word. In Jesus' name. Amen.*

SATURDAY - A PRAISING CHURCH

Scripture: Romans 15:9-11; Revelation 19:4-6

As mentioned earlier in the week, the giving of praise to God was a key component of the regular gathering together of the early Believers. This could be done in prayer or in song and most likely was done in both. Granted, they didn't have hymnals or LCD projectors or keyboards, but they could raise their voices together in praise and thanksgiving to God. No doubt the Hebrew songbook, the book of Psalms, was used. Repeatedly, we read of people whose hearts were overflowing with gratitude.

When people are super happy, they sing and dance. This is true universally. It is a human thing and is done in all kinds of secular gatherings. When people are spiritually happy, they also sing and dance, but the singing and dancing is an offering of praise to God.

Jesus has set us free through his grace, by the cross. There is reason for rejoicing. There is reason for singing. Where the love of God is flowing freely, there will always be joyous singing. Cynical, critical, soreheads don't sing. A singing church is a growing church, a caring church, a gospel sharing church. It all runs together.

In recent years, there has been a wave of new praise songs written, as more and more churches have been awakened to the possibilities of praise and adoration. Unfortunately, it has brought division in some churches, but it has generally revived churches all across America. Major stores in every city now have sections of praise music in their music aisles. Hundreds of Christian radio stations broadcast 24/7 praise music. It is truly God's Spirit moving across our land as massive Christian concerts bring people together from all denominations and Christian groups.

Prayer: *Father, I want to praise You for all eternity. I want to praise You with others who have also come to know You. Oh Lord, You are worthy of our praise. In Jesus' name. Amen.*

SUNDAY – GOD'S SPECIAL DAY – THE LORD'S DAY

"I will bless the Lord at all times; His praise shall continually be in my mouth. My soul will make its boast in the Lord; the humble will hear it and rejoice. O magnify the Lord with me, and let us exalt His name together."

Psalm 34:1-3

THE INFANT CHURCH

WEEK #39: WINESKINS BROKEN

MONDAY - A MODEL FOR ALL TIME

Scripture: Acts 2:7

Almost two thousand years have passed since the explosive birth of the Church. At no other time throughout these two millennia have we witnessed such magnitude of church growth. Some people theorize the earth came from a "big bang" in the universe. In a similar way, the church of Jesus Christ was born, with a sudden burst of men and women filled with the Holy Spirit. Without a doubt, when Peter stood and preached the first Christian message on the Jewish Day of Pentecost, he had no idea of the seismic numbers of people who soon would be baptized and received into the company of Believers.

This kind of church growth has been studied, analyzed, and put under the microscope in every way possible. Every generation of Christians wants to duplicate the first century church. Many denominations have been started with this vision in mind. Almost every mission agency has a new strategy to plant churches, thinking they have discovered the New Testament way of church growth.

Without hearts being convicted of sin, there is no real church growth. Good marketing can draw crowds, as will paved parking lots or entertainment for the children. It must be more than simply counting heads. Without changed hearts, church growth is meaningless and possibly even a stumbling block to the real presence of God in peoples' lives.

God's Spirit was the key to the growth of the early church. It is the key to all church growth today. Because such a move of the Spirit is difficult to analyze, measure, predict, or control, and requires huge doses of humility and spiritual discipline, it is rare. This moving of the Spirit must be desired above all petty turf battles with churches and denominations.

Prayer: *Oh Lord, give us pastors and church leaders who love You far more than they love themselves. Give us shepherds who are hungry to see Your true presence convicting hearts and breathing life into dead souls. Come Holy Spirit. In Christ's name. Amen.*

TUESDAY - ESSENTIAL COMPONENTS: PREACHING & TEACHING

Scripture: Acts 2:14; 5:42

The public proclamation of God's word has been central to all church growth. It is a tradition rooted in the Old Testament with all the prophets. Remember Ezekiel when he prophesied over the dry bones? He proclaimed, *"Now hear the word of the Lord"*. Everyone who opens the Bible to speak the gospel of our Lord Jesus Christ should be gripped by that very same spirit, the Spirit of God, the Holy Spirit, or as some say, the Holy Ghost.

The Spirit of God can grab hold of the human heart to the point that tears flow. Many times in reviewing a message before preaching this happens to me. On Sunday morning, I introduce every sermon with the same words God instructed Ezekiel when preaching to the bones, *"Now hear the word of the Lord."*

Preaching always involves two basic elements – Biblical story and current life application. It is telling the story of the cross through different Biblical texts and then persuading people through examples and illustrations to either follow Jesus through repentance and faith or to deepen their walk with Christ.

To teach is to instruct or to impart knowledge. In the Great Commission, Jesus said *"teaching them to observe all that I have commanded you."* Every growing church will have a strong teaching aspect to its life. This can be done in a variety of ways, but it must be done. Believers must take on the mind of Christ by sitting at the feet of Godly men and women, learning the Bible.

Many churches have no means of training good teachers. It is easy to exalt preaching above teaching. Teaching was a key component of the early church and is just as much of a key component today.

Prayer: *Father, I praise You today for all who have taught me Your word, the Bible. Lord Jesus, may I continue to learn more and more about how You did life. In Jesus' name. Amen.*

WEDNESDAY - ESSENTIAL COMPONENT: BAPTIZING

Scripture: Acts 2:38; 16:32-34

It is worth noting that in the very first Christian sermon, the one preached by Peter on the Day of Pentecost, when challenging the people to repent, he challenged them to be baptized. Later the number of 3,000 is given for those who did repent and were baptized. It would be difficult to read the book of Acts and avoid the subject of water baptism. On more than one occasion, it mentions that one's whole household was baptized.

In chapter 8 of Acts, we read of Philip and a man from Ethiopia, a man he had just met for the first time in his life. The man was reading from the book of Isaiah. Philip explained to him what it meant as it related to faith in Christ, repentance, and baptism. As his chariot went along the road, he saw a small stream and said, *"Look! Water! What prevents me from being baptized?"* Philip instructed him to believe. He did and was baptized there on the spot.

The Bible gives little in the way of specific instruction as to the amount of water to be used in baptism or restrictions as to age. This leads me to put my emphasis on the actual act of baptism rather than the kind of details that many Christians divide over.

We should not be shy in regularly challenging people to be baptized. Every congregation is blessed when people are constantly being baptized as they come to faith in Christ. Many churches sincerely believe infants of Believers were baptized in the first century church and do likewise.

To the person reading this devotion today, have you been baptized? If not, why not? Why wait? You know the Bible teaches it. Isn't that enough?

Prayer: *Oh Father, when people surrender their will to Your will it is beautiful. May more and more people across our land and throughout the world repent and be baptized. In Jesus' name. Amen.*

THURSDAY - ESSENTIAL COMPONENT: THE LORD'S SUPPER

Scripture: Acts 20:7; I Corinthians 10:16

Giving the celebration of the Lord's Supper its proper place in the Lord's Day gathering has been quite the controversy over the years. The Roman Catholic Church has given it the most prominent place in their gathering, believing it to be the literal body and blood of Christ.

The Lutheran position is similar, only they believe the mystical, not literal, presence of Jesus Christ is in and through the bread and wine. They maintain the high point of worship is the proclamation of the Word of God but also put a great emphasis upon the presence of Christ in communion. Most other Protestant groups see the bread and wine as symbols, announcing the Lord's Supper as a meal of remembrance, putting an emphasis on Jesus' words, *"Do this in remembrance of Me."* Most of these groups celebrate communion either monthly or quarterly.

In the book of Acts, chapter 20, we read of the Apostle Paul and his missionary team coming to Troas. Here it states that on *"the first day of the week, when we were gathered together to break bread."* It appears their purpose of gathering was not to sing praises to God or to hear the Scriptures expounded but to *"break bread"*. This also fits well with Paul's words to the Christians at Corinth as he explains in great detail the practice of sharing the Lord's Supper.

In the Gospels, we do have detailed accounts of Jesus taking his last supper with the disciples and unequivocally stating that the bread is his body and the wine, the *"new covenant in My blood"*. I see the early church sharing in this sacred meal when they met every Sunday. It was an important part of their gathering.

Prayer: *Father, thank You for giving us the presence of Your Son, our Lord Jesus Christ. Though I know He is with me each and every day, every hour, I look forward to His special presence when His body, the Church, meets in His name. Amen.*

FRIDAY - ESSENTIAL COMPONENT: PRAYER AND THE HOLY SPIRIT

Scripture: Acts 4:31; 9:40; 12:5

Who can accurately describe the role of prayer in the early church? It was made possible through the Holy Spirit and was the Believers' most noticeable practice. Through prayer, houses were literally shaken as people were filled with the Holy Spirit. Peter raised a woman from the dead by prayer. Later on, the Believers were crying out to God for Peter, as he had been put in prison for his faith. As an answer to prayer, an angel of the Lord appeared and set him free. Those praying were stunned to learn their prayers were answered. The God who raised Jesus from the dead was now powerfully present among them, sending a shockwave of awe and wonder throughout their community.

I would like to have been at one of the early church gatherings where one of the Apostles was teaching about prayer. Can you imagine how they retold the story of Jesus teaching His followers about two of them agreeing in prayer? In the same teaching, Jesus explained how He would always be present in their midst, if two or three were gathered in His name. Those early Believers learned to pray boldly in Jesus' name, which meant they prayed for those things brought to mind by the Holy Spirit, things that were clearly aligned with God's will.

Today, especially in poverty and disease stricken countries, Believers are experiencing the same awe and wonder as recorded in the book of Acts. Entire communities are being changed as Believers unite in the power of the Holy Spirit. God's blessing is being poured out in amazing and mind boggling ways, such as droughts coming to an end, land becoming fertile again, and rivers suddenly being populated with large numbers of fish.

Prayer: *Father, forgive me when my faith is too small. Forgive me when I lose sight of Your power, when Your people unite in prayer. Stir my heart, Lord. In Jesus' name. Amen.*

SATURDAY - ESSENTIAL COMPONENT: FELLOWSHIP

Scripture: Acts 2:46-47; 4:32-33

Christian fellowship is the horizontal aspect of Christian faith. Many times people will limit their understanding of Christianity to a *"me and Jesus"* mentality, resulting in only a vertical approach to the faith. This individualistic, privatized version of Christianity lends itself to a loner mentality which has no Biblical basis, being quite different than the Christianity we see lived out in the early church. The faith of the early Believers had both a vertical and horizontal aspect. It was both a relationship with God and relationship with others.

There are people who have high social skills, who easily get along well with others and who are comfortable engaging with others. We describe these people as extroverts. They have *"never met a stranger"*. On the opposite end of the spectrum are introverts, those who are more at peace being by themselves, those who struggle with socializing and connecting with others and are, by nature, more contemplative. Few of us have a good balance between these extremes.

Christian fellowship is not just for those with high social skills. Christian fellowship is the art of learning to care and appreciate one another in meaningful ways. It is seeing Christ in another person of like faith. It is the Christ in you recognizing and serving the Christ in your Christian brother or sister.

The Believers I read about in Acts did more than verbalize or simply talk about faith. They truly recognized Jesus in one another and were able to humbly serve the Christ they saw in one another. The love of God had come to them, and they were able to give that love back and forth, one to another. Authentic Christian fellowship is one of God's powerful tools in changing lives.

Prayer: *Father, help me to see You in the eyes of other Christians, especially those of my own church. Help me to share with them in practical ways the love You have given me. In Jesus' name. Amen.*

SUNDAY – GOD'S SPECIAL DAY – THE LORD'S DAY

"I will give You thanks in the great congregation; I will praise You among a mighty throng." Ps. 35:18

THE INFANT CHURCH

WEEK #40: ON BOARD WITH GOD'S MISSION

MONDAY - DISCOVERY OF THE GOLDEN THREAD

Scripture: Acts 13:2-3

Like a child slowly learns the mind and heart of his parents, the Christian is slowly learning and embracing the thinking pattern of his or her heavenly Father.

For the first few years of the early church, all Believers were Jews. They were people who were well acquainted with the stories of the Old Testament. The first non-Jewish Christian congregation was the church of Antioch, the one mentioned in today's text. These people would have known little or nothing of the grand stories of the Old Testament. They would have leaned heavily upon the teaching of their senior leaders – Barnabas and Paul and the others named in Acts 13.

Through the Holy Spirit, God was revealing to them His mind and heart. After much prayer and fasting, their leaders sent out their two senior pastors to take the message of Christ to other people groups in other countries. I think this is quite revealing. We can make some certain conclusions about their teaching when we look closely at how the people responded and what they did, after they were taught the ways of God. I believe they heard much teaching about Jesus' last words to His Disciples, instructing them to make disciples of all the nations. I believe they heard about God's plan to bless all the peoples of the world. This plan is thought of like a *"golden thread"* woven throughout the entire Bible. It is full blown in Genesis and subsequently in every book of the Bible. It is the subject of Jesus' final command and the subject of the last book of the Bible.

As you grow to know the mind and heart of God, may you begin to see this *"golden thread"*. It is precious.

Prayer: *Father, thank You for allowing me to know Your mind and heart. Help me to love the things You love and to care for the things You care about. In Jesus' name. Amen.*

TUESDAY - CATCHING THE VISION

Scripture: Matthew 28:18-20

Yesterday I introduced the phrase *"golden thread"*. God's global theme is like a thread in a shirt or blouse that stands out from all the other threads. It weaves its way through every aspect of the garment and is quite noticeable. The plan of God to bless all the peoples of the world is like that. Look closely at every book of the Bible, and you will see it. It is there. It is golden. It is the Bible's main theme.

Today's text is known by Bible students as the *"Great Commission"*. It is one of the most obvious examples of the *"golden thread"*. This teaching was fundamental in the thinking of the early church and remains fundamental in the thinking of everyone who values the teaching of Jesus. It is the banner verse for my own denomination, the North American Lutheran Church.

Read again the first part of vs. 19. Do you see a period after the word *disciple*? Do you? One little dot after that word would significantly change the meaning of the sentence. If there would have been a period after the word *disciple*, the early church would not have sent its top leaders to other nations. If there would have been a period after the word *disciple*, Thomas would not have gone to India, and Mark would not have gone to Egypt. Both died preaching the gospel in a foreign land. If there would have been a period after the word *disciple*, the main mission thrust of the early church would have turned inward to its own community and its own people. Christianity would have remained a small, ethnic bubble, rather than the world's largest global movement.

Prayer: *Lord, give me the vision You shared with the Disciples and the early church. Put that vision in my mind and heart until the last breath goes from my body. In Your name. Amen.*

WEDNESDAY - GUIDANCE BY THE SPIRIT

Scripture: Acts 13:2; 15:28; 16:6

Most all church leaders seek to be guided by the Holy Spirit, but not all are confident that they have been guided by the Holy Spirit. Many times, the agendas of powerful, influential people rule the day with little sincere effort put forth to hear from God.

A good read of the book of Acts will reveal amazing church growth amidst hardships, intense suffering, egos, pride, and disappointments. All of the men and women of the early church were flawed people with their share of weaknesses, personality disorders, and embarrassing moments. In spite of this, they sought and desired, more than anything else, the leading of the Spirit to reach the world with the message of Christ. Things like personal comfort, pensions, benefits, popularity, and wealth seemed to be absent, as to controlling factors in decision-making. Above anything and everything, the Apostle Paul, Barnabas, Priscilla and Aquilla, James, Peter, Timothy, and many other men and women were willing to lay down their very lives for the sake of God's kingdom coming into the lives of people everywhere.

The three verses in today's readings are illustrations of how the Holy Spirit guided the early church. At times He spoke a clear and distinct message. At times church leaders came to a unified conclusion as to how they sensed God leading. And at times they got it wrong yet the Holy Spirit intervened, prevented them from going here or there and redirected them. In the end, we find the greatest church growth story in two thousand years of church history. In the end, we see God's thumbprints everywhere.

God did it back then and is doing it today – transforming lives through churches guided and directed by the Holy Spirit.

Prayer: *Father, thank You for guiding people who genuinely desire and seek the leading of Your Holy Spirit. Thank You for the many places around the world where this is happening today. Lord Jesus, come. Amen.*

THURSDAY - BECOMING A SENDING CONGREGATION

Scripture: Acts 13:2-3

From chapter 13 on to the end of the book of Acts, we are confronted with stories of men and women who were called by God and sent out by a local congregation for the distinct purpose of taking the gospel story to other nations and peoples. Barnabas and Paul were "sent" by the church of Antioch. Because of this risk-taking move by a church, many other nations were blessed.

Barnabas and Paul were the senior pastors of the church of Antioch. They were not anti-social misfits who struggled to find themselves in any other role in society. They were highly gifted, intelligent, educated, influential, well-loved people. No church in their right mind would want to send these kind of leaders away. Churches today would offer pastors like this attractive compensation packages to stay, not to go away. It would take the intervention of God for such a thing to happen. This is precisely the picture of today's reading – the intervention of God – the Holy Spirit speaking a very clear message. The leaders of the Antioch church were spiritual men, not worldly men. They were fasting and praying. They were prepared to hear the Holy Spirit. Upon hearing the Holy Spirit, they obeyed. And guess what? The church continued to grow and grow and grow. Individuals were blessed. Families were blessed. Marriages were strengthened. Churches were planted. Multitudes heard the life-changing story of Jesus Christ.

Many Christians are going on mission-trips but few churches are actively "sending" and "equipping" their brightest and best for full-time, cross-cultural missionary work, taking the gospel where it has never been. This is unfortunate. Few Christian leaders are praying and fasting as the result of their burden to *"make disciples of all the nations"*.

Prayer: *Oh Father, burden my heart with the Great Commission. Give my church leaders a desire to fast and pray because of the burden they have to make disciples of all the nations. In Jesus' name. Amen.*

FRIDAY - THE WORLDWIDE CHRISTIAN MOVEMENT

Scripture: Acts 15:12; 17:6

The story of the New Testament church is similar to the man who gets one plate spinning on a pole while keeping another plate spinning, while keeping another plate spinning. Clusters of new believers sprouted forth in almost every city visited by early missionaries. These clusters were nurtured by itinerant pastors/evangelists, as they matured into churches with appointed elders. In chapter 19:10, we find this stunning statement, *"so that all who lived in Asia heard the word of the Lord . . ."*

In chapter 17, we find another revealing statement, *"These men who have upset the world have come here also . . ."* The verse in chapter 19 mentions all of Asia. The verse in chapter 17 mentions all of the world. The Spirit of God moving in the lives of the first century church was shaking many cultures and many nations. It was an incredible movement prophesied throughout the Old Testament, even all the way back to Genesis where God told Abraham that all the nations of the earth would be blessed.

Peter was a dynamic, spontaneous, highly spirited man. Paul was the intelligent scholar, the able administrator and methodical practitioner. Yes, the early church had its share of high octane people but the movement they led was not personality driven, not built around the charisma of one or two people. It was much bigger than that. . . and still is.

There have always been people with winsome personalities who attract crowds. This is just as true with politics as it is with religions. The worldwide Christian movement has its share of colorful people, but a closer look reveals a startling picture of society after society transformed and lifted up by the power of God.

Prayer: *Oh Lord, You have done a great work through Your people throughout the history of civilization. Praise You for what You have done. Praise You for what You are doing today in many nations. In Jesus' name. Amen.*

SATURDAY - ENGAGING THE CULTURE AT THE HIGHEST LEVELS

Scripture: Acts 17:16-17

The leaders of the first century church did not find refuge in a religious, stained glass ghetto. They went out into pagan society unafraid to sit at the table with the leading philosophers and intellectuals.

Athens, Greece, was the philosophical epicenter of the known world. The Apostle Paul did not shy away from philosophical reasoning. He did not condemn their thinking but instead, respectfully challenged their truth claims and philosophical arguments. Neither the Apostle Peter nor the Apostle John engaged the Greek philosophers, as they were not schooled in Greek philosophy and knew little of Greek culture. As Hebrew fishermen, they would have been quite uncomfortable making a philosophical/religious argument in the midst of the Areopagus in Athens. . . , but not the Apostle Paul.

C.S. Lewis was a novelist, poet, academic, medievalist, literary critic, essayist, and Christian apologist – one of the intellectual giants of our day. Authoring such books on the Christian life as *Mere Christianity* and *The Screwtape Letters*, he wrote fictional novels such as *The Chronicles of Narnia* and *The Lion, the Witch and the Wardrobe*. Born and raised in an Anglican, Christian family, he abandoned the faith of his parents, becoming an atheist. Through study of the Bible, he converted to Christ and used his intellectual ability to engage a pagan culture.

We need Christians at every level of society today to boldly engage the culture. We must not retreat to our stained glass ghettos in fear. There are those in our midst who are qualified intellectuals who can take their place around the table of our society's greatest thinkers and make the case for the Christian faith, calling people of the highest levels to repentance.

Prayer: *Father, help me to find ways to use my ability to the utmost for Your glory. Teach me, Lord, to interact and engage my own culture. Help me to be respectful but uncompromising. In Jesus' name. Amen.*

SUNDAY – GOD'S SPECIAL DAY – THE LORD'S DAY

"For where two or three have gathered together in My name, I am there in their midst." Matt. 18:20

THE CHURCH THE BODY OF CHRIST

WEEK #41: AN AMAZING STORY

MONDAY - BIRTHED IN PERSECUTION

Scripture: Acts 4:1-3

When the disciples heard Jesus saying, *"If anyone wishes to come after Me, let him take up his cross and follow Me . . ."*, they probably did not give it much serious thought. After Jesus was crucified and the church was born, one doesn't have to wonder why the cross became the symbol for the Christian faith. It was not attractive jewelry, it was a crude symbol of human brutality. In many countries, such as India, every church has a cross on its steeple and many churches have crosses which are lit at night. The cross has become a universal symbol for compassion and faith in God.

Within a few days after the coming of the Holy Spirit on the Day of Pentecost, Peter and John were put in jail. Through their prayer, God healed a crippled man and subsequently used this display of his power to bring several thousand people to repentance. News of this was spreading rapidly around Jerusalem. The Jewish priests and religious leaders were quite threatened by such an outpouring of excitement and fervor by the multitudes. By crucifying Jesus, they thought they had this Jesus movement thwarted, but now his popularity had expanded even more.

Though the early disciples were not criminals and had broken no laws, they were treated as criminals. Jesus had warned his followers about persecution. Now that he was gone from the scene, they faced a harsh reality; if they stood for the things Jesus stood for, they would be treated as he was treated. This was the "cross" Jesus spoke about. Jesus gave his life so others might hear news of eternal salvation and truth, and he called those who followed him to give their lives as well.

Prayer: *Father God, thank You for Peter and John. Thank You that they chose to be obedient. Thank You for those who have sacrificed for me to hear the news of eternal salvation. Teach me the value of a crucified life. In Jesus' name. Amen.*

TUESDAY - SPEAKING THE MESSAGE OF LIFE

Scripture: Acts 5:18-20, 40-42

Might doesn't always make right, but few power-brokers of this world understand that. The top leaders of Judaism decided to imprison the apostles. They did this for one reason – to silence them. It seemed the spoken proclamation of the gospel of Jesus Christ was the problem. This proclamation had power. It transformed guilt-ridden, defeated people into confident lions. It engaged the powers of heaven to overturn evil and establish integrity, morality, and justice.

It is interesting that we have the very words of the angel who opened the gates of the prison to release the apostles. The angel said, *"Go, stand and speak to the people . . . the whole message of this Life."* The apostles obeyed. After they were beaten, they were ordered not to speak in the name of Jesus. Did they want sympathy for their suffering? Were they intimated by prison bars and whips? Did they ask the Christian community to pray for them that they might not be persecuted? No. No. and No. They rejoiced that they had been *"considered worthy to suffer shame for His name"*.

Rhonda and I felt the same way when I was taken into custody by the Immigration Department of the government of India and deported. Yes, I felt the shame, the humiliation, and embarrassment. I was treated like a criminal. My only crime was in speaking the gospel of Jesus Christ. Today when I read this text, I resonate with the apostles. I rejoice that I was considered worthy to suffer shame for the name of Jesus.

We are not called to a life of comfort. Believers see time as valuable to complete the task of world evangelization. People cannot believe in a gospel they never hear.

Prayer: *Father, thank You for the high privilege of speaking the greatest news ever spoken. You put this task before every person who repents and believes in You. Father, give me the courage and passion to live a life, not of comfort, but of significance. In Jesus' name and for His sake. Amen.*

WEDNESDAY - BLOOD IS SPILLED

Scripture: Acts 7:58-60

The early church recognized Stephen to be a man *"full of faith and the Holy Spirit"*. It would be quite the honor to have that distinction. Though he was chosen to be a servant of the church in compassionate ministries, he did not limit his service to the Lord to good works but powerfully spoke the gospel message. Because of his preaching he was arrested, tried, convicted, and stoned to death. He was the first Christian to die as the result of his Christian testimony and message. We recognize Stephen as the first martyr.

Scripture tells us that on the day Stephen was martyred, a great persecution began against the church in Jerusalem. This persecution forced many Christians of the Jerusalem church to move away in areas more friendly to the message of Christ. Because of this scattering, many surrounding areas heard the gospel.

A famous pastor in the second century wrote, "the blood of martyrs is the seed of the Church . . ," Throughout the history of Christianity, some 2,000 years, this is the picture one sees. Whenever the gospel comes to a nation or people group, sacrifices are made. People leave their comfort zones. They leave their relatives and known surroundings. They submit to training. They learn languages. They give up many conveniences so other people would come to know Christ. Many Christians downsize their lifestyle so they can financially support those who do go. Christians cry out to God and in prayer in tears.

The Christian life is all about sacrifice at many levels. Sometimes, the ultimate sacrifice happens. The result is many lives changed for eternity. No other movement has shaped and transformed the world like Christianity, and it is still happening today.

Prayer: *Father, some 1,500 years ago, missionaries came to Ireland, came to many parts of western Europe. Thank You, God, for these brave men and women. Thank You for blood that was shed so I might have the opportunity to know You. In Jesus' name. Amen.*

THURSDAY - SACRIFICE THAT MAKES A DIFFERENCE

Scripture: Acts 9:1-2

Before Paul (also known as Saul) was converted to Christ, he was a prosecuting attorney for the Jewish state. He purposely targeted Christians, having the authority to arrest them and even stone them. Remember Stephen's death? Paul was present at the stoning, giving his approval. I'm sure the look on Stephen's face, in his final moment of life, remained with him for many years.

The story of Paul is the story of a relentless persecutor of Christians making a complete turnabout, committing his life to the very enterprise which he earlier opposed. He was Christianity's first missionary, taking the message of Christ to much of Asia. This turnabout did not go unnoticed. It inspired and motivated others to make sacrifices for the gospel. Paul was a living example of the crucified life. In one of his letters, he states, "*I have been crucified with Christ. It is no longer I who live but Christ who lives in me.*"

Years ago, I had the privilege of teaching the pastors of the Malto people group in northern Jharkand state, India. The story of the Malto people receiving the gospel of Jesus Christ is a typical missionary story. Thirty years ago, missionaries went to the Maltos, learned their language and customs, and shared the message of Christ to them. Initially they resisted. Gradually their interest grew. On one night, a father and son missionary team died of a tropical disease. This touched the Malto people deeply. After that sad loss, entire Malto villages came to Christ. Today, 560 of the some 900 Malto villages have churches.

Many Christians believe they can make this world their heaven and also enjoy heaven in the next life. It just isn't so.

Prayer: *Father, I want the joy of a life of service and sacrifice. Oh Father, keep me away from the lure of entertainment and comfort each day of my life. May I always choose You and Your way. Forgive me when selfish dreams interfere with Your gospel work. In Jesus' name. Amen.*

FRIDAY - ON ITS KNEES

Scripture: Acts 12:1-2, 5

King Herod was enraged by the threat posed by so many people becoming Christian. After having James killed, he imprisoned Peter. In our story today, we read about the church "fervently" praying for Peter. After the brutal death of James, the church was well aware of what might now happen to Peter.

We will never understand, this side of glory, why God intervenes in some situations and others he doesn't. He didn't intervene with Stephen and James, but as the church was fervently praying for Peter, God intervened. An angel showed up and miraculously set him free. Peter immediately went to the house where people were praying for him. When he stood before them in the doorway, they were stunned. They thought they were seeing a ghost!

Fervency in prayer is missing in many churches and in the prayer closets of many people. Lengthy, majestic prayers are plentiful, but heart-felt prayers in tears and loud crying are few. A couple of months ago, I mentioned how Jesus' prayers are described in the book of Hebrews – *"with loud crying and tears"*.

When no sacrifice is being made, one can be flippant about praying. When no one's safety is being threatened and everyone is living nice, comfortable lives, little passion is evident in prayers. When everyone is healthy and wealthy, why cry out to God for anything?

God doesn't suggest that maybe, if it is convenient, to take the gospel to the ends of the earth; he commands it. When his commands are taken seriously and huge sacrifices are made, huge opposition will be rallied . . . and persecution and suffering will happen. This is when people cry out to God with fervency, with loud crying and tears.

Prayer: *Father, thank You for the thousands of great missionary stories. Thank You for bringing life, light and love to this world of death, darkness and hate. Help me more and more to be one of Your true ambassadors. In Jesus' name. Amen.*

SATURDAY - SUFFERING, REJOICING, GROWING

Scripture: Acts 16:22-26

One of the most inspiring things about the suffering in the early church is the joy that was also evident amidst all the pain and problems. At one point in Paul's first missionary journey, we read the statement, *"And the disciples were continually filled with joy and with the Holy Spirit"* (13:52). This is a strange twist. Typically when people encounter persecution and suffering, they don't rejoice. Instead they complain, weep, and are depressed. The opposite is true with the early church. And it is true wherever and whenever people suffer for the cause of Christ.

Another mystery is the incredible growth of the early church. At one point we read that *"all who lived in Asia heard the word of the Lord."* When Paul and his missionary band came to Thessalonica, the city authorities shouted, *"These men who have upset the world have come here also . . ."* The word was out. Neither death, torture, nor prison could stop these passionate men and women who were determined to take the message of Life to the world.

As the book of Acts comes to an end, the Apostle Paul is in house arrest in Rome but planning to take the gospel to Spain. Legend has it that he was executed in Rome. We think Peter was also executed in Rome, hung on a cross. He asked to be hung upside down because he was not worthy to die as Jesus died. Mark is thought to have gone to Egypt and Thomas to India. They thought globally because their Lord thought globally. Christians today who think globally share the passion of Christ and the passion of the early church. Deep, inner joy is their trademark.

Prayer: *Father, just when I think I give up a lot for Your cause, I find that I get more than I could ever give. Lord, thank You for that precious joy and peace that follows those who truly follow You. In Jesus' name. Amen.*

SUNDAY – GOD'S SPECIAL DAY – THE LORD'S DAY

"Praise the Lord! I will give thanks to the Lord with all my heart, in the company of the upright and in the assembly." Ps. 111:1

THE CHURCH THE BODY OF CHRIST

WEEK #42: A TRANSFORMING FORCE IN THE WORLD

MONDAY - THE AMAZING WORK OF THE HOLY SPIRIT

Scripture: Matthew 16:17-18

Jesus told His disciples, ". . . *I will build My church; and the gates of Hades will not overpower it.*" They most likely did not begin to comprehend the full ramifications of his words. Though such worldwide expansion was foretold by several Old Testament prophets, no one really could wrap their mind around such a movement that would shape and mold most all of what we now know as modern civilization.

Few professors on college campuses dare give credit to Christianity for everything from the invention of the printing press to modern medicine to industrial advances. The credit is usually given to man, not God. The world would be a dangerous and barbaric planet without God's revelation of Law to the Hebrew people and God's revelation of Himself in the person of Jesus Christ in the New Testament. The Holy Bible remains the number one bestseller of all time. It has been translated into more languages than any other book and has influenced more societies than any other book.

Wherever the Holy Bible has been embraced by a large percentage of a society, that society has prospered and risen to high levels of education, advancement, and human compassion. It is no accident that the industrial and technical revolution happened at the same period of history as the explosion of Christian missions. Civilization has greatly advanced whenever and wherever Christian missions has happened. History is truly "His story". God has a plan. God has a purpose.

God told Abraham that through him all the nations of the earth would be blessed. God is doing a great work throughout human history, and we are privileged to have a tiny part of that work.

Prayer: *Father, You are so great, so loving, and so good. I am humbled that an insignificant being such as I could be considered worthy enough to partner with someone as great and good as You. Thank You, Father. In Jesus' name. Amen.*

TUESDAY - THE AMAZING WORK OF THE HOLY SPIRIT (China & S. Korea)

Scripture: Matthew 24:14

The western part of Europe and North America is known as the "West". The "East" is normally thought of as China. Within in a few hundred years after Christ's birth, the gospel of Jesus Christ did reach China and quickly spread throughout much of the country, but was short-lived. From then to the era of Protestant Missions (more than a thousand years), China and its surrounding smaller countries were considered unreached.

After William Carey awakened much of the church in England to the barbaric idolatry in India, Hudson Taylor, born of Methodist parents, bravely began a work in China that would expand to hundreds of young missionaries by 1900. By the 1940's, about every mission agency had missionaries serving in China, totaling in the thousands. When China succumbed to the Communist Party, all these missionaries were sent out with many Chinese pastors either killed or jailed and churches burned and most seminaries closed. Atheism was imposed on the people. It appeared all was lost. The future of Christianity in China certainly looked dim.

Fifty years later we began to hear of the "underground church" in China. Much to the amazement of church leaders, Christianity had flourished through a secret house-church movement. Today it is estimated that there are more Christians in China than anywhere else in the world with over 30,000 Chinese converting to Christ every day.

In 1900, Korea had zero Christians. Today, South Korea is 35% Christian boasting the two largest churches in the world. South Korea is second only to the U.S. in the number of missionaries sent out to other countries.

The story of the growth of Christianity in the "East" is still unfolding. Truly, it is amazing. Truly, it is a work of God.

Prayer: *Father, thank You for the sacrifice and tears of so many missionaries dedicated to the telling of Your love and grace to the people of the East. We know You love those people. We praise You for Your work in that part of the world. In Jesus' name. Amen.*

WEDNESDAY - THE AMAZING WORK OF THE HOLY SPIRIT (Africa & India)

Scripture: Hebrews 12:1-2

The colonizing efforts of Western European countries such as Portugal, Spain, France and England paved the way for Christian missions in Africa, India, and other parts of the world. Christian leaders began to see that if secular business people could "go for gold" they could "go for God". The Catholic missionary, Francis Xavier, was commissioned to India in the middle 1500's and had much success along India's southwest coast. He and other Catholic Jesuit missionaries influenced Protestants, who slowly began in the 1700's with the Moravians and then led to explosive missionary work during the 1800's.

Africa was about 3% Christian in 1900 but by 2000 was 40% Christian with several of its nations in the central and southern half of the continent being 70, 80 or 90% Christian. This is phenomenal growth. One would think the religion of the Europeans, who took their land and gold and sold many of their people into slavery, would not have become popular among African people. The Africans resented European rule but embraced the light of the gospel of Jesus Christ.

Many missionaries did not take refuge in European trading colonies like the business merchants. The missionaries ventured deep into the country, lived with the people, gave them a written language, started schools and medical clinics, and by their love and sacrifice, won the hearts of the people. Many of these missionaries died of tropical diseases within a few years after arrival.

The Bible speaks of a "great cloud of witnesses". Certainly the men and women who literally sacrificed their lives so others might hear the story of Jesus are in that cloud. We have a legacy to carry on. Now go. Do your part.

Prayer: *Father, I am just one and the needs are so great. Help me not to make excuses but to give my all for things which are eternal. Help me not to be seduced by comfort and wealth. In Jesus' name. Amen.*

THURSDAY - THE AMAZING WORK OF THE HOLY SPIRIT

Scripture: Acts 1:7

Though North and South America have 30% of the world's land mass, they have only 12% of the world's population. Within that 12% is about 40% of the world Christian population. South America is considered 91% Christian with North America being 77% Christian.

South America was evangelized by the Spanish Catholics in the 16th century. In the last thirty years, Pentecostalism has rapidly spread throughout much of South America, especially in Brazil. Today, Brazil is number three in sending missionaries to other countries.

When the Europeans first landed on the shores of South America, they unknowingly brought diseases which the indigenous peoples had never been exposed. These diseases wiped out 30-50% of the population. The hope of eternal life was a precious hope offered to the dying masses. Almost all of South America quickly converted to Catholicism which today remains the majority Christian expression.

Some Christian leaders recognize the Catholicism as being a valid Christian faith and therefore are not comfortable sending missionaries to South (Latin) America. Others recognize that Christianity is only a thin veneer to most of Latin America and for all practical purposes, the people are without a true understanding of what it means to follow Jesus. Pentecostals are obviously of the latter mindset and have sent thousands of missionaries there with remarkable success.

What was Jesus thinking when he told the Disciples they would be his witnesses *"even to the remotest part of the earth"*? Did he understand the unfortunate circumstances which would pave the way for the Gospel? We don't know many things but we know he visioned the gospel story for all the people of every continent, tribe, and tongue, and this story has spread by various means.

Prayer: *Father, indeed You are very serious about Your plan to bless all of humanity. I see it is not Your will for people to perish but for them to have eternal life. Help me, Lord, to join this mighty cause. Help me to be one of Your ambassadors to the world. In Jesus' name. Amen.*

FRIDAY - THE AMAZING WORK OF THE HOLY SPIRIT

Scripture: Mark 16:14 – 15

When the church of Jesus Christ emerged on the Day of Pentecost, in Acts 2, the Romans ruled much of the world. Italy and Greece were world powers for many years. Much of our governmental structure came from these civilizations. Their people worshiped many gods but within 300 years after Christ's death, the Greeks and Romans were the hubs for Christianity. In 325, Christianity was given an official endorsement by the Roman Empire. Within a few hundred years, the Roman Empire weakened and eventually crumbled. Tribal people from what is present-day Germany, England, and France gained control of western Europe and at the same time, embraced the Christian faith. These countries along with Spain and Ireland were significantly influenced by Christian teaching, propelling them to the forefront of education and civilization. By the year 1,000, Christianity had also spread to much of central Asia and Eastern Europe. There it was known as the Orthodox Christian Church. Western Europe was considered Roman Catholic.

The Roman Catholic Church was governed by a central figure, the Pope. The Pope had enormous political power in addition to ruling the church. He was looked upon as being Christ's representative on earth.

Christians, at that time, viewed people who were truly spiritual as people who would not marry but commit themselves to Christ totally in celibacy. They lived together in community as monks and nuns, refraining from sexual activity. The monks lived in retreat-like places called monasteries, and nuns lived in convents. They resisted participation in the world and sought a pure, holy life, completely devoted to Jesus. Many of them learned skilled crafts and pursued knowledge through rigorous, academic discipline. The concept of the modern educational system was born through their efforts.

Prayer: *Oh Father, throughout history You have been doing a marvelous, stunning work. In spite of wars and barbaric moments, Your mission has continued to advance. You are in the background of all scientific inventions and of modern medicine and technology. To You be all glory. In Jesus' name. Amen.*

SATURDAY - THE AMAZING WORK OF THE HOLY SPIRIT

Scripture: Acts 5:29

By the 16th century, the Roman Catholic Church had evolved into something far different than the first century church. Services could only be held in Latin. Only priests, monks, and nuns could take the cup in communion and sing hymns. The Bible was restricted to Latin, making it impossible for the common person throughout most of Western Europe to read it. Forgiveness of sins was thought to be possible only through baptism by the Catholic Church and by receiving communion.

As more and more people were literate and more and more books were translated into other languages, people began to desire the Bible in their own language. One monk, Martin Luther, led a huge movement challenging the authority of the Pope and many of the teachings of the Catholic Church. Through his study of the book of Romans, he began to see that forgiveness of sins could only come about by faith in Christ's work on the cross. He translated the Bible into German so the common people could read the Bible. He wrote hymns for the common people to sing. He taught that every believer was a priest and therefore had a right to partake of the cup in communion. In the eyes of the Catholic Church, this teaching was a protest against true doctrine. Though the Catholic Church vigorously opposed this revolt, it rapidly spread throughout all of Western Europe, resulting in great enthusiasm and passion in Christian faith rooted in the teaching of the Bible. This significantly changed the landscape of Christianity and today is referred to as the "Protestant Reformation".

Before the 16th century, Christianity had two major branches - the Roman Catholic Church and the Eastern Orthodox Church. After the Protestant Reformation, there were three.

Prayer: *Father, thank You that I am able to have the Bible in my own language, take the cup in communion, and sing to You songs of praise and thanksgiving. Thank You for the mystery of faith and salvation. In Jesus' name. Amen.*

SUNDAY – GOD'S SPECIAL DAY – THE LORD'S DAY

"I will give You thanks in the great congregation; I will praise You among a mighty throng." Ps. 35:18

THE CHURCH THE BODY OF CHRIST

WEEK #43 A CLOSER LOOK

MONDAY - THE COMMUNITY WHO PROCLAIMS JESUS AS MESSIAH

Scripture: Matthew 16:15-16

The Hebrew word for messiah means a very special anointed one, like a special king. Present day Jews still believe an anointed king will come and will be a political force for good, unlike any king ever born. He will be of the lineage of King David and will restore Israel as the supreme nation.

Our story today is an encounter with Jesus and his closest followers. Jesus inquires of them as to who people think he is. They respond with various names of great men of God. Jesus quickly gets to the point, pressing them with the question, *"But who do you say that I am?"*.

Peter answered, *"You are the Christ (Messiah), the Son of the living God."* This would have been quite an alarming statement for any Jewish leader. Since childhood, Jesus' disciples lived in the hope of seeing the "Messiah". The followers of Jesus, throughout history, have unapologetically made this statement as their defining proclamation. Every Christian, regardless of denomination or church group, sees Jesus as the messiah of the Old Testament, the Hebrew people. The word, Christ, is the English word for messiah. When we say Jesus the Christ, we are really saying Jesus the Messiah.

In a deeply personal way, Christians hear Jesus asking the same question, *"But who do you say that I am?"* This question is personal and to the point. It is not enough to say he was a great moral leader, a Ghandian sort of crusader for justice and equal rights. It is not enough to say he was a great prophet. To the Christian, Jesus is the one and only Messiah. He is the one and only "Son" of the living God.

Prayer: *Father, the sending of Your only Son to be the Jewish Messiah is a truth that I will value to my grave. The proclamation of this truth will be on my lips throughout my life. Thank You, Lord. In Jesus' name. Amen.*

TUESDAY - THE COMMUNITY WHO HAS RECEIVED REVELATION

Scripture: Matthew 16:17

I wish I could have been there when Jesus stated the words in our verse today. I wish I could have seen the countenance on his face, heard the joy in his voice, and witnessed his animation. It must have been one of the peak moments of his ministry.

After saying, *"Blessed are you"*, he immediately informed Peter of one of the most amazing truths – the identity of Jesus. When the undercover cop reveals his identity, he purposely allows people to see and understand who he is. He may do this by showing his badge, his gun, or some other identification. Then and only then do we really know the cop's identity. In the story of Joseph, as recorded in Genesis, Joseph was a high ranking government official with great power. His brothers did not recognize him, as they had not seen him or heard from him in many years. At one point in the story, Joseph reveals his true identity. He stands up at the large meal table and proclaimed, "I am Joseph!". His brothers were stunned. They didn't have a clue. He was their brother, and Joseph revealed it to them.

When Peter proclaimed Jesus as the Messiah, Jesus lit up. Jesus knew that the unfolding of his life was now in process. Like the undercover cop or like Joseph, the Father exposed the identity of Jesus. It was not because of their high intelligence or their clever wit. The revelation didn't happen because they were handsome or honest or kind. Because of God's love and grace, he simply chose to reveal this amazing truth to them. Theologians call this divine revelation. It is God's gift to the church, the community of believers.

Prayer: *Father God, I am one of them also. Without You, I would never have recognized the Lordship of Jesus. Thank You for working in my sin-stained heart. Thank you for revealing Jesus to me. In the name of the Messiah, Jesus. Amen.*

WEDNESDAY - THE COMMUNITY OF THE ROCK

Scripture: Matthew 16:18

Every building constructed upon a foundation of rock will most likely have a firm foundation and a long life. The imagery surrounding the word "rock" implies durability, strength, density, and longevity.

Three weeks ago, we purchased a house here in Wabash. It is almost 100 years old. If you go to the basement, you will easily see the rock foundation. It has lasted a long time. If a foundation of wood was used, what would the house be like today? Would it even be standing? If a foundation of sand would have been used, what would it be like today? Would it even be standing?

Jesus purposely selected a new name for Simon. The name was Peter, which means rock. Jesus then exclaims that *"upon this rock, I will build My church"*. The actual Greek word for church is ekklesia, which means assembly. Towns and villages had assemblies for political purposes. The word ekklesia was a commonly used Greek term that had no specific reference to a religious gathering. Jesus was stating that this incredible revelation, just witnessed, would be the foundation for the future gathering of people known as the people of God, the body of Christ, the bride of Christ. This is why most all churches put great emphasis upon a profession of faith.

Every true Christian builds his faith upon the rock, upon the profession of *"You are the Christ, the Son of the living God."* Every true church is built on that same rock. It is not jello. It is not sand. It is not cardboard. It is a rock that will never decay, never deteriorate, never weaken, and never crumble. This is the foundation for our faith and for the church.

Prayer: *Father, the gift of faith is most incredible. Thank You for this strong foundation. This is why Your church stands today and continues to spread throughout the world. In Jesus' name. Amen.*

THURSDAY - THE COMMUNITY CONSTRUCTED BY JESUS

Scripture: Matthew 16:18

In this famous encounter, Jesus makes several light-bulb statements. Let's examine the one which says, *"I will build My church"*. The ramifications of those words are huge.

Take note of what he didn't say. He didn't say, *"great men and women will build My church."* He didn't say, *"people of high moral character will build My church"*. He didn't say, *"famous preachers, evangelists, missionaries, and theologians will build My church"*. The architect of this building is God the Father. The contractor is Jesus. It is him and no one else. He didn't sublet certain components of the construction. The building is his from top to bottom, inside and out. Jesus is the master carpenter, the master builder.

The most amazing aspect of this building is the material used in construction. Though Jesus is perfect, the material he chose is not. It is you and me, those who have professed him, repented, and received forgiveness of sins. Warts and all, we are the building. Throughout the ages, the church has suffered through serious and shameful scandals. Church leaders have embezzled funds, sexually abused women and children, manipulated and deceived thousands of people, yet it goes forth. Some people, like the famous author, C.S. Lewis, were at one time professed atheists. They studied the Bible, contemplated its truth, were convicted by the Holy Spirit and went on to become giants of faith. Some people, like Billy Graham, have lived lives above reproach and are examples to the world of integrity and sacrifice. None of these people have been perfect. In spite of them all, Jesus called them and has taken their offering of time and talent and constructed a movement that has revolutionized life on planet earth.

Prayer: *Father, thank You for taking me as I am, forgiving me, and including me in this great assembly, known as the body of Christ, the bride of Christ. I am not worthy yet You called me and forgave me. I will give thanks to You for all eternity. In Jesus' name. Amen.*

FRIDAY - THE COMMUNITY VICTORIOUS

Scripture: Matthew 16:18

Immediately upon stating the church would be his and that he would build it, Jesus gives us valuable information as to the existence and future of this great community or assembly. He makes the powerful statement that *"the gates of Hades (or hell) will not over power it"*. One modern paraphrase of the Bible, The Message, puts it this way, *"I will put together my church, a church so expansive with energy that not even the gates of hell will be able to keep it out."*

This strong word of victory should be remembered by all who give of their time to the Church of Jesus Christ. Many things in life fail, but the Church of Jesus Christ is not like all those things. The Church may be persecuted and may suffer unimaginable things. Just this month, children of Christian parents were beheaded in northern Iraq. Never before in the history of Christianity have so many people been jailed or martyred because of their faith in Jesus. Though it makes no sense on the surface, with Christ there is always a resurrection after a crucifixion. About the time it looks like evil is winning, God turns the tables, just as he did with the death of his only Son.

Because of control issues and selfishness, many innocent people have been hurt and churches closed, but the Church of Jesus Christ marches on. God's kingdom continues to expand in much of the world.

We must keep in mind that the bottom line to life is how it ends. Just like a book with a scary chapter, everything is ok in the end. The endgame should be fixed in our minds. The church of Jesus Christ is victorious.

Prayer: *Father, may I not lose sight of the endgame. Forgive me when I can't see beyond my own pain and disappointment. Thank You, again, for Your victorious Church. In Jesus' name. Amen.*

SATURDAY - THE COMMUNITY WITH THE KEYS

Scripture: Matthew 16:19

Jesus informs Peter that he will one day give him the keys to the kingdom of heaven. Jesus went on to explain that his resurrection power will be visited upon Peter, giving him the power to bind or to unbind. Some churches have taken this to mean that this power was only given to Peter and those who succeeded Peter. Since Peter was the Bishop of Rome, which eventually became known as the Roman Catholic Church, Peter is viewed as the first Pope (father or papa in Latin). Those who come after Peter are viewed as having that same power.

Protestants have viewed this promise to Peter meaning a promise to all believers everywhere. We don't see it as magic. We see the gospel as being the entry to the kingdom of God. If you have the gospel, you have the keys. If you refuse to share the gospel, it is a very serious matter with eternal consequences. You have the keys. You must open the door. You open the door by sharing the story of the cross.

The Apostle Paul says the gospel is the power of God for salvation. If you have the gospel, you have the power. If you have the gospel, it is for a reason. If you have the gospel, God has given you a tremendous responsibility.

My mother, Reba Curry, gave me the gospel. She received Christ in her younger years, professed faith in Christ, and was baptized. She gave all three of her children the gospel of Christ. Little did she realize at the time, when she told us about Jesus, the impact this faith would have upon us. She had the keys and opened the door for us.

Prayer: *Father, Your gospel continues to go forth around the world changing lives and giving hope. Thank You for the one who gave me the gospel. Help me to share it with everyone I know. In Jesus' name. Amen.*

SUNDAY – GOD'S SPECIAL DAY – THE LORD'S DAY

"Come and hear, all who fear God, and I will tell of what He has done for my soul." Ps. 66:16

THE CHURCH THE BODY OF CHRIST

WEEK #44 THE BODY OF CHRIST IN ACTION

MONDAY - NURTURING THE YOUNG

Scripture: I Peter 2:1-3

We begin our Christian life as a babe in Christ. We begin in the nurture and care of more mature Christians. This usually happens in a congregation. We learn to worship with other believers. We learn to study with other believers. We share communion with other believers. The church is God's design. It is the institution founded by Christ and put together by Christ. Participation in church is not optional for those who hunger for a Biblical faith.

Infants first need milk, then, after a certain amount of growth, solid foods. Infants start out by crawling and later on begin to walk and finally to run. This is a picture of the Christian life. When we give up trying to be our own god, when we finally humble ourselves in submission to the One who created us, when we repent of sin and receive Christ into our hearts, God accepts us. He forgives us, and gives us new life. In that sense, we start out as a spiritual infant.

As an infant, we are dependent on nourishment given to us by mature adults for a period of time. New Christians know little about the Bible. They must learn. They know little about prayer. They must learn. They know little about the schemes of the devil. They must learn. Learning to trust God in the face of disappointment and despair is not easy for the most mature adult. Many things can be confusing to the new Christian and can easily lead a person to severe depression and disillusionment. All Christians face these moments. When the storm comes and the new plant is not deeply rooted, it desperately needs the support of others.

Prayer: *Father, thank You for the church. Thank You for mature believers who know You and are firmly rooted in You. Oh Lord, teach me Your ways. Grow me. Deepen me. In Jesus' name. Amen.*

TUESDAY - PRUNING THE MATURE

Scripture: Proverbs 27:17

Today's verse is one of my memory verses. It is short and pithy. It can be applied to daily life quite easily.
Have you ever tried to sharpen a knife with a sharpening stone or with another piece of iron? If you do, you will find the sharpening process will heat up the blade. Friction between the stone and the blade causes the heat. Without friction, the knife can't be sharpened.

This is God's analogy for Christian growth. Though spoken by an ancient king, God preserved its use for every generation. It is quite fitting for 21st century believers maturing in the faith.

Remember how Nathan confronted David concerning David's sin with Bathsheba? That was a classic picture of iron sharpening iron. Nathan had a strong and trusting relationship with David. He cared about David. He cared about the people of God. Because Nathan cared, he took a great risk. He approached the King of Israel about the King's personal sin. Wow. Talk about risky. Did Nathan create an awkward moment? Did emotions run high? Yes and yes, but the momentary heat and friction resulted in a humbled man who cried out in confession, seeking forgiveness and restoration.

This is how the church is to work. Like the gardener who cuts off branches to save the larger tree, in our calling to be priests to one another, we are to be Nathans. We are to risk awkward moments, and in deep love correct one another, helping one another to grow, though painful at times. This can only happen when believers develop strong and trusting relationships. Intentional pruning is the by-product of every healthy relationship. This should be the norm, not the exception, for every congregation.

Prayer: *Father, I confess that many times I am blind to my own sin. In order to grow into Your Son's image, I need the pruning. Oh Lord, give me Christian friends who will help me. In Jesus' name. Amen.*

WEDNESDAY - TRAINING FOR BATTLE

Scripture: Ephesians 6:10-12

One of the reasons the followers of Christ desperately need one another is the opposition from the enemy they face. If you are in sync with an enemy force, you will have no opposition from that force. If you oppose it, the opposition will be intense.

The Bible states, *"The Son of God appeared for this purpose, to destroy the works of the devil."* In following Jesus, we are called to carry on the work he began. He strongly opposed demonic activity on all fronts. He opposed disease, poverty, injustice, arrogance, envy, jealously, adultery, dishonesty, deceit, blatant demonic oppression and death. To put it mildly, Jesus gave the devil a serious migrane. We are called to do the same.

The problem comes when we go forth to do this type of battle. Upon arriving on the frontline, we are faced with vigorous push-back. Doing war requires armor and weapons. The Apostle Paul described different aspects of the Christians' armor – Scripture, faith, prayer, and righteousness. He wrote that with these weapons, we may stand strong against the *"flaming arrows of the evil one"*. Without these weapons, we are no match and are doomed for defeat.

Having the prayer cover, encouragement, support, and accountability offered by a healthy church is God's way of equipping us to maintain the offensive in this bloody conflict. All around us are wounded and weary people. Through drug or alcohol abuse, through physical and sexual abuse, through hatred, through the deceit and scheming of the world, the death-count is staggering. The sad stories are real.

Sooo . . where are you in the battle? Do you have the cover of a healthy church? Are you on the frontline, well equipped?

Prayer: *Oh Father, many times I fail to see this life as a war zone and fail to see the casualties. Forgive me. Open my eyes. Help me to receive the support from my church and to give support to others. In Jesus' name. Amen.*

THURSDAY - TRAINING FOR THE HARVEST

Scripture: Matthew 9:37-38

Harvest training is one of the primary functions of the church. Jesus described the situation of the world as a mighty harvest. In doing this he also mentioned a huge crisis – lack of workers. With any kind of harvest, there must be some type of basic training. This is precisely where believers can help equip one another.

Growing up on a farm in Union County, harvest time for the Curry family was an exciting and busy time of the year. All farmers who have a plentiful harvest are happy farmers. It is their hope and joy for much of the year. With every rain the anticipation rises. Driving a large combine down through a corn field and witnessing the golden corn rolling into the bin is quite special. If I live to be a hundred, I will never forget that feeling of satisfaction and reward.

At the end of the Bible we read of a great cloud of witnesses too large to count, people from every tribe, tongue and nation. This is the harvest Jesus described in Matthew 9. When that moment arrives, I believe God will be feeling that same special feeling of satisfaction, times ten, that I felt when harvesting corn many years ago.

For us, that moment is yet to arrive. As long as God gives us life, we are to be workers in the field. Lack of workers has been a historic problem in the church in every period of history. The prophecy uttered by Jesus is stunningly true. Jesus explicitly tells his people to pray to the Lord of the harvest to send out workers. This prayer focus should be big for every congregation, for every Sunday service.

Prayer: *Father, thank You for every church that is training field workers for the coming harvest. Through others and through Your Holy Spirit, teach me how to reach my co-workers, friends, and neighbors. Oh Father, send more workers to my church. In Jesus' name. Amen.*

FRIDAY - COMMISSIONING THE SAINTS

Scripture: Acts 6:6

Having the Bible as one's guide, it would be unthinkable to be a Christian and not be an active part of a church. Throughout the book of Acts and most of the New Testament one reads of many churches and church situations. Acts chapter 6 records the first major church crisis and reveals the solution. The Apostles instructed the congregation to select men of *"good reputation, full of the Holy Spirit and of wisdom"* to handle the distribution of food to widows. Upon learning of their selection, the Apostles *"after praying, they laid hands on them"*.

This story speaks volumes on several fronts. A big one is the commissioning act. Imagine how those seven men felt when prayed over by the Apostles with laying on of hands. Imagine the support felt from the whole church. It would have been interesting to hear their prayers. Do you think they asked God to powerfully anoint them with the Holy Spirit for this task? I do.

In many churches today, this is not taken seriously. When church officers are elected, formalized prayers are offered with little passion or intensity. I'm not sure God is that impressed. Recently our congregation here in Wabash had a husband and wife go to Jamaica as team members to lead a retreat. The Sunday before they left, the entire congregation surrounded them in prayer and laying on of hands. It was important for the congregation. It was important for them. Though the retreat was not formally conducted through our church or denomination, their ministry in Jamaica was an extension of our church's ministry.

As workers are raised up within a congregation, they should feel strong support from their faith family. This is the body of Christ.

Prayer: *Father, thank You for every church in America and around the world that is truly Christ's body - His arms, His eyes, His mind, His hands, and His feet. This is Your will. It is precious in Your sight. Thank you. In Jesus' name. Amen.*

SATURDAY - COMFORTING THE WEARY

Scripture: II Corinthians 1:3-4

Jesus comforted the weary when he was here on this earth. Upon preparing his followers for his absence, he described the Holy Spirit as the *"Comforter"*. This comfort given by God through his Spirit is critical when faced by the disappointment and pain of this life. In addition to that, the comforting arms and words of loving friends can soothe the aching soul in powerful ways.

In August of 1978, heart-wrenching tragedy came our way, as one morning Rhonda and I discovered our three month old baby lying in the crib unresponsive. Words can't begin to describe the pain we felt in the coming hours, days, and weeks. At our church, two days later, over a hundred people came to express their condolences. Rhonda especially remembers one of her friends who didn't say a word but simply held her and wept for several minutes. Her friend didn't have to say words. Her actions and love were quite loud. Though the Holy Spirit was very much at work comforting Rhonda and me, the people of our little church that evening were *"Jesus with skin on"*. They were Jesus' arms and hands. The body of Christ was at work.

The Bible says to *"weep with those who weep"*. There is a dynamic in sharing another person's pain that is almost mystical. We are instructed to *"bear one another's burdens and thus fulfill the law of Christ"*. These words of direction to congregations can lead to acts of love and kindness which keep people from giving up and are the pathways to healing and wholeness. The therapeutic factor in healthy congregational life is profound. It is God's design to carry us through until he calls us home.

Prayer: *Father, again today I thank You for Christ's church, His body. Oh Lord, may I be "Jesus with skin on" to the weary and weak. In His name. Amen.*

SUNDAY – GOD'S SPECIAL DAY – THE LORD'S DAY

"I was glad when they said to me, 'Let us go to the house of the Lord.'"
Ps. 122:1

THE CHURCH THE BODY OF CHRIST

WEEK #45 THE REAL THING

MONDAY - GOD'S HOUSEHOLD

Scripture: Ephesians 2:19-20

Paul gives us an interesting picture of the Church. He describes her as a household of which Jesus is the cornerstone. In this analogy, he views the apostles and prophets as the foundation of the house and the believers as the visible building. This building is an ever-changing building. It is *"growing into a holy temple"*. By being included in the many parts of the building, the believers are no longer strangers and aliens but are fellow citizens with the saints.

When I think of the church, I don't think of my small group of churches or denomination. I think of all the people around the world who bow at the foot of the cross, all people in every nation who confess to Jesus, *"thou are the Christ, the Son of the living God"*. Every day in my morning prayer, I thank God for this massive body of people, the household of God. I pray for the leaders of all these churches – the Russian Orthodox Church, the Greek Orthodox Church, the Coptic Orthodox Church, the Syrian Orthodox Church, the Roman Catholic Church, the Anglicans, the Lutherans, the Methodists, the Presbyterians, the Evangelicals, the Fundamentalists, and the Pentecostals. Most all these groups have their distinctive view of baptism, communion, and worship. They all look to Jesus as God and recognize his work on the cross for salvation. For me, that is enough. I ask God to bless them, protect them, and to fill them with his Spirit.

Like a building that is visible with the eye, these churches are visible institutions. Whether anyone else understands or recognizes them to be Christian, they understand themselves to be Christian and carry the Christian label in the eyes of the world.

Prayer: *Father, thank You for Your wonderful household. Thank You that all the parts of the house are not the same and there are many rooms. May Your people all around the world rise up and continue to be salt and light. In Jesus' name. Amen.*

TUESDAY - AN INSTITUTION FOR EQUIPPING

Scripture: Ephesians 4:11-12

It would be unthinkable to send an army out to do battle without equipment and training. One of the primary purposes for the church is to equip and train. The saints are to overcome evil with good. The saints are to make disciples of all the nations. This does not happen without great effort and sacrifice. Indeed the church is a worshiping body, but to view it as only a worshiping body is to want the icing and not the cake. The task of training and equipping is not an easy task, but a needful task.

In today's verses it refers to the *"building up of the body of Christ"*. This happens when the many parts of the body are functioning properly. We read of apostles, prophets, evangelists, pastors, and teachers. In other New Testament letters, we read how God has gifted everyone in the church with certain gifts for the proper functioning of the church. Learning to recognize one's gifting and to practice that gifting is a huge step of faith for many believers.

The body of Christ is to be built up, not torn down. It is a work in progress fueled by the Holy Spirit. Because it is a work in progress, an unfinished product, it is far from perfect. To be active in the body of Christ is to be vulnerable. One runs the risk of getting hit with a two-by-four or hammer and being hurt. People say things they shouldn't say and sometimes are jealous and critical. Don't forget, this imperfect body is the body of Christ. As the training goes forth, as real battles of eternal significance are fought, the lives of the saints are poured out for God's glory.

Prayer: *Father, thank You for giving me a congregation where I can labor in the vineyard. Lord, help me to be a blessing. Help me to be always forgiving and an encouragement to others. In Jesus' name. Amen.*

WEDNESDAY - PROPER CONDUCT AMONG THE SAINTS

Scripture: Ephesians 4:29-30

You may know of someone who has been hurt deeply by church involvement. More than likely, words were said that put a gashing cut to the heart. Those words were replayed in the mind of the wounded like a rewinding tape that won't stop for days, weeks, months, and sometimes years. James in his letter writes, *"But everyone must be quick to hear, slow to speak and slow to anger . . ."*

Our verse for today reads, *"Let no unwholesome word proceed from your mouth but only such a word as is good for edification . . ."* If all believers of a congregation would take those words to heart, the kingdom of God today would be much larger. Pastors and church leaders need to be especially careful with their words. Unwholesome words or critical words uttered thoughtlessly destroy and demean people. The church is for the building up of the body of Christ not for tearing it down. When Christians are not restrained in their talk, the Holy Spirit is grieved.

All church leaders should be proactive in teaching the proper use of words to encourage people and to edify the congregation. The popular saying, "sticks and stones will break my bones but words will never hurt me" first appeared in a Christian magazine in 1862. It was well intended but how foolish the statement. Deep psychological harm is done by parents trying to shame or embarrass their children. Words are used as weapons by bullies to inflict emotional pain. Such words have absolutely no place in the life of a believer. As our world was created by God's words, we should learn to realize the power of words to empower and inspire one another.

Prayer: *Father, thank You for giving me the ability to build up people with wholesome and caring words. Help me, Lord, to be careful in the things I say. Help me remember the importance of encouragement. In Jesus' name. Amen.*

THURSDAY - THE MONUMENTAL TASK OF ONENESS

Scripture: John 17:20-21

All of John chapter 17 is a prayer, an actual recorded conversation between Jesus and God. This long prayer gives us great insights into Jesus' heart and mind just before he was crucified. Only the Gospel writer, John, records this prayer. In it, Jesus prays for his present followers and for his followers to come years later. The question immediately surfaces, "Ok, what were his requests?" Today's verse gives us one of those requests, ". . . *that they may all be one.*"

Jesus is referring to his future followers. God must have given him a glimpse of the future. He must have looked forward two thousand years and seen a divided, fractured church. He must have seen how this would seriously derail the spreading and acceptance of the gospel message. Jesus enjoyed very close intimacy with his heavenly father. He wanted his future followers to enjoy that same intimacy. Since God is one, the people who become intimate with God will inevitably realize a oneness. In Jesus' mind, this was huge. It was important, and with that he cries out to the Father.

I have wondered why God did not issue a ten-point statement of faith for all Christians to accept and believe. This would have solved a lot of church splits. I have wondered why God did not issue a manual on congregational life and structure, giving detailed instructions for the role of pastors, elders, deacons, etc. Again, this would have solved many church divisions. I have concluded that God wants us to know him most of all. He wanted us to gather around the cross, not a set of documents. His love for men and women to share eternity with him, as one, cannot be overemphasized.

Prayer: *Father, teach me more and more about how I can be one with You and one with other people who know You. Take away any divisiveness in my heart. Forgive me Lord. In Jesus' name. Amen.*

FRIDAY - THE MONUMENTAL TASK OF ONENESS

Scripture: John 17:22-23

As if Jesus did not make the point well enough in his prayer to God in the previous verses, he takes it a step further. The intimacy Jesus enjoys with the Father surfaces again. Jesus then expresses his desire that his future followers would be perfected in one specific way – doctrine? ideology? dress? nationality? church polity? race? You may have guessed it – unity - ". . . that they may be perfected in unity. . ." This merging together of mind, heart, and soul needs to be top priority for every true follower of Christ.

It is also interesting to note that he again makes the connection with masses of men and women around the world coming to faith and the oneness experienced by his followers. To flip this the opposite direction, one would conclude that the more divided the body of Christ is, the fewer people will come to Christ. There has been great emphasis upon world evangelism in the last century, but few evangelism plans include unity among God's people. The one exception to this is Billy Graham. With every one of his crusades, he has put forth much effort to bring the churches together. Could this be a key to his success?

So let's get personal. What about you? You are involved in a church, but have you given much thought to the importance of Christian unity? Think about the intimacy between Jesus and God. To become one with God and to partake of that intimacy is to be one heart and soul with other followers of Jesus, even those of different churches. Intimacy demands transparency and honesty, which flows freely between God and his son and should flow freely within the circle of God's people.

Prayer: *Father, I will eternally thank You for bringing me into the circle Your people. Lord take me deeper. Give me that same mind and heart which was in Christ Jesus, Your Son. In His name. Amen.*

SATURDAY - ONE BODY

Scripture: I Corinthians 12:12-14

Almost all of the New Testament letters were written to churches encountering some issue or controversy. This is most true with Corinthians. The church of Corinth was a very divided, dysfunctional church, experiencing serious problems. It was no accident that the Apostle Paul wrote in detail about how the members of the church were to be one, though many. Most of chapter 12 is given to the analogy of a human body as compared to a congregation.

No one thinks of himself as many different parts. We think of ourselves as one unit, though we do have many parts. My foot is just as important to me as my hand, my eye or my ear. Though it is not visible and may be considered not as important as other parts of my body, it is still is very important. I value both feet and would put up glaring, violent resistance to anyone wanting to remove either one of my feet.

Congregations, likewise, have many parts or members. There are those members who do things which are more visible, such as music leaders, Scripture readers, and Sunday School teachers. Within every church there are also people who are not as visible, such as those who prepare the communion elements or those who do worship planning or maybe prepare slides for the powerpoint or prepare bulletins. Within the dynamics of church life, there is great potential for jealousy and envy, as we all are insecure in some way. If the men and women of a church are not very aware of the importance of loving and forgiving one another as Christ loves and forgive us, the church is a recipe for disaster, waiting to happen. When it does, it is always tragic.

Prayer: *Father, teach me to love and support the other members of my church, regardless of what position they hold. Teach me to forgive quickly when offended and to be relentless in my efforts to maintain the unity of my church. In Jesus' name. Amen.*

SUNDAY – GOD'S SPECIAL DAY – THE LORD'S DAY

"The heavens will praise Your wonders, O Lord, Your faithfulness also in the assembly of the holy ones."

Psalm 89:5

THE CHURCH THE BODY OF CHRIST

WEEK #46: AND WHAT ABOUT MONEY?

MONDAY - ALL FOR GOD'S GLORY

Scripture: Mark 12:42-43

The Gospels of Mark and Luke provide the story of a widow giving her offering in the Jerusalem Temple treasury. Jesus observed the amount of money being offered and the financial status of those bringing gifts. The people who gave large amounts of money are described as "rich" yet his eyes become fixed on a poor, widow, and the small amount she gave. He comments that she gave out of her poverty whereby the rich gave out of their surplus. Jesus concludes that she gave more than the rich people gave. Wow.

If Jesus didn't care about money, why this story? If the subject of money is off limits for the church, why does Jesus address the subject of money and its proper handling numerous times? Money can be loved. It can be worshipped. Money is power. It controls many things and many people. Is it any wonder Jesus addressed this subject numerous times?

I would argue that money, in and of itself, meant nothing to Jesus. Jesus cared about people, not gold or silver or dollars or pounds or rupees. Jesus cared about money because of what it can do. It has the power to corrupt people or institutions, and it has the power to do wonderful things. For example, think about wood from trees. One can use it to carve out a weapon for murder, or one can use to make a house for urgently needed shelter. All the things given to us by the Lord are to be used for good and not evil, whether it be wood, soil, food, drink, animals, or money. In this way, the proper use of everything God has given us matters to him. Money is no exception.

Prayer: *Father God, thank You for the widow in today's story. Thank You for her love for You as showed by her sacrifice in giving. May I use everything You have given me for Your glory. In Jesus' name. Amen.*

TUESDAY - MONEY: THE NEW TESTAMENT CHURCH

Scripture: Acts 4:34-35

The church in her infancy was incredibly vibrant, passionate, and generous. Congregations met to worship and share meals daily, pooled their resources, cared for one another, and shared life as followers of Jesus. Such living was certainly counter-cultural yet attracted others and transformed societies. This attempt at communal living did not last too long, as history records.

It does make one wonder what it would be like for believers to share all possessions and wealth, eliminating the need for some to be rich while others remain poor. Some would say such thinking is Pollyannaish, not practical, but only wishful thinking. Churches and Christian groups throughout the ages have experimented with communal living or some form of it.

The early church did view the use of their financial resources as a means of furthering God's kingdom. They approached this with great sincerity. Chapters 4 and 5 of Acts offer several references to entire tracts of land given to the church. One story describes a husband and wife who promised the Lord a piece of property but later on changed their mind. Their deed is referred to as a "lie to the Holy Spirit". For this, God took their lives. He struck them dead, resulting in great fear throughout the Christian community. Withholding money in the face of a world of human hurt gets the attention of God.

In writing to his young friend, Timothy, the Apostle Paul explains, "Instruct those who are rich in this present world not to be conceited or to fix their hope on the uncertainty of riches, but on God". He also gives this stunning comment, "the love of money is the root of all evil". These are strong words with profound implications.

Prayer: Father God, all I have is Yours – my health, my time, my talent, my property, my bank account. It is for Your glory. Help me to learn that in the giving, nothing is truly lost. In Christ's name. Amen.

WEDNESDAY - AN UNAVOIDABLE SUBJECT FOR EVERY CHURCH

Scripture: I Corinthians 16:1-2

Receiving offerings from God's people was the norm for the early church and for every church throughout history. This is true across the board regardless of church or denomination. Investing one's life in the kingdom of God is not limited to occasional pious prayers. True discipleship demands all of one's being, which includes time, talents and treasures.

Some churches have a "stewardship campaign" at a certain time of the year, which usually is the budgeting time of the year. Some pastors will address the subject through a sermon series. Many churches ask their people to think, plan, and pray about their financial giving, leading to an actual weekly pledge.

Many believers get rather prickly about the subject, which does reveal a certain level of maturity. These Christians would prefer that giving would never be mentioned, thinking one's spiritual life is a completely separate compartment from the use of one's financial resources. To the other extreme, some churches raise the subject of giving all too often. When this is done, the implication is that the church is money hungry, just like all other organizations. Some who do consider themselves Christian, refuse to join a church fearing they will be required to give a certain amount.

Tithing is understood by most churches to be an acceptable and reasonable amount to commit to the Lord weekly. A tithe is understood to be 10% of one's gross salary. This is specifically taught by many pastors. Tithing was the law under the Old Testament covenant and has since been adopted by most New Testament groups. Tithing requires discipline and great trust. Bringing one's tithe to the Lord should be a joyous moment, celebrated by all of one's church family.

Prayer: *Oh Lord, teach me to trust You in all ways. Guide my church leaders. Give them wisdom in knowing how to handle the financial resources entrusted to their care. In Jesus' name. Amen.*

THURSDAY - YIKES! SOMETHING TO PONDER

Scripture: Malachi 3:8-9

Disobedience to God can come in many ways. One way is in the arena of the giving of tithes and offerings. In today's text, we read that God was very angry with his people. They were "tipping" and not "tithing". Malachi poses the question, *"Will a man rob God?"* He then quotes God as saying, *". . . you are robbing Me!"* Because they had become greedy and withheld a proper tithe, God felt cheated. Much needed work of his kingdom had to be foregone because of their greed. God told them they were *"cursed with a curse"* for this act of disobedience. One certainly gets the feeling that God was deeply offended by their behavior and could not overlook it.

Have you ever thought that by tipping rather than tithing you might be robbing God? Who me? Me robbing God? That is certainly the implication when one seeks to give application to today's text. Yes, it is strong, but something we should all ponder.

Also in Old Testament teaching we find the concept of *"first fruits"*. Upon bringing a grain offering or animal offering to the Temple, the people were to give the first of the fruit of produce at harvest or the first-born of the womb. They were not to bring a sickly animal or one that was weak but their very best. In the same way, Christians today have adopted the practice of setting aside their 10% tithe first, before any other bills are paid. The gift brought to the Lord on Sunday morning is even that much more special when it is looked upon in this light. A tip would be a gift from what is leftover. A first fruit tithe would be taken off the top.

Prayer: *Thank You for this opportunity in my lifetime to give back to You a portion of what You have given me. Forgive me, Lord, if I have ever robbed You. Again, I need Your grace. In Jesus' name. Amen.*

FRIDAY - GIVING, TRUSTING, RECEIVING A BLESSING

Scripture: Malachi 3:10

This verse offers a very clear challenge concerning tithing. God is challenging his people to test him. In other parts of the Bible, we are warned not to "test God", but with this aspect of our faith, we are told to test God.

So ok, what does the test look like? It is quite simple. Obey . . . and then see how God blesses. God says to see *"if I will not open for you the windows of heaven and pour out for you a blessing until it overflows."* If you want to see what an apple tastes like, you do what? Right. You taste it. If you want to see how God will bless you, if you faithfully tithe your salary (give 10%), try it and see what happens.

Everyone who has trusted God in this way has stories to tell that will amaze you. Our faith is unique as compared to other world religions in that our God is a living god. He is not a stone or piece of gold nor is he a cosmic policeman waiting for us to step out of line so he can punish us. He wants to be our best friend. He wants to know us intimately. He wants us to enjoy his presence daily. He wants to bless us. In many instances, people call out for his blessings but refuse to obey him in tithing. Tithing is God's avenue, his strategy for blessing. Tithing pulls the trigger for blessing, and it is exciting. God wants us to use 90% of our regular income for our personal needs, not wants, and to use a minimum of 10% of our income for the church.

Prayer: *Lord, You are so amazing. How You give back to those who give is a mystery to my mind. Your blessings come in many shapes and sizes. Help me, Lord, to learn to simply obey and trust. In Jesus' name. Amen.*

SATURDAY - KEEPING PERSPECTIVE

Scripture: I Timothy 6:9-10

I once had a close friend who wanted to be very rich and wanted his children to be very rich. Yes, he was a Christian, had trusted Christ as Savior and Lord, and had an active prayer life. But oh how he wanted to have a big bank account. Most of his time and mental energies were given to this effort. He even encouraged his son to set a goal of being a millionaire by the age of thirty.

In retrospect, I believe I failed him as a brother in Christ. I never took the time to personally point out the truth of today's verse. He read the Bible daily, but did he ever read today's verse? I have since wondered. At the end of verse ten, the Apostle Paul tells young Timothy what happened to many believers who could not discipline their financial desires – ". . . *some . . . have wandered away from the faith and pierced themselves with many griefs."*

My friend had great discipline in all other areas of his life. He would be the ideal church member in most churches. His sin was not noticeable, certainly not like adultery or theft. It was very subtle and even misunderstood to be good by some. He was charitable, kind, faithful to his wife, and quick to pray if called upon in public. He could even give a good sermon and testimony. Everything was in place but this one little, but not so little, aspect. Because of unrestrained greed, the man caused himself, his family, and many others *"many griefs"*.

Maintaining perspective in all areas of one's life is big in God's eyes. It is the key to real success, happiness, and purpose.

Prayer: *Father, put out any desire to get rich that You see in me. I know that only You have the true riches. Help me to long for those true riches more and more. In Jesus' name. Amen.*

SUNDAY – GOD'S SPECIAL DAY – THE LORD'S DAY

"Praise the Lord! I will give thanks to the Lord with all my heart, in the company of the upright and in the assembly."   Psalm 111:1

THE CHURCH THE BODY OF CHRIST

WEEK #47: THE BODY IN ACTION

MONDAY - ADMONISHING AND LOVINGLY CORRECTING

Scripture: Acts 18:25-26

The early church had noticeable qualities which allowed her testimony concerning Christ to be widely known. Upon looking more closely at her practices, one sees why she was so powerful.

Our verses today give brief mention of a Christian man who was a gifted debater and was committed to the cause of Christ. He is described as being *"fervent in spirit"*. The most admirable quality about him was his openness to correction. An older husband and wife team learned that he was not teaching the full story of God's Holy Spirit. They took him aside and *"explained to him the way of God more accurately"*. When confronted with this problem, he did not get defensive and angry but made adjustments and continued to boldly go forth in ministry. He was teachable. What a lesson for church leaders today.

I am quite passionate about the truth of God and how it can give people vibrant life and hope. In my more passionate moments, I confess that I have not been that teachable or open to correction. After many years of following Christ, I do have some regrets. This is one.

There is much wisdom in giving respect to the senior, more mature people among us, especially in the household of God. We Americans pride ourselves in independence and charting our own course in an entrepreneurial spirit. Indeed this has been a strength, but it has also been a weakness. It takes humility and a teachable spirit to sit at the feet of older more experienced people. This can be done in a classroom setting, mentoring relationships, and/or by reading the writings of respected, Godly people. This is an important aspect of spiritual growth.

Prayer: *Father, give me humility like I see in today's story. Make me teachable, Lord, that I might further be sharpened for effective ministry in my day-to-day world. In Jesus' name. Amen.*

TUESDAY - ASKING THE RIGHT QUESTIONS

Scripture: Acts 19:1-2

Today's story is a follow-up of yesterday's story. It highlights the same problem – weak teaching on the Holy Spirit. Take note of the inquiry offered by the Apostle Paul. He inquired about their faith. He went to the heart of the matter and asked a rather pointed question, *"Did you receive the Holy Spirit when you believed?"*

The thought police of today would not look kindly upon the Apostle Paul's approach. In our society, one's spiritual convictions are viewed by most people as private and personal. Any inquiry into this arena of life is considered rude and inappropriate. The wise believer will take heed of his cultural atmosphere, but not let societal pressure stop much needed gospel teaching. The wise believer wanting to disciple people will prayerfully and respectfully go forth asking the right questions.

It is no secret that the early church was fixed on the Holy Spirit. Every church which puts great emphasis upon the Holy Spirit will make continual references to the book of Acts and the early church. The coming of the Holy Spirit gave birth to the church on the Day of Pentecost. The anointing of the Holy Spirit was key to preaching and teaching with authority and boldness. The leading of the Holy Spirit is found in all of Paul's missionary journeys. The continual filling of the Holy Spirit is evident in everyday Christian living as recorded throughout the book of Acts.

Every church and every Christian should be vigilant as to authentic inquiry in major doctrinal matters. It should be our concern. It should be the focus of our prayers. A good understanding of God, Jesus Christ, and the Holy Spirit is essential for maturity in Christian faith.

Prayer: *Oh Father, give me a good understanding of the Holy Spirit. I want Your Spirit every day. Your Spirit brings my spirit to life and gives me Your presence and guidance. In Jesus' name. Amen.*

WEDNESDAY - LOVING ONE ANOTHER

Scripture: Acts 20:36-38

A well respected church leader, Tertullian, who lived about 150 years after Jesus, made an acute observation of Christians who gathered to worship. He wrote, "see how they love one another". In a world of so much hatred and violence, this deep love attracted attention and grew to be the trademark for early Christianity. We get a glimpse of that deep love in our verses for today.

Ephesus had been a city where Paul spent much time. He called together the church leaders and announced to them his plans of leaving, which meant they probably would not see him again. At his farewell gathering, we read of them weeping and repeatedly kissing him. The love they had for Paul was obvious.

Though our world today is much different with staggering advancements in technology, medicine, and education yet in regards to humanity, it is much the same. We still see brutality and hatred raising their ugly heads on a regular basis. Power and wealth still go hand-in-hand and are restricted to a small percentage of most societies with greed and envy plaguing every corner of the globe. Sex still sells and permissiveness is still rampant. Will it ever change?

Many organizations compete for our time and energy, but one organization stands tall above all the others – the church of Jesus Christ. Why does it stand tall? There is a mysterious and supernatural love flowing through the body of Christ, the Church. Love attracts attention regardless of where it is found. It is the foundation of every family, every healthy marriage, and every healthy parent-child relationship. Where the love of God is found, embraced, and experienced, the Church always grows. And the world takes note.

Prayer: *Father, because You first loved, we can love. Because You came to us in love, we know love. May Your love invade every congregation which bears Your name. Through Christ. Amen.*

THURSDAY - LIFE AND PEACE

Scripture: Romans 8:6

For the last few days of the month we are camping on Romans 8, known by many as the victory chapter of the Bible. This chapter is like a mountain peak of the whole book of Romans. God wants his people to walk in victory, not defeat and not guilt. Yes, we are sinners, but through Christ we are winners. I am an optimist only because of the grace of God. I know how the book ends for God's people, and it is good.

We know that non-Christians can have fun, be somewhat happy and fulfilled, honest and good, but most non-Christians won't allow themselves to contemplate where it all ends, what is next. The message of the Bible is very troubling to some people because it says the ship is sinking. Like the Titanic, we can have first class cabins with the finest of food and entertainment, but it is short-lived. The end is coming and only those few with life-rafts will survive.

In today's Scripture reading, it speaks of the mind in several places. It addresses where we focus our thinking, be it on fleshly, worldly things or on God's Spirit. In other words, our minds will either be headed down the road which results in death or on the road which results in life. When the Holy Spirit is directing our thinking, there is true life and peace.

I have seen people get pumped up and excited about God by attending a Christian concert, a camp or retreat, or church service with intense emotional appeal. But if a Spirit led life doesn't follow, the emotion and excitement fades. Led by God's Spirit, we are not destined for death but for life.

Prayer: *Father, my mind is so fickle, so vulnerable to daily frustrations and interruptions. Lord, I want life and peace, not guilt, defeat and death. Help me, Father. Help me to learn how to set my mind on Your Holy Spirit. In Jesus' name. Amen.*

FRIDAY - TRUE LIFE

Scripture: Romans 8:11

The indwelling of the Holy Spirit is quite the mystery. The union of God's Spirit with our spirit gives us a new beginning, a spiritual birth. We all know and have experienced a fleshly birth but not all people have experienced a spiritual birth. Those who have truly repented of their sin and put their faith in Christ as Savior have experienced a second birth. The well-known evangelist, Billy Graham, describes this new birth as being "born again".

Martin Luther, in 16th century Germany, while preparing to teach a class on Romans, spoke of justification by faith. In describing this new birth, he wrote these words, "*When I discovered that, I was born again of the Holy Ghost. And the doors of paradise swung open, and I walked through.*"

Another famous church leader, John Wesley, two hundred years later in London, England, attended a Bible study on the book of Romans and later wrote in his diary, "*About a quarter before nine, while he was describing the change which God works in the heart through faith in Christ, I felt my heart strangely warmed. I felt I did trust in Christ, Christ alone for salvation, and an assurance was given me that he had taken away my sins, even mine, and saved me from the law of sin and death.*"

Life given to us by the Holy Spirit is the heartbeat of Christianity. No other religious faith offers this inward work of God at the point of faith. All other religions lead people through exhaustive and complicated religious practices in the hopes of finally achieving a heightened spiritual state. With Christianity, the work is already done by Jesus. This work empowers the Christian to live a new life.

Prayer: *Lord, I marvel at the work You do in the hearts of men and women. Your Holy Spirit in me, changes me. Thank You for Your Holy Spirit in me. Continue to transform me, daily, into the likeness of Your Son. In His name. Amen.*

SATURDAY - THE FACE THAT SHONE

Scripture: Exodus 34:29

A couple of months ago we looked at great characters of the Old Testament. Moses certainly stands out as one of the greatest of the greats. Let's bring closure to this week by looking at Moses.

After being on the mountain and hearing from the Lord God, beholding God's incredible glory, we read that the skin of Moses' face glowed or shone, as he came down to be with the people. Some translations read that his face became radiant. It is clear that the change in the look on his face was indicative of the change in his heart and mind. He had been with God, the God of the universe. He would never be the same again. Such an encounter would change any one of us.

When Jesus was transfigured on the mountain, the Bible says his face shone like the sun. Moses and Elijah appeared with Jesus.

Those who do not believe in the miracles of the Bible would, no doubt, scoff at this phenomenon. It is hard to imagine the God of the universe revealing himself to any one human being, let alone an entire nation.

Every June for many years, I would direct a week of youth camp. In a spiritual sense, many of those young people would *"go to the mountain"*. In our worship and prayer times, they would sense the presence of the Lord in a powerful way. The glory of the Lord descended upon many of those young people to forever change their lives. Many of us adults witnessed a work of God we will never forget. When these young people returned home, their parents and friends would often comment how the look on their faces had changed.

Prayer: *Father, thank You for revealing Yourself to Moses and the people of Israel, and to multitudes of people around the world and throughout history, and to me. I am forever changed. In Jesus' name. Amen.*

SUNDAY – GOD'S SPECIAL DAY – THE LORD'S DAY

"I will proclaim Your name to my brethren, in the midst of the congregation, I will sing Your praise."

Psalm 22:2

WEEK #48: THANKSGIVING, THANKSLIVING

MONDAY – LOOKING UP WITH PRAISE

Scripture: Psalm 100:1-2

The Bible says, *"Shout joyfully to the Lord, all the earth."* One scholar translating this opening verse states it like this, *"On your feet now – applaud God."* There is no better way to start the day.

One might think, "Yeah, but what about all the bills I owe? Why am I not talented and smart like some people? Why is my family dysfunctional when all around me are families that seem to have it together? Why can't I get the right job or the right opportunity to make something of myself?" In spite of all the yuck in the world, there are ample reasons to recognize God's goodness and to honor him as God, giving thanks and praise. I couldn't do this until I heard the story of Jesus Christ and how he died on the cross for my sins. I wondered at the time, "Could this really be true? Could it really?"

Everyone who hears the Gospel story is confronted with that question. If it is true, it changes everything. It changes the way one views their own life. It changes the way one views other people and relates to other people. It changes the way one views the world and people of other nations. And it changes the way one thinks about his reason for living and hope for the future. I can't think of any other decision in life that results with these kind of seismic changes.

Yes, I did respond to that message, the Gospel. I repented, and received Jesus Christ as Lord and Savior of my life. Because of that decision many years ago at age thirteen, I am thanking and praising the Lord God today.

Prayer: *Father, I give this day to You. I can't see very far down the road, but You can. I know enough about You to trust You with my future, believe in You, and faithfully follow You. Thank You, Lord. In Jesus' name. Amen.*

TUESDAY – ADORATION WITH JOY

Scripture: Psalm 100:2

Verse two indicates that knowing the Lord is anything but drudgery. In the first part of vs. 2, we find the proper condition whereby one is to give himself to the Lord – gladness. In the second part of the verse we find there is a proper state of the being to sing to the Lord – joyful.

God's word to us is not bad news or sad news. It is not depressing news or news that brings grief. God's word of victory should raise our spirits. God's promise of his presence with us and his power in us, through the Holy Spirit, should put a smile on our faces.

I have been around people who were giddy about following the Lord, displaying a rather superficial or cosmetic happiness. They felt compelled to be happy and so to be a "good Christian". They forced themselves to smile and to put on a show. This is quickly recognized as disingenuous.

To serve the Lord in one's daily life is a very high calling. This can be done through one's chosen profession or career or job. It is one thing to provide service to an employer or to the public; it is quite another thing to view that service as service to God. This can make even mundane work exciting.

I will never forget riding the Metra train one day going from Round Lake down to Union Station in Chicago. The conductor had a special joy about him. That joy radiated throughout the car as he went seat by seat checking tickets. He didn't have to tell me. It was the joy of the Lord. I could recognize it. Without saying a word about Jesus, he was giving testimony with his life.

Prayer: *Father, when we smile down deep inside, it is hard to hold it in. Thank You for taking away our guilt and shame. Thank You for setting us free from the chains of addictions and fears. Thank You again for giving us Jesus. In His name. Amen.*

WEDNESDAY – EXPLOSIVE KNOWLEDGE

Scripture: Psalm 100:3

No other religious movement in the world has had the emphasis upon education as the Christian movement. A very important aspect of our faith is learning – learning about God. Christians should not be afraid of knowledge and truth. We believe God is truth and the source of all truth.

In verse 3, we are commanded by the Psalmist to "know". We can know because God has revealed himself. God has pulled the curtain back by giving us the story of creation, the story of the fall of mankind, the story of God's people throughout history, and the story of redemption and grace through Jesus Christ. A key component in giving thanks is knowledge of God. The middle verse of Psalm 100 addresses this key component. It is the basis for all worship and praise.

A few months back, a member of our church gave us a pickup. We expressed to him our thanks. We verbally communicated our feelings of gratitude. We weren't thanking him for nothing. We were thanking him for a specific act of kindness. Christians are not thanking God for nothing. They are not spewing out words for mental gymnastics. They have something specific in mind. Deep inside, they feel a sense of gratitude and want to express it verbally.

If we were the products of human invention and effort, we would have no reason to praise and thank God. As it is, we have much for which to thank God. He created every man, woman, boy and girl alive today and in history. God has claimed us to be his people. The analogy of a sheep is used over and over again throughout Scripture and here it is again. We are the *sheep of his pasture*.

Prayer: *Thank You, Lord, for giving me life, for giving all of us life. Thank You, Lord, for claiming us as Your people. We are privileged to be sheep in Your pasture with Jesus as our great Shepherd. In His name. Amen.*

THURSDAY – ATTITUDE OF GRATITUDE

Scripture: Psalm 100:4

With today's verse, we find specific instruction as to how to approach a worship gathering. It is impossible to have an attitude of thanksgiving without having something in your mind that you have feelings of gratitude about.

Years ago, in my senior year of high school, I won a pig at the Indiana State Fair Greased Pig Contest. I was proud to represent the Liberty FFA Chapter that day, and upon wrestling to the ground a squealing, oily, panic-stricken pig, I was overwhelmed with joy. Something good had happened to me, something so good that it motivated me to do and say things that I would not normally have said or done. When interviewed by the reporter for the Cincinnati Enquirer, I said thanks to about everyone I could think of – my parents, my agriculture teacher, my friends in my FFA chapter and on and on. I had something for which to be thankful, and it was bubbling over, as shown by my face and as expressed by my lips.

Imagine church on Sunday morning if people came to worship with the same kind of joy that I had when winning a greased pig. We have something much greater to shout about than a greased pig! We have been ransomed from darkness to light! That very same Spirit that is mentioned in Genesis 1, in the creation story, is now in us! That very same Spirit that conceived a son in Mary's womb is in us!

We should raise our voices when we praise. We should shout "Hallelujah!" We are not at a funeral or memorial service. We are approaching the very one who gave us life, to be counted among his people, giving him the fruit of our heart and lips.

Prayer: *Father, forgive me for every time I have entered a church to worship, weighed down with worries or cares, and not aware of Your goodness. Help me to take the time to adjust my attitude upon entering to worship, to participate in such a sacred act. In Jesus' name. Amen.*

FRIDAY – AWESOME GOD

Scripture: Psalm 100:5

Two things about God's goodness are mentioned at the conclusion of this famous Psalm – lovingkindness and faithfulness.

His love is not temporary, not here today and gone tomorrow. It existed before creation, as love going from God the Father - to God the Son - to God the Spirit. Love demands an object. If God is love then he must have someone to love. It is this kind of love, from one part of the Godhead or the Trinity to another, which we know is eternal. It was before creation and will be in existence when the world is no more.

If you think you have nothing for which to thank God, due to this unfortunate circumstance or that, think of his eternal love. You can never in this lifetime thank the Lord enough for his love.

God's faithfulness, as another aspect of his goodness, is there also to motivate us to giving thanks. It is there for you, for the generation coming after you, and the next generation and on and on. This reminds me of an incredible truth. The ramifications of a decision to repent and believe in the Lord Jesus Christ go far beyond the person making the decision. The ramifications go to the person's children, and to his children's children, and to his children's children's children, and so forth.

Few people will let themselves think this far down the road. We are such a "me" generation. The older we get, the more we should begin to think beyond "me". Most of us do this when we have children. Then we think of what is best for them. Then grandchildren come, and we think about what is best for them. God's faithfulness is not a one-generation faithfulness.

Prayer: *Father, thank You for Psalm 100, such a powerful reminder to me of many things concerning worship. For every day, Lord, I want to be among those who praise and thank You and do it every Sunday. In Jesus' name. Amen.*

SATURDAY – MEDITATION

Scripture: Psalm 119:147-148

Most of us are better at keeping busy doing things than taking time to ponder the deep meaning of life, God, and all he has created. We are meant to be human "beings" but most of us are human "doings". We are good at keeping busy or keeping entertained.

Pastors even fall prey to the busy syndrome. It is so easy to keep busy doing things for the Lord that you really never take time to know the Lord intimately. It is possible to know a lot about the Lord but not know the Lord.

The Psalmist reveals a deep longing to understand the ways and thoughts of God. His search to know God more intimately starts early in the morning and goes throughout the day, late into the night. The word, "meditate" is used. One might also use the word "reflect" or "ponder". This daily exercise profoundly impacted his life.

Reflecting on God's promises and his faithfulness to his people brings great peace and assurance. Pondering his truths brings great confidence in his ability to care and protect his people. We typically want the rewards of meditation and reflection but find it difficult to devote time to this simple discipline.

Last June, I went through our old family pictures, which made me stop and remember my father and mother, what they were like in their younger years, when they were raising a family with high hopes and dreams. This time of reflection reminded me of just how fortunate I am to have had such loving parents. It moved me deep within.

Meditating on God and his mighty deeds throughout history has that same effect and even greater. It is the trademark of a soul at peace.

Prayer: *Father, slow me down and help me to take the needed time to reflect upon You, Your greatness and goodness. May I be like the Psalmist, and ponder Your ways early in the day. In Jesus' name. Amen.*

SUNDAY – GOD'S SPECIAL DAY – THE LORD'S DAY

"Praise the Lord! Sing to the Lord a new song, and His praise in the congregation of the godly ones."

Psalm 149:1

WEEK #49: ANCIENT PROPHECIES

MONDAY - THE CHRISTMAS PROPHET

Scripture: Matthew 1:21-22

Isaiah was used mightily of God to announce the coming of his Son, Jesus, some seven hundred years before he was born. No other prophet is directly quoted by an *"angel of the Lord"* in the announcement and birth of Jesus. For this reason, Isaiah is called the Christmas Prophet. Out of the three Old Testament prophecies, which are traditionally thought of as being clear references to Christ's birth, two of them are found in Isaiah.

The New Testament is inseparably linked to the Old Testament with many various quotations pointing to the life and ministry of Jesus Christ. Christians read and interpret the Old Testament through the lens of the New Testament. Anyone who recognizes the New Testament as inspired by God sees the Old Testament as the foundation for all Christian belief.

The Israelite people looked forward with great expectation to the birth of a Messiah or great king. As centuries would come and go, talk of this saving King increased. Neighboring nations were aware of this prophecy as is evidenced by the "magi" (as recorded in Matthew 2) from the east who came to see the newborn king. They were evidently searching the skies for some sign of his birth. With the people of Israel taken captive as far away as Persia some three hundred years before Christ, the Messiah talk had spread to many nations.

For much of the history of the church, the season of Advent is observed the four weeks leading up to Christmas Day. Advent comes from the Latin word, *adventus*, which means coming. During this time, the focus is on the coming of the Lord in his birth and in his coming again to usher in God's Kingdom in its fullness.

Prayer: *Father, Your plan to redeem fallen humanity is truly awesome. History shouts of Your existence and Your love for the world. All praise and glory to You. In Christ's name. Amen.*

TUESDAY – GOD WITH US

Scripture: Isaiah 7:14

Today's verse stands quite tall as a clear reference to Christ's birth. When an angel of the Lord came to Joseph in a dream to speak with him concerning Mary's pregnancy, the angel quoted this verse. In addition to quoting the verse, the angel put emphasis upon the name "Immanuel" by translating its meaning as *"God with us"*.

The belief in God being with his people was nothing new. Throughout the Old Testament there are occasional references to God being with this individual or that individual. Joseph in the book of Genesis is a good example. Moses would be another example, as he argued with God to go with the people of Israel. So why is the angel drawing attention to this aspect of Christ's birth? Why is *"God with us"* worth mentioning?

Think of the wise men falling to their feet in wonder. Think of the shepherds going back to their flocks rejoicing. Being in the presence of the babe of Bethlehem was being in the presence of God. When Mary kissed the cheek of her newborn child, she had kissed the face of God. In seeing Jesus, they had seen God. And their lives would never be the same again.

Not only did Isaiah cause the people to stop in their tracks by saying a *"virgin will be with child"*, but he really got their attention when he announced the name of that child – Immanuel. Though there are many names for Christ found throughout Scripture, this one spoken to Joseph by an angel, as he was tossing to and fro in the night, pierced his heart. The role of Old Testament prophecy in the birth of Jesus Christ is quite amazing.

Prayer: *Father, today I am humbled by Your plan which is so perfect. Isaiah was probably not aware of just how important his obedience to You would be in the grand scheme of things. Help me, Lord, to find my place in Your perfect plan. Take me again to the Bethlehem manger. In Jesus' name. Amen.*

WEDNESDAY – HIS MANY NAMES

Isaiah 9:2, 6-7

Some say there are over one hundred names for Jesus in the Bible. I haven't counted them, but I know there are many. In chapter 7 of Isaiah, he speaks of this great light coming to illuminate the way for people who live in darkness. This light is a "child" to be born, who will have names that reveal much about his role – "*Wonderful Counselor, Mighty God, Eternal Father, Prince of Peace*".

There is no other person in human history who has brought as much spiritual harmony and restoration to people than Jesus. Today almost one-fourth of the world's population identify with him in that way. They proclaim him to be Savior and Lord, the One who stands between God and man to mediate and to save.

He is to me the prince of peace. Through this prince, in my alienated state, God reached out to me through the death of his son on the cross and brought me into a harmonious relationship with my creator. Because of my sin, God was offended. The relationship was broken, severed. If God would have embraced me, he would have embraced evil, because sin is evil. Jesus took that sin and nailed it to the cross. He paid a debt I could never pay. He brought about reconciliation between me and God. He will forever be my prince of peace.

As the darkness of December descends upon me every year, I am reminded of the true Light spoken of by Isaiah, some two thousand seven hundred years ago. I am reminded of the darkened state of my soul that is transformed by the Light. The world is still full of darkness, but through Jesus, I celebrate the Light.

Prayer: *Oh Lord, the darkness can be overwhelming in many ways. Lord Jesus, You promised that those who follow You would not walk in darkness but would have the light of life. May that light forever invade my heart, mind and soul. In Your name. Amen.*

THURSDAY – BIRTH AND DEATH

Scripture: Micah 5:2

The prophet, Micah, utters the third major Old Testament prophecy concerning the birth of Christ. He prophesied at the same time as Isaiah. Micah gives the specific town, Bethlehem, where this great ruler of Israel will be born. The magi or wise men from the east who studied the stars to determine the birth location of this great king eventually made their way to Bethlehem. Matthew records the Jewish chief priests and religious leaders referring to the Micah passage to determine where this king would be born. Because of this, King Herod had all the male babies in Bethlehem two years old and under murdered. It must have been an awful scene with much weeping and wailing.

In the Christmas story we have birth, and we have death. It is a strange contradiction. We see a power hungry, insecure king willing to shed much innocent blood to protect his petty, little hold on status and wealth. We also see our heavenly Father willing to send his Son into this world of violence and bloodshed, knowing that he would die a brutal, gruesome death. With all of that as a backdrop, we find a baby wrapped in swaddling clothes, lying in a manger.

In recent years, I have concluded that a young infant is the nearest thing to God this side of glory. While in India, Rhonda and I saw young babies of Indian couples in our apartment building. They were completely innocent, having no knowledge of Indian culture, dress, food, language, etc. Every baby of every race speaks the same language at birth. In their innocence, they are incredibly beautiful. This is how our Savior started his journey on this earth, speaking the same language as you and me.

Prayer: *Father God, the wonder of Christmas grips me today. I too was born into a world of much violence and greed. I too am loved by You. Thank You, Lord. In Jesus' name. Amen.*

FRIDAY - THY KINGDOM COME

Scripture: Daniel 2:44; 6:27

Jesus prayed for a "kingdom" to come, as many of his parables and much of his teaching were about the *"kingdom of heaven"*. His miracles were live demonstrations of this kingdom, which had come upon them. He stated the *"gospel of the kingdom"* would be preached throughout the whole world and then the end would come. The Bible ends with graphic details of this kingdom having come.

I find it amazing that this very kingdom was mentioned numerous times in the book of Daniel by secular kings. Daniel speaks of this kingdom in the interpretation of King Nebuchadnezzar's first dream. In response to Shadrach, Meshach, and Abednego's miraculous escape from the heat of the fiery furnace, King Nebuchadnezzar himself describes this kingdom as an *"everlasting kingdom"*. Then King Darius joins the chorus calling Daniel's God the *"living God"* whose kingdom is *"one which will not be destroyed"*. The coming of this kingdom, being ushered in by the *"Ancient of Days"*, the Messiah, is the main theme throughout Daniel's life.

This kingdom is the same kingdom Isaiah visioned, as the time when men will *"beat their swords into plowshares"* and never again will there be war and killing and hatred. Isaiah also said in that day the lion will lay down with the lamb and a little child will play by the cobra's hole. In other words, there will be peace among all of God's creatures like never before seen. This was the hope of Israel, a real and living hope.

The last words of Jesus in the Scriptures are in the final verses of the Bible in Revelation 22, *"Yes, I am coming quickly"*. Following this statement is the Bible's last prayer, *"Come, Lord Jesus"*.

Prayer: *Lord Jesus, we long for Your return to earth to bring God's Kingdom in its fullness. We long for that time when there is no hate, no war, no sickness, no poverty, no crying, and no death. Come, Lord Jesus. Amen.*

SATURDAY - IN THAT DAY

Scripture: Malachi 4:1, 5

Throughout past months, we looked at several Old Testament characters and related their life stories to our lives. Today, I highlight a phrase that one finds on the increase as the Minor Prophets bring the Old Testament to its end.

The phrase *"in that day"* is mentioned several times in Isaiah and then like a snowball that starts quite small and quickly gets much larger, the phrase is found in most all the smaller prophets. For example, it is found seventeen times in the little book of Zachariah, the next to last book of the Old Testament. And it is the main theme of Malachi, the last book. The final chapter of Malachi opens with the announcement of the coming of the *"day of the Lord"* and ends with an even more graphic description, *"the great and terrible day of the Lord"*. It will be great - hope in full color - for God's people who know him and obey him. It will be terrible - unspeakable wrath - for those who reject God.

The coming of the Lord was partially fulfilled in the birth of Christ and will be completely fulfilled in Christ's coming again, the theme of the Bible's final chapter. In the Lord's prayer, Jesus prays for the coming of the kingdom. This kingdom is *"that day"*. This kingdom is the theme of many of Jesus' parables and in almost all of his teaching. In *"that day"*, God's eternal kingdom will finally come. The crucifixion and resurrection of Jesus Christ was the capstone for God's kingdom. Every student of the Bible should see this. This is the *"gospel"*. It is God's message for all the peoples of the world. It is the true message of Christmas.

Prayer: *Father, the story of the Bible is refreshing water to my dry and desolate soul. I want to be within Your family in "that day". This is the hope of my life, the hope of this most precious season. In Christ's name. Amen.*

SUNDAY – GOD'S SPECIAL DAY – THE LORD'S DAY

Praise the Lord! Praise God in His sanctuary; praise Him in His mighty expanse. Praise Him for His mighty deeds. Praise Him according to His excellent greatness."   Psalm 150:1-2

WEEK #50: THE TIME HAS COME

MONDAY – JOSEPH'S DILEMMA

Scripture: Matthew 1:19-20

Years ago, Rhonda and I had a foster girl who showed no progress after being in our home for many months. We realized that our home was not helping her. The dilemma was do we keep on trying or do we have her removed from our home and placed in another home that might fit her needs better. For weeks we discussed, prayed, and agonized as to what to do.

Joseph faced a much more serious dilemma. He had become engaged to Mary. Now he learns she is pregnant. How did he learn this? Mary must have told him. Can you imagine that conversation? He knows they have not been sexually intimate. How could she betray him like this? Who was the father? What would Joseph's family think? Adultery would bring great shame to both families. Legally, he could have her stoned. Should he? I can imagine him having many sleepless nights agonizing over the situation.

I have often wondered, "Why didn't God also reveal this to Joseph at the same time and manner that he did to Mary, preventing all the struggling and questioning?" As we see with most other Biblical characters, God is forever testing his people. It appears that God wants them to see just how much they really do trust him and are willing to walk by faith. God came to Joseph in a dream and revealed to him the true picture. Joseph believed the angel, trusted God for the impossible, and moved forward in obedience, taking Mary as his wife. Wow.

This Christmas season, how is God testing you? What dilemma are you facing? How is your obedience and trust being put on the line? Are you truly seeking to hear from the Lord?

Prayer: *Father, thank You for giving me Joseph as an example to follow. Help me, Lord, to seek Your will above my own, even at the risk of shame and embarrassment. In Jesus' name. Amen.*

TUESDAY – HE REALLY DOES KNOW BEST

Scripture: Matthew 1:24-25

All parents want their children to obey them. Many years ago there was a long-running television series called, *Father Knows Best*, starring Robert Young and Jane Wyatt. It was American pop culture at its best. Robert Young played a faithful, caring, sacrificing, honest father in everyday family life. The show did a good job of capturing the Biblical concept of our heavenly Father as he relates to his children.

Disobedience comes with a price, whether it be the little girl touching a hot burner or man setting his own standards for living. In the story of Joseph and Mary, we read of God commanding Joseph to take Mary as his wife. God's word to Joseph was not a suggestion or something for him to ponder. It was a command. He would either obey or disobey. It was that simple. God had spoken, and the rest is history.

It is possible to obey his/her parent out of fear. In a healthy relationship, it is a mixture of fear and love. In early childhood, fear of a swat in the pants is the big motivation. Later on, it is hoped that obedience would come more from love and respect. John tells the early church that obeying God's commands shows our love for him.

In light of the coming of Christ, what area of your life might you be missing the mark in obedience? Do you resent God's commands? Do you see them as means of making your life miserable or a means of making your life better and more purposeful? Do you see obedience as a way of showing God your love for him? God has spoken. Now is our chance to show our love for him by obeying.

Prayer: *Father, You do really know best. Many things in life don't make sense. Thank You for Your commands that give me direction in this world filled with so much confusion and chaos. In Jesus' name. Amen.*

WEDNESDAY – BELIEVE

Scripture: Luke 1:18-19

It is frustrating to limit preaching and teaching about the coming of Christ to four or five services. There is so much more to the story. During these weeks of daily devotions, you may learn parts of the story you never knew. Today's story may be case in point.

If we call Isaiah the Christmas prophet, we probably should call Luke the Christmas Gospel. Out of the four Gospels, Luke gives us the Bethlehem story in detail. He begins it with the story of John the Baptist's conception. It was miraculous in its own way.

John's parents, Zacharias and Elizabeth, were unable to have children and were past child-bearing years. Zacharias was a Jewish priest, a pious and faithful servant of God. While Zacharias was in the Jerusalem Temple performing his priestly duties, the angel Gabriel appears and gives him a lengthy message about his son to be born and his role in preparing the way for the Messiah. Zacharias was stunned, full of fear and disbelief. Because of his disbelief, he was unable to speak until the day of the actual birth of his son. How excited he must have been to learn how God was blessing him with a child, but how discouraging it must have been to not speak for nine months! He probably wondered if he would ever speak again.

God expects his children to believe him. And he does discipline them and allow them to suffer the consequences when they don't. Zacharias' disbelief didn't thwart God's plan, but it made life quite awkward for several months. God's plan for you is to bless you, but are you making it difficult for yourself by not fully embracing his word? Be not afraid. Believe. Believe. Believe.

Prayer: *Father, I confess that sometimes Your word to me seems too good to be true. The story of Christ's birth and Your plan for the world is almost beyond belief yet You call me to believe. Oh Lord, I believe. I believe. In Jesus' name. Amen.*

THURSDAY – BE IT DONE TO ME

Scripture: Luke 1:34-35

The angel, Gabriel, played a major role in the story of Christ's birth. Here we read of another visitation by Gabriel. This time it is not to an old man but a young woman – Mary.

Mary must have been in her home. She may have been sewing, preparing food, or praying. Luke gives us the very words spoken by Gabriel, just as he did with Zacharias. Gabriel tells her not to be afraid. Most of us are frightened by appearances of unknown people or unknown voices. After all the talk about having a child, Mary questions the angel as to how this will happen as she has not been intimate with any man. This tells us she was thinking and, though a bit frightened, not too afraid to question the angel. Gabriel explains how this miracle will happen. Wow, we have it in print! We know how it happened.

Unlike Zacharias, an older, wiser, educated man in the Temple, this young woman - probably uneducated, going about everyday life, certainly not a religious leader of any kind - believes God. What a contrast. Her response was not, "Do you realize what people will think of me?" or "What will Joseph say?" Her response was ". . . *may it be done to me according to your word.*" Is it any wonder why God chose her to bring his Son into the world?

This season I am reminded again how precious in God's sight are the everyday people, the common people, who learn to live by faith, love God, and love their neighbor. Those are the people usually chosen by God for really great things. I see this every Christmas. Oh, the wonder of it all.

Prayer: *Father, I look forward to meeting Mary and Joseph some day. What examples of faith You have given me. Purify my heart, Lord, to serve You in simplicity and faith. In Jesus' name. Amen.*

FRIDAY – GOD IS GOD

Scripture: Luke 1:36-37

After telling Mary the Holy Spirit would overshadow her as she conceived God's Son, the angel Gabriel gives young Mary a fitting reminder – *"For nothing will be impossible with God"*. Gabriel probably knew she needed to hear that, as the skepticism in her mind must have been running wild.

Humans are forever putting God in a box. God is God. He can do anything he wants as he is not limited by the same boundaries we are. In recent years the saying, "think outside the box" has been popular. Taco Bell did a take on that saying by coming up with their own promotional lingo to "think outside the bun", meaning don't limit yourself to traditional fast food such as burgers. When one surrenders to the Lordship of Jesus Christ, he lives life "outside the box". He is a believer. He believes that God cares and wants to have a relationship with the people of his creation. The believer accepts that God intervenes in daily life and situations and sometimes does so in ways that defy logic, such as a virgin having a baby. Jesus' birth is not only out of the box, it is not within sight of the box. Nothing is impossible with God, as correctly stated by the angel Gabriel.

Mary's "God-moment" must have stayed in her mind a long time. When they were in the town of Bethlehem, and she was heavy with child, hours before she would go into labor, they could not find a guest room. Did she remember the word from Gabriel, *"nothing will be impossible with God"*? I wonder. There are many times in one's life when that kind of assurance is needed. Christmas is all about God being God.

Prayer: *Father, help me to live outside the box with my faith. Forgive me for limiting You in any given situation. Oh Lord, I want to abandon my boxed-in world to walk in the moment of letting You truly be my God. In Jesus' name. Amen.*

SATURDAY – PREPARING THE WAY

Scripture: Luke 4:1-2; 13-14

As John the Baptist was the forerunner to Christ, announcing his coming, he did so from the rough and tumble of a harsh wilderness, not from ivory towers wearing soft clothing adorned with gold. We typically think of God leading one into safety and comfort, but the Holy Spirit led Jesus into this excruciating time of fasting and temptation. Many people see the Holy Spirit leading people into moments of uncontrolled ecstasy in babbling tongues or wild gyrations. That is not the picture we see of Jesus, nor of Paul, nor of Peter.

God wanted to prepare Jesus for victory over evil in healing people, in casting out demons, and in teaching the multitudes. God knew Jesus would face unimaginable opposition in his ministry. God knew Satan would throw every ounce of his artillery power at Jesus.

When Jesus emerged from the desert, he was walking in the power of the Holy Spirit. Yes, he was hungry. Yes, he was tired, but above the physical weakness he might have suffered, his spirit was soaring.

Denying oneself of worldly pleasure for the purpose of seeking God's wisdom and leading usually leads to walking in God's power. It is through sacrifice and suffering that many of God's saints over the years have been deepened and their ability to discern right from wrong, good from evil, sharpened.

During Advent many people go to parties and family gatherings. It is easy to put on weight in December only to be depressed in January. Why not try a different approach this December? Why not do an occasional fast in preparation for a high and holy celebration of Christ's birth and to move into the new year without the same ole, same ole resolutions.

Prayer: *Father, the way of the cross has never been easy. Teach me to walk in the ways of Jesus, above all else. Teach me, Lord. Teach me to fast and pray and grow deep in my faith. In Jesus' name. Amen.*

SUNDAY – GOD'S SPECIAL DAY – THE LORD'S DAY

"With my mouth I will give thanks abundantly to the Lord; and in the midst of many I will praise Him."

Psalm 109:30

WEEK #51: JOY TO THE WORLD

MONDAY – MORE AND MORE OF THE SPIRIT

Scripture: Luke 1:39-41

God's precious Spirit, who is mentioned in creation in Genesis, plays a very major role in the Christmas narrative. The Holy Spirit overshadowed Mary when conception happened and then moved mightily in the hearts of the other Christmas characters. Elizabeth, the mother of John the Baptist, is one. Mary went to Elizabeth's house for a visit while in her sixth month of pregnancy. Upon hearing Mary's greeting, Elizabeth was *"filled with the Holy Spirit"*.

When thinking about the birth of Jesus and the Holy Spirit, I think of the birth of the church, as recorded in Acts. The church was miraculously conceived. People involved were *"filled with the Holy Spirit"*. As the church grew, more and more people were *"filled with the Holy Spirit"*. When the Spirit comes, the mouth opens in praise to God.

It is as true today as it was then. When God has taken up residence inside the heart, the mouth is animated. Praise to God is inevitable, regardless of culture, race, or nationality. It is universally true. It is during the Christmas season that some of the greatest choral productions surface. God's Spirit stirs and Christians enjoy singing Christmas hymns with great confidence.

I well remember, just last Christmas, a Christmas concert Rhonda and I attended in the chapel of Wabash College, in Crawfordsville, Indiana. Here on the campus of a secular, educational institution was a heart-stirring choral and brass presentation on the birth of Jesus Christ. The chapel was a packed house. The singing was moving.

"Joy to the world, the Lord is come! Let earth receive its King. Let every heart prepare him room and heav'n and nature sing and heav'n . . . "

Prayer: *Father God, praise You and thank You for the moving of Your Spirit this season. Fill me every day, Lord, fill me up to overflowing with You, with Your Holy Spirit. In Jesus' name. Amen.*

TUESDAY – INCREDIBLE WOMEN

Scripture: Luke 1:46-47

Mary's visit to Elizabeth is quite the animated encounter. Elizabeth's excitement is very obvious. Baby John leaped in her womb upon hearing Mary's greeting. The Spirit of God that overshadowed Mary in conception now speaks through her with words that appear to be much more mature than a young, uneducated Jewish girl might speak.

As she stayed with Elizabeth for the following three months, I can imagine they had long conversations about the Living God, and how incredibly exciting it is to know and serve Him. They must have talked about the future and what it would be like to raise the Messiah in childhood and the coming kingdom. Did they talk about whether he would do miracles, walk on water, heal the sick, and raise the dead? Did they talk about how the Jewish religious leaders would react? Did they consider that Jesus might be the sacrificial lamb and possibly killed?

This young woman was chosen by God to bring his Son into the world to give eternal life to people of all nations. Indeed she was special. Some Christian groups have exalted her to the point of worship, saying she herself was without sin, even calling her the mother of God. The Bible, though, portrays her as a normal human being and does speak of Jesus having brothers and sisters. We must keep the focus on Jesus. I think Mary would have wanted it that way. In the New Testament, Jesus is the focal point. The shepherds and wise men came to see Jesus, to bow before him and adore him.

O come, let us adore him. O come, let us adore him. O come, let us adore him - Christ, the Lord.

Prayer: *Father, the story of Mary touches my heart. I can only wonder all the things that went through her mind as she was carrying Your baby. Today I bow at the manger with the shepherds. Oh precious Jesus. In Your name. Amen.*

WEDNESDAY – HIS NAME IS JOHN

Scripture: Luke 1:57-63

Most people don't realize there are two very important births in the Christmas story. The one so easily glossed over is the birth of John the Baptist. John was not conceived by the Holy Spirit, like Jesus, but his conception happened only because of a divine touch through answered prayer.

Mary must have stayed with Elizabeth until baby John was born. As with many ancient cultures, babies weren't named until after the birth. Relatives would select and announce the name at a family gathering. Indian culture is much the same today. According to Jewish custom, the male baby would be circumcised the eighth day and also named. Though the relatives had decided on a name common to their family, Elizabeth emphatically protested saying he would be called John, as that was the name the angel had given to her husband, Zacharias. Remember how Zacharias had been unable to speak because of disbelief? The story is that he scribbled on a tablet that his son shall be called, "John". At that moment, Zacharias' tongue was loosed and he could speak again. What a joyous moment! Imagine! What did he then say? Being filled with the Holy Spirit, he gave praise to God and uttered a powerful word of prophecy. Everyone present knew this was a special moment and that God's hand was upon this baby boy in a special way. John would later be known as John the Baptist. He would call people to repentance in preparation for the coming of Jesus. John was chosen by God to baptize Jesus.

Oh come, oh come Emmanuel. And ransom captive Israel. That mourns in lonely exile here. Until the Son of God appears. Rejoice! Rejoice! Emmanuel shall come to you, O Israel.

Prayer: *Praise You, Father, for orchestrating the birth of Your Son in a way that is far beyond human comprehension. All the angels in heaven were amazed. All glory to You this day. In Jesus' name. Amen.*

THURSDAY – GOD'S PLANS UNFOLDING

Scripture: Luke 1:67-70

Wouldn't it be special to have the actual words which Zacharias spoke on that day when John was born, that day when Zacharias' tongue was loosed to speak again? He was *"filled with the Holy Spirit"*. Well, guess what? We do have his words. Verses 67 through 79 give us the entire prophecy word for word.

Remember, Zacharias was a Jewish priest. God did not circumvent Judaism to bring his Son into the world. He had made a covenant with them many years ago. Though they had been disobedient, and he had punished them for their disobedience, he remained committed to them. He promised Abraham to bless all the peoples of the earth through him and his family. God keeps his promises. In spite of man's disobedience and rebellion, God is doing a great work throughout history. The weakness of man will not thwart God's plan.

Zacharias had nine months of silence, not able to speak a word. He must have given much thought about his son to be born. I could see him having extended times of prayer. I could see him in deep thought, pondering about the coming Messiah and kingdom, pouring over Old Testament Scriptures. His prophecy carries a very similar tone as Isaiah's prophecy of the coming Messiah. This incredible event was now in process.

Zacharias spoke of God remembering his covenant with Abraham and the Jewish people. He spoke of his son as a prophet who would prepare the way of the Lord. Wow.

Oh come, blest Dayspring, come and cheer, our spirits by your advent here. Disperse the gloomy clouds of night, and death's dark shadows put to flight. Rejoice! Rejoice! Emmanuel shall come to you O Israel.

Prayer: *Father, I join the heavenly chorus in that my spirit rejoices at the thoughts of Your coming kingdom. By giving us Your Son, salvation has come to us, and we have tasted of Your kingdom. You have pierced the darkness. In Jesus' name. Amen.*

FRIDAY – BETHLEHEM HERE WE COME

Scripture: Luke 2:6-7

After all the Old Testament prophecies, after the story of Joseph and Mary, Zacharias and Elizabeth, and the baby John, we finally make our way to Bethlehem where our wondering couple had no Day's Inn, Motel 6, Best Western or Comfort Inn. If Bethlehem would have had all those places of lodging, they would have been full. There was simply, *"no room for them in the inn"*. Think about that a little bit more - no Redi-Med, no ER, no 9-1-1, no doctor, no nurse practioner, but only Joseph, a barn, a few sheep, a few cows and maybe a donkey. Talk about panic. On the inside, I would have been screaming, "Where are you God? You got me into this. Now where are you?" It is interesting that at this moment, Gabriel is nowhere to be found.

The faith of young Mary and Joseph was being tested again. It was God's plan that his Son be of lowly birth. God didn't want him born in a five-star Hilton or Hyatt Regency. He didn't care that he was not surrounded by elitist, upscale wealthy and powerful people. We need to understand that God is not into most of the things the world values. It is not his nature. He can be found in the simple things. Christmas is the most graphic illustration of God's economy. It turns the world's way of thinking upside down. I like it.

O little town of Bethlehem, how still we see thee lie! Above thy deep and dreamless sleep the silent stars go by; yet in the dark streets shineth the everlasting light. The hopes and fears of all the years are met in thee tonight.

Prayer: *Father, the Bethlehem story never gets boring and stale. Every year, it comes alive even more. Oh, the wonder of it all. Praise Your holy name. Amen.*

SATURDAY – SHEPHERDS AND ANGELS

Scripture: Luke 2:8-11

The story of the shepherds is quite colorful. Within it we find a message from "*an angel of the Lord*", possibly Gabriel. The shepherds actually make their way to the manger scene and behold the Christ-child. Whew, a lot in this story!

Years ago, when visiting a rural seminary in Karnataka, India, Rhonda and I actually observed shepherds bedding down and keeping watch over their flocks by night. To make it even more amazing, it was during the Christmas season. The shepherds had small fires lit and were cooking. Tents were scattered about the area. Small children were playing as the sheep were being rounded up. We were informed that shepherds were considered to be of very low social standing. Every time I read of the shepherds in Luke 2, I think of that little rag-tag community going about everyday life. It is just like God to include the shepherds.

The message from the angel to the shepherds is consistent with the global theme of the Bible – the good news of a great joy will be "*for all the people*". Directed to Bethlehem to a baby wrapped in cloths, lying in a manger, this baby would be "*a Savior, who is Christ the Lord*". As if this was not enough, we then have a sudden appearance of a multitude of angels praising God and singing, "*Glory to God in the highest . . .*"

What child is this, who, laid to rest, on Mary's lap is sleeping? Whom angels greet with anthems sweet while shepherds watch are keeping? This, this is Christ the king, whom shepherds guard and angels sing; haste, haste to bring him laud, the babe, the son of Mary!

Prayer: *Father, what a display of Your glory the shepherds must have witnessed that night while keeping their flocks. Oh how I would like to have been with them as they beheld Your Son in the manger. Praise be to Your name. Amen.*

SUNDAY – GOD'S SPECIAL DAY – THE LORD'S DAY

"I will give thanks to You, O Lord, among the peoples, and I will sing praises to You among the nations."

Psalm 108:3

WEEK #52: THE BIRTH THAT CHANGED THE WORLD

MONDAY – FINDING THE WAY TO THE MANGER

Scripture: Luke 2:16-18

God intervened in the day and life of the shepherds. The shepherds wasted no time in going to Bethlehem. We don't know how many shepherds nor do we know if their wives and children accompanied them. We do know they were in the same region, and it was night. Their sheep probably had been put down for the night. My guess is the men went and left the women and children back at the camp with the sheep. The shepherds were amazed and shared their story of the angels with Joseph and Mary. Mary was touched. This confirmed all she knew in her heart. The last picture we get of the shepherds is them returning to the flocks "*glorifying and praising God*".

I have often wondered what happened to those shepherds, their wives and children. Did they witness any of Jesus' miracles? Were they in the large crowds when Jesus miraculously fed thousands of people? Were they in Jerusalem the day he was crucified? Were any of them a part of the first three thousand to hear the gospel message and be baptized? We might learn that some day when we get home, but probably not in this lifetime.

Making one's way to the manger is a journey all of us have made, all who have come to know God through Jesus Christ. God spoke to our hearts. We were drawn to the Savior. And now we go our way "*glorifying and praising God*".

The first Noel the angel did say, was to certain poor shepherds in fields as they lay; in fields where they lay keeping their sheep, on a cold winter's night that was so deep. Noel, Noel, Noel, Noel! Born is the King of Israel.

Prayer: *Father, thank You that I am one who made his/her way to Bethlehem. Thank You, Lord, that I can glorify and praise You until that moment You call me home. In the name of the One in the manger on that very special night. Amen.*

TUESDAY – FOLLOWING THE STAR

Scripture: Matthew 2:10-11

Matthew's gospel has the unique story of the magi or as we know them, the wise men from the East. Most scholars believe these men were Zorastarian astrologers who were known for identifying great political leaders by studying the stars. The U.S. National Aeronautics and Space Administration keeps a database of every constellation of stars throughout history. Chinese and Korean astronomers wrote of some type of comet with no tail that stood still in the sky at 4 BC. Dr. Grant Mathews, a theoretical astrophysicist at the University of Notre Dame, has identified an alignment of the sun, moon, Jupiter, and Saturn on April 17th, 6 BC. This would have caused all astronomers to take note and especially would have been pursued by Zorastarian astrologers. This may have been the Bethlehem star.

It is especially worth noting that these men were not Jews. They most likely were the first Gentiles to worship Jesus. The gifts they brought could very well have been from what we now know as India. It remains today a huge custom of the East to offer gifts when visiting or receiving guests. Mary and Joseph must have found a house in Bethlehem where they stayed for a few months and maybe even a year or two. Mathew does say the magi came to a "house", not a stable or manger.

The birth of God's Son was a cosmic event. Today, calendars around the world measure time based upon the birth of Christ.

We three kings of Orient are, bearing gifts we traverse afar. Field and fountain, moor and mountain following yonder star. O Star of wonder, star of night, Star with royal beauty bright. Westward leading still proceeding guide us to thy Perfect Light.

Prayer: *Father, I praise You today for these magi from the East. I look forward to meeting them someday. Each Sunday when I follow the Star to bow down and worship, like the magi, I offer You my gifts. In Jesus' name. Amen.*

WEDNESDAY – LOVE AND LIGHT

Scripture: John 3:16-17

God's love looms mighty big in the Christmas story. Some have said that God so loved the world that he didn't send a committee or appoint a task force. God is highly invested in humanity. He has a plan and will bring it to pass. He wants to create a people for himself, to enjoy eternity with him. His plan is his Son. His plan is his Spirit. His plan is the Church. His plan is people from Europe, Asia, the Orient, Africa, South and North America, and the Middle East. His plan is you and me.

It would not be love for a parent to see his son or daughter drowning in a pool and walk away. True love is more than a feeling. It demands action. God could not love this world, be all powerful, see the world on a downward spiral, and remain passive. Because of God's deep love for people, he sent his Son. God did not come as fire, like in the case of Moses or Elijah. But in Jesus, God came down to us as man. He not only came to us but became one of us. Because of Jesus, he knows what it is like to laugh, to cry, to suffer, to die. He understands our plight in life. He is with us in our frustration, our anxiety, our disappointment and pain.

There is more love and compassion shown this time of the year than any other season. In the darkest month of the year, we celebrate the Light. Some people find it difficult, as they miss their loved one over the holidays. For the Christian, the hope of everlasting life shines brightly through the pain of loss.

Prayer: *Father, Your love and light dispels the darkness in my soul. I can't imagine a world without Christmas. Thank You for coming to earth to give Your life that we may live. In Jesus' name. Amen.*

THURSDAY – THE WONDER OF IT ALL

Scripture: John 1:14

Every year on our tree is a special ornament that reminds Rhonda and me of our baby daughter, Joni Annette, who is with the Lord. We also have an ornament made in childhood by our son, Jim, and our daughter, Jenny. We like to have our closest family members with us each Christmas, but that is not always possible.

We celebrated Christmas in India for several years. I never thought I would miss the storefront decorations and what I have even criticized as the "commercialization of Christmas", but I did. It was not the same without hardly any decorations up along the street or in the stores. I saw how the rest of the world stood up and took notice when western Europe and America went all out for Christmas. Hindu families in our neighborhood tried to get in the act by putting up lights. There is something about Christmas celebrations that attract people, even people without faith in Christ. Now I get excited when stores put up decorations, even if they don't directly speak of Jesus. I am even happy to see Santas go up. I know that doesn't sound very spiritual, and I can't fully explain it.

How can it be that a Jewish, peasant boy born in a barn in a small, rural village could impact the world so much? Maybe if he would have been born in London, Paris, or New York City, one might understand. Maybe if he would be the great grandson of the British crown, one might understand. Maybe if he would have had a PhD from Harvard or would have been a summa cum laude graduate of West Point, one might understand, but a hometown boy from Bethlehem? How did this happen?

Prayer: *Father, the wonder of Christmas is truly of You. May that special love flow in and around every neighborhood, especially those who are missing loved ones. In Jesus' name. Amen.*

FRIDAY – ONE SOLITARY LIFE

Scripture: Hebrews 1:1-2

If you land a jet in Tokyo, you must use a calendar based on the birth of Jesus Christ. The same for an Air India jet in Delhi, or Saudi Arabia. This "great light" prophesied by the prophet, Isaiah, has shined forth in every major part of the world.

One Solitary Life, by James Allan Francis.
He was born in an obscure village, the child of a peasant woman. He grew up in still another village, where He worked in a carpenter shop until He was 30. Then for three years He was an itinerant preacher. He never wrote a book. He never held an office. He never had a family or owned a house. He didn't go to college. He never traveled more than 200 miles from the place He was born. He did none of the things one usually associates with greatness. He had no credentials but Himself. He was only 33 when public opinion turned against Him. His friends deserted Him. He was turned over to His enemies and went through the mockery of a trial. He was nailed to a cross between two thieves. When He was dying, His executioners gambled for His clothing, the only property He had.. . . on earth. When He was dead, He was laid in a borrowed grave through the pity of a friend. Nineteen centuries have come and gone, and today He is the central figure of the human race, the leader of mankind's progress. All the armies that ever marched, all the navies that ever sailed, all the parliaments that ever sat, all the kings that ever reigned, put together, have not affected the life of man on earth as much as that One Solitary Life.

Prayer: *Father, that one solitary life has given me life and hope. He will forever be the Light of my life. May I never be ashamed of Him. May I stand strong to my last breath as His witness. In His name. Amen.*

SATURDAY – BOUND FOR EGYPT

Scripture: Matthew 2:13-14

Today's verse is the sole Biblical reference of baby Jesus and his parents going to Egypt. We do know that many Jews fled to Egypt during that same time period out of fear of King Herod. Most likely they joined a caravan and traveled by donkey. King Herod died about four years after the birth of Christ, which must have been the time Joseph and Mary made their way to Nazareth.

Presently in Egypt there is a church dedicated to the place when Joseph and Mary took refuge. The Coptic Church, which is the Christian church in Egypt, puts great emphasis upon the holy family visiting their land. There are many miracle stories told about the baby Jesus. Stories like the baby Jesus smiling at a barren fruit tree and suddenly there is fruit. One story speaks of his bath water having miraculous healing powers. None of these can be substantiated, but it does make one wonder.

God could have miraculously protected the holy family there in Bethlehem, but he chose otherwise. I'm sure it was very difficult and frightening for Mary and Joseph to go to a foreign land as refugees, especially traveling that far by donkey. I'm sure the parents of the babies who were ruthlessly butchered by Herod's soldiers wondered why God would have allowed their innocent babies to die. I can't imagine being in Bethlehem with all the weeping and wailing.

When I think of these events, some of them rather sobering, I am reminded that God doesn't always exempt his people from facing injustice, brutality and difficult, worrisome times. Even with Joseph and Mary, God did not make the path smooth. He was with them through it all, and he is with you.

Prayer: *Father, Your presence means everything. In spite of the brokenness and pain of this life, You have given me hope and light. I end this year praising You and giving You glory. Through Christ. Amen.*